Alexander Hamilton on
Finance, Credit, and Debt

# ALEXANDER HAMILTON ON FINANCE, CREDIT, AND DEBT

Richard Sylla and David J. Cowen

Columbia University Press
New York

Columbia University Press
*Publishers Since 1893*
New York   Chichester, West Sussex   cup.columbia.edu
Copyright © 2018 Museum of American Finance
All rights reserved

Library of Congress Cataloging-in-Publication Data
Names: Hamilton, Alexander, 1757–1804, author. | Sylla, Richard Eugene,
editor. | Cowen, David Jack, 1959– editor.
Title: Alexander Hamilton on finance, credit, and debt / [edited by]
Richard Sylla and David J. Cowen. ·
Description: New York : University Press, [2018] | Includes
bibliographical references and index. |
Identifiers: LCCN 2017053353 (print) | LCCN 2017056270 (ebook) |
ISBN 9780231545556 (ebook) | ISBN 9780231184564 (cloth : alk. paper)
Subjects: LCSH: Finance—United States. | Credit—United States. |
Debt—United States.
Classification: LCC HG181 (ebook) | LCC HG181 .H219 2018 (print) |
DDC 332.0973—dc23
LC record available at https://lccn.loc.gov/2017053353

Columbia University Press books are printed on permanent
and durable acid-free paper.
Printed in the United States of America

Cover design: Noah Arlow

To our spouses and children, with gratitude and love
Richard: Edith, Anne, and Peggy
David: Beth, Andrew, and Ethan

# Contents

# Acknowledgments

WE THANK ESPECIALLY our colleague and long-time collaborator, Professor Robert E. Wright of Augustana College, for his research and analysis of Alexander Hamilton's writings on finance. We are also grateful to Myles Thompson of Columbia University Press, who had the initial idea for this book. Myles's colleagues at Columbia—Ryan Groendyk, Marielle Poss, and Stephen Wesley—provided important support at various stages of the project.

The Museum of American Finance will benefit from any and all authorial proceeds of this book. We are grateful for the longstanding and continuing support of the Museum's dedicated senior staff: Kristin Aguilera, Tony Critelli, Jeanne Driscoll, Maura Ferguson, Chris Meyers, Sarah Poole, Linda Rapacki, and Mindy Ross.

For many years, John E. Herzog, the Museum's founder and chairman emeritus, stimulated and encouraged our interest in Hamilton and America's financial foundations by his enthusiasm for this subject, by his donations of documents to the Museum's collection, and by sharing with us his own extensive collection. Other members of the collecting community, in particular Ned Downing and Ira Unschuld, also shared with us their remarkable documentary collections.

Friends and Hamilton aficionados provided us with important insights from their own research. In particular, we recognize the assistance of Douglas Hamilton, a direct descendant; Michael Newton, a meticulous scholar; and Rand Scholet, founder of the Alexander Hamilton Awareness Society.

Writing a book manuscript is one thing—and for this we must thank Alexander Hamilton, who did most of the work—but producing a book from that manuscript is another. For this, in addition to the folks at Columbia University Press, we thank Ben Kolstad and Peggy Tropp of Cenveo Publisher Services for excellent support in the late stages of the project. Much earlier, Spencer Cowen provided assistance in preparing the Hamilton documents for us.

Last and hardly least, we thank Lin-Manuel Miranda, a friend of the Museum, whose immensely popular show, "Hamilton: An American Musical," continues to create a resurgence of interest in the life and work of Alexander Hamilton in the United States and throughout the world.

Alexander Hamilton on
Finance, Credit, and Debt

# Introduction

---

*Hamilton and the U.S. Financial Revolution*

---

Hamilton was without doubt the best and most foresighted
economic policy maker in U.S. history. . . . As Treasury Secretary
[he] put in place the institutional basis for the modern
U.S. economy.
—BEN BERNANKE, FORMER FEDERAL RESERVE CHAIR, 2015

ONE OF THE most important, yet least acknowledged, developments in the entire history of the United States occurred during just
a few short years at the start of the 1790s. We call it the U.S. financial
revolution. During those years, the new nation saw the emergence
of virtually all of the key components of a modern financial system.
Before 1790, it essentially had none of them.

Why did this matter? It mattered because modern financial arrangements, along with modern technologies, are the drivers of economic
growth and national power. Only in recent decades have economists
and economic historians come to understand and document that
finance is a driver of growth and power. That this connection has only
recently achieved acceptance among academic specialists may account
for its failure, so far, to make much of an impression on more general
historians.

We think it interesting that Alexander Hamilton, the real author of
this book, made the connection running from finance to growth and
power more than two centuries ago. During his relatively short life
(1757–1804), Hamilton, after making the connection when he was a

young soldier in the Continental Army, went on as the nation's first Secretary of the Treasury from 1789 to 1795 to engineer the U.S. financial revolution. He did so to promote economic growth and national power. He was ahead of his time. Indeed, since we have only of late come to appreciate what he knew long ago about finance's or credit's connection to growth and power, he remained ahead of his time right down to the present.

In the case of the United States, modern economic growth appears to have emerged at the time of the financial revolution of the 1790s. By modern economic growth, we mean sustained increases in economic output (or income) per person of 1 percent or more a year on average. The best estimates we have indicate that such rates of growth began in the 1790s, gradually accelerating to around 2 percent per year on average by the middle decades of the twentieth century.[1] Sustained modern growth began at the time of the financial revolution. Indeed, quite recent research suggests that the United States, not Great Britain with its pioneering industrial revolution (as many historians until recently have contended), may have been the first country to achieve modern economic growth.[2]

Rates of economic growth of 1 to 2 percent per year may not sound like a lot, but when they continue for more than two centuries, the results can be astounding. In real, inflation-adjusted terms, the average American in the early twenty-first century has an income some fifty times greater than the average American of 1790. Meanwhile, the United States, in 1790 a country of fewer than 4 million people on the periphery of a Western European–centered world, grew to a nation of more than 325 million. It quadrupled its territory, mostly in its first century, in good measure because its excellent finances made it easy to pay the costs of acquiring more land. It became a country of enormous wealth and power. The numbers given here imply that the output of the modern American economy is more than 4,000 times what it was in 1790. It is likely that no other country comes close to an expansion of that size during the same period, or just about any other lengthy period of modern economic history.

Hamilton would have been pleased. His main goals for the United States, along with constitutional government and national security, were wealth and power. His policies that modernized U.S. financial arrangements, as we hope readers of this book may discover, got the ball rolling toward all of those goals.

The U.S. financial revolution was hardly unprecedented. Italian city-states introduced some of the key components of modern financial systems in the late Middle Ages and Renaissance. Roughly two centuries before the United States gained independence, the Dutch Republic (the United Provinces), the modern-day Netherlands, had its own financial revolution. It helped that small country to win its independence from Spain, a seemingly larger and more powerful country. Armed with modern finances and an entrepreneurial mercantile spirit, the Dutch Republic became the leading and richest economy—some term it the first modern economy—of the seventeenth century. Amsterdam became the world's leading financial center, and it was where Hamilton floated loans in the 1790s to restructure U.S. debts. New Amsterdam was Dutch before it became New York.

Great Britain, the mother country of the United States, followed in the footsteps of the Dutch by handing its throne to a Dutch prince, Willem of Orange, in the Glorious Revolution of 1688. As William III of Britain, he brought over experienced Dutch financiers, who together with Britons launched an English financial revolution. Similar to the ways in which the Dutch exploited credit to defeat the Spanish, England used it to win all of its protracted wars with France, a larger county, between 1688 and 1815.[3]

Hamilton knew all this financial history, as his writings in the early chapters of this book will show. It is what led him to realize that credit was a new and great power in the affairs of nations and individuals. If the United States was to become a great nation, its governments—federal, state, and local—needed to have public credit. So he restructured the national debt, eased the financial burdens of the states, and founded the first central bank. These measures established public credit. If America's economy was to grow, individuals and business enterprises needed to have private credit. So Hamilton had his central bank lend also to them; he helped to found other banks and nonfinancial corporations; and he fostered the growth of securities markets to encourage investments in economic infrastructure and new technologies by making the stocks and bonds representing them attractive, liquid investments.

But we may be getting a little ahead of our story. Hamilton is better known to historians and those who read their works as a political reformer and spearhead of the movement for the Constitution than as a founder of the U.S. financial system. In truth, he would not have been able to execute his financial revolution unless he and others had first achieved the reform of American government represented by the Constitution. In his letter to James Duane (chapter 2), Hamilton had indicated that the Articles of Confederation, America's first constitution, were defective even before they were ratified because they failed to provide the national government with adequate revenues. Without adequate revenues, the government would not be able to establish its credit, and without good public credit, it would be difficult to establish private credit on firm foundations.

So the first task after winning the War of Independence, or even before that was accomplished, was to reform the national government. In the 1780 letter to Duane, seven years before the Philadelphia convention that drafted the Constitution, Hamilton says that Congress should immediately call a convention of the states to come up with a better plan of government. Although Hamilton was a twenty-three-year-old lieutenant colonel and General Washington's principal aide at the time, he was the first American leader (in his case, perhaps, a leader in the making) to call for such a convention. Then, in his *Continentalist* essays of 1781 and 1782 (chapter 4), he went public with his analysis of the defects of American government.

Thereafter, Hamilton served a term as a New York State delegate to the Confederation Congress, where an inability of that body to get much of anything done hardened his views on the need for governmental reform. Even less was done at the Annapolis Convention of 1786, where several states sent delegates—they included Madison from Virginia and Hamilton from New York—to ease trade disputes between states. The one thing that was accomplished at Annapolis was to agree to, and appoint Hamilton to draft, a request to the states to ask Congress to call a convention of all the states the next year to reform an increasingly ineffective plan of government.

The request met with success when Congress asked the states to send delegates to Philadelphia in 1787, leading to the new Constitution. Hamilton was one of New York's three delegates at the Philadelphia convention, and the only one to sign the Constitution. To help get it ratified, Hamilton then organized *The Federalist*, a series of eighty-five newspaper essays (he wrote fifty-one of them, with James Madison and John Jay penning the others) explaining why the new Constitution should be adopted and how its ratification would make the U.S. government far more effective. And he was a leader of the forces that were successful in getting New York State to adopt the Constitution at its state ratification convention in mid-1788.

A year later, President Washington appointed Hamilton Secretary of the Treasury, and he launched the financial revolution. In what did that revolution consist? To our mind it had six key components:

1. Establishing effective institutions of public finance—revenues and spending—and public debt management to finance the government, restructure its unpaid debts, and establish public credit so the U.S. government would always be able to borrow on good terms.
2. Founding a central bank to aid the government's finances and serve as the central node of the country's emergent banking and financial systems.
3. Creating the U.S. dollar as the country's unit of account and medium of exchange, and basing it on gold and silver as the monetary base into which banknotes and deposits were convertible, to give it the stability of value that would make it a safe basis for long-term contracts (such as bonds) and a safe asset in which to hold savings.
4. Fostering the growth of a banking system by encouraging state governments to create more banks to aid their own finances and lend to businesses and individual entrepreneurs—i.e., to establish private credit and bank money.
5. Fostering the growth of securities markets to make financial assets—government bonds, private sector bonds, and company equities (stocks)—liquid and transferrable, for the benefit of issuers and investors.
6. Fostering the growth of business corporations, both financial (such as banks and insurance companies) and nonfinancial (such as utilities; road, bridge, and canal companies; and manufacturers), to pool the capital of individuals to allow large enterprises to be created and economies of scale to be achieved.

As Treasury Secretary from 1789 to 1795, Hamilton had direct authority concerning the first three items on the list. Public finance and debt management are the subjects of the documents in chapters 6, 7, 8, 9, 10, 16, and 17 of this book. The central bank, the Bank of the United States, is the subject of chapters 10 and 12. The U.S. dollar is the subject of chapter 11.

Hamilton had to rely on others—state authorities and private entrepreneurs—to flesh out his financial revolution by implementing components 4, 5, and 6, but he prompted them to do that with his work on components 1, 2, and 3. The reforms of public finance established a government of law, order, and justice across the nation. The national debt restructuring and assumption of state debts allowed the states more easily to encourage development via tax cuts or spending on economic and social infrastructure, and it created a lot of new and prime debt securities—$63–64 million of domestic debt and $12–13 million of foreign debt—to foster the emergence of securities markets and stock exchanges, which happened in major cities in the early 1790s. Foreign investors viewed U.S. Treasury securities as safe and profitable investments, and their purchases, which Hamilton welcomed, transferred foreign capital to the United States.

The Bank of the United States issued more securities—$8 million of stock in public hands—and that also encouraged securities market development. The Bank also lent to private borrowers, fostering private credit. And Hamilton's Bank Report (chapter 10), by making the federal government a part owner of the Bank and saying that it would be a profitable public investment, encouraged state legislatures to follow that example by chartering more and more state banks. Hamilton's charter for the Bank became a model emulated by American and, later, Canadian banks.

By defining the U.S. dollar in his Mint Report (chapter 11), Hamilton gave the country a standard unit of account, creating a nationwide currency union. That facilitated interstate trade and economic growth.

States, as Hamilton had hoped, chartered more and more banks. In 1790, there were three local banks, in Philadelphia, New York, and Boston, and they were hardly a system because they had few if any connections. By 1795, some twenty additional banks had been created, and the Bank of the United States had established branches in several cities, giving the country interstate banking. The Bank kept large reserves of specie, and its notes were treated as good as gold and silver by other banks, which held them as a part of their reserves. That expanded the monetary base for lending and credit.

With all the new public and private securities, private brokers and dealers developed regular securities markets to trade them. Philadelphia and New York brokers established exchanges in 1790 and 1792, respectively. The New York Stock Exchange, long the world's largest by market capitalization of its listed securities, traces its founding to May 17, 1792, when some twenty brokers met under a buttonwood (syca-more) tree on Wall Street and agreed to form a private traders' club to launch a more reliable trading system. In the chapters that follow, the reader will note that Hamilton a number of times stresses the impor-tance of securities' being negotiable—i.e., tradable—because by being liquid they, in varying degrees, were almost a substitute for money.

Finally, Hamilton did all he could to promote corporations with limited liability. His first mention of a Bank of the United States in 1780 (chapter 1) made it a large trading company. His letter to Robert Morris a year later (condensed in chapter 3) mentioned, in the detailed outline of a proposed charter (the detail is left out of our condensa-tion), that the bank would "be erected into a legal corporation," with a comment to Morris, who no doubt understood such things, that "This article needs no illustration." Morris, like Hamilton, knew that limiting stockholders' liability to the amount of their investment would be attractive to investors, making it easier to raise larger amounts of capital.

Then we see Hamilton himself drafting company charters in chap-ters 5, 10, 13, and 18. Two of these (Bank of New York and Merchants Bank) called for the companies to have limited liability even before they had obtained state charters of incorporation, which both even-tually did. This was a controversial, but apparently legal, maneuver. Corporations have always been controversial in U.S. history, no less today than when they first emerged in large numbers during the finan-cial revolution of the early 1790s.

The texts that follow were downloaded from the National Archives' Founders Online website, https://founders.archives.gov. We have condensed the longer documents to omit detail that mattered more to readers of Hamilton's writings when they came out than they would to readers more than two centuries later. Most of the documents are available in hard copy in the twenty-seven-volume series, *The Papers of Alexander Hamilton*, edited by Harold C. Syrett et al. and published by Columbia University Press (1961–1987). We have also modern-ized some of Hamilton's eighteenth-century spellings and punctua-tion, often quite heavy on commas, to make this volume easier for a modern reader to read and understand. Hamilton's writings that were not edited and copied by others—for example, his opinion on the constitutionality of the Bank of the United States and his Defense of the Funding System in this volume—are both clearer and less comma-laden than his state papers, such as the reports on public credit, manufactures, and the national bank, which were edited and copied by government scribes. One wonders if they were paid by the comma!

For more than two centuries, much has been written about what Hamilton stood for, said, and thought. Those who told his story sometimes had their own agendas, leading to inaccuracies and distortions of what Hamilton actually wrote. An example is the oft-stated argument that Hamilton wanted the federal government to assume state debts primarily to enlarge the body of Treasury bondholders, who then would be beholden to and supportive of the federal government and less beholden to the states. The argument did occur to Hamilton (see chapter 17), but he deemed it a weak one because an enlarged federal debt would require more unpopular taxes to pay the interest, because the debt was to be extinguished "in a moderate term of years" and in the interim much of it would be purchased by foreign investors. To Hamilton, then, the oft-repeated argument "was the consideration upon which I relied least of all. . . . Had this then been the weightiest motive to the measure [assumption], it would never have received my patronage."

What Hamilton himself wrote is a better guide to his thought and his economic policies than what others have said he thought and believed. We hope that readers of this volume will agree.

# CHAPTER ONE

# To— (December 1779–March 1780)

*The necessity of a foreign loan
is now greater than ever.*

THIS LETTER REPRESENTS Hamilton's first serious foray into the subject of finance. Neither the recipient nor the exact date is known. The editors of *The Papers of Alexander Hamilton (PAH)* give the date range above based on when Hamilton was known to have been in Morristown, NJ, from which the letter was sent, and on its contents. They consider suggestions of various scholars that it may have been sent to Robert Morris, John Sullivan, or Philip Schuyler, but find the evidence inconclusive.[1] The financial problem that motivated Hamilton's letter was the inflation, bordering on hyperinflation, of prices during the War of Independence—or, in other words, the rapid depreciation of the Continental currency issued by Congress and of currencies issued by individual U.S. states. As the war had dragged on for five years, during most of which Hamilton was a soldier, both types of paper currency had been issued to excess. By early 1780, they had lost most of their value. That prompted Hamilton, as he says at the end of the letter, to engage in "some reading on the subjects of commerce and finance" and "occasional reflections on our particular situation." From Hamilton's references in the letter to the 1720

Mississippi scheme and John Law in France, it seems apparent that one of his sources was Sir James Steuart's *An Inquiry into the Principles of Political Economy* (1767), which has similar descriptions and phrasings.

After noting that even the richest of European states had to resort in wartime to foreign loans or subsidies, Hamilton said the United States could do no less. But how should such a loan, assuming it could be arranged, be best employed? One plan would be to use the proceeds of the foreign loan to buy up and retire most of the superfluous American currency issues and hope that would end the inflation. Hamilton doubted that would work because Americans had lost all confidence in their currencies. His discussion is couched in terms of what economists now call the quantity theory of money, and when he says that American currencies depreciated much more than might have been expected according to the simplest version of this theory, he implies that the public's lack of confidence in those currencies led them to spend them as fast as they could, which modern quantity theorists would term an increase in the "velocity" of spending.

Hamilton discussed a second plan that he thought had a better chance of success—using the foreign loan to purchase imported commodities, especially ones militarily useful, which he thought would allow the Americans to carry on the war for two to three years—but he doubted it would restore confidence in the currency.

Hamilton then unveils his own plan, which is most interesting because it presages a key part of the program of financial reform he would execute a decade later when he became the first Secretary of the Treasury of the United States. His plan is to use the foreign loan proceeds to capitalize an American bank, which Hamilton already in 1780 calls the Bank of the United States, the name he and Congress would give the national bank in 1790–1791. The proposed bank was to be a modern bank based on European precedents, which Hamilton had studied in his crash course of reading about financial history in the period before this letter was written. There was no such modern bank in the United States in 1780. Indeed, there had never been one. Hamilton was ahead of his time.

This first version of Hamilton's central bank has a number of similarities to the Bank of the United States he would recommend to Congress in 1790 and which Congress would approve in 1791 (see chapter 10). The confederation Congress would own half of the bank's stock and be entitled to half of its profits. The government would have the right to inspect the bank's books, an early form of financial regulation. The bank would lend to Congress and also to private commercial borrowers. It would issue a new and better currency, which Hamilton implies would be convertible into specie (gold and silver coins, presumably obtained in the foreign loan). The convertibility of bank money into specie is what would restore confidence in American currency.

To induce private investors, "the principal monied men," to invest in the bank along with the government, Hamilton calls for giving them incentives to invest. But he is against giving the bank exclusive privileges, as were given to European trading companies, because such privileges would "fetter that spirit of enterprise and competition on which the prosperity of commerce depends." Hamilton believed in free enterprise and free markets, but hardly in an extreme libertarian fashion. Enlightened government policies could be used to encourage and sustain free markets and free enterprise.

In this letter we see the beginnings of a far more comprehensive plan of financial reform and modernization that would be more fully formed when Hamilton hit the ground running as Secretary of the Treasury in September 1789. In his discussion of the national debt toward the end of the document, we also see the germ of his idea that a national debt could be a national blessing. This idea became explicit in his letter a year later to Robert Morris (see chapter 3).

We have condensed the 6,418 words of this document to 2,555 words.

[Morristown, New Jersey, December 1779–March 1780]

Sir,
The present conjuncture is by all allowed to be peculiarly critical. Every man of reflection employs his thoughts about the remedies proper to be applied to the national disorders; and everyone from a partiality to his own ideas wishes to convey them to those who are charged with the management of affairs. . . .

The object of principal concern is the state of our currency. In my opinion all our speculations on this head have been founded in error. Most people think that the depreciation might have been avoided by provident arrangements in the beginning without any aid from abroad, and a great many of our sanguine politicians 'till very lately imagined the money might still be restored by expedients within ourselves. Hence the delay in attempting to procure a foreign loan. . . .

The public expenditures from the dearness of everything necessarily became immense, greater in proportion than in other countries and much beyond any revenues which the best concerted scheme of finance could have extracted from the natural funds of the state. No taxes which the people were capable of bearing on that quantity of money which is deemed a proper medium for this country (had it been gold instead of paper) would have been sufficient for the current exigencies of government.

The most opulent states of Europe in a war of any duration are commonly obliged to have recourse to foreign loans or subsidies. How then could we expect to do without them and not augment the quantity of our artificial wealth beyond those bounds, which were proper to preserve its credit? The idea was chimerical. . . .

The ordinary revenues of The United Provinces amount to about 25.000.000 of Guilders or 2.250.000 £ Sterling per annum. This is in proportion to its territory and numbers the richest country in the world, and the country where the people sustain the heaviest load of taxes. Its population is about equal to ours, 2000000 of souls. The burthens on the subject are so great that it is by some held almost impracticable even on extraordinary emergencies to enlarge the revenues by new impositions. It is maintained their dependence in these cases must be on the extraordinary contributions of wealthy individuals, with the aid of which in some of their wars they have raised 4000.000 Stg. a year. In a country possessed of so vast a stock of wealth, where taxes are carried to such a height and where the means of paying them so infinitely exceed those in our power, if the national revenues only amount to the sum I have stated, how inadequate must have been the product of any taxes we could have levied to the demands of the service? Loans for the reason before hinted would have been out of the question; at least they would have been so trifling as to be an object of little importance. . . .

From these reasons it results that it was not in the power of Congress when their emissions had arrived at the 30,000,000 of dollars to put a stop to them. They were obliged, in order to keep up the supplies, to go on creating artificial revenues by new emissions; and as these multiplied their value declined. The progress of the depreciation might have been retarded but it could not have been prevented. It was in a great degree necessary.

There was but one remedy, a foreign loan. All other expedients should rather have been considered as auxiliary. Could a loan have been obtained and judiciously applied, assisted by a vigorous system of taxation, we might have avoided that excess of emissions which has ruined the paper. The credit of such a fund would have procured loans from the monied and trading men within ourselves, because it might have been so directed as to have been beneficial to them in their commercial transactions abroad.

The necessity of a foreign loan is now greater than ever. Nothing else will retrieve our affairs. The wheels of government without it cannot much longer be kept in motion. Including loan-office certificates and state emissions, we have about 400.000.000 of dollars in circulation. The real value of these is less than 7.000.000, which is the true circulating medium of these states. . . .

The hope of appreciating the money by taxes and domestic loans is at an end. As fast as it could be received it must be issued in the daily expenditures. The momentary interval between its being drawn out of circulation and returning into it would prevent its receiving the least advantage.

These reasons may appear useless, as the necessity of a foreign loan is now acknowledged and measures are taking to procure it. But they are intended to establish good principles, the want of which has brought us to the desperate crisis we are arrived at and may still betray us into fatal mistakes.

How this loan is to be employed is now the question, and its difficulty equal to its importance. Two plans have been proposed: one to purchase up at once in specie or Sterling bills all the superfluous paper and to endeavor by taxes, loans and economy to hinder its returning into circulation. The remainder it is supposed would then recover its value. This it is said will reduce our public debt to the Sterling cost of the paper. . . .

A great source of error in disquisitions of this nature is the judging of events by abstract calculations, which though geometrically true are false as they relate to the concerns of beings governed more by passion and prejudice than by an enlightened sense of their interests. A degree of illusion mixes itself in all the affairs of society. The opinion of objects has more influence than their real nature. The quantity of money in circulation is certainly a chief cause of its decline, but we find it is depreciated more than five times as much as it ought to be by this rule. The excess is derived from opinion, a want of confidence. In like manner we deceive ourselves when we suppose the value will increase in proportion as the quantity is lessened. Opinion will operate here also, and a thousand circumstances may promote or counteract the principle.

The other plan proposed is to convert the loan into merchandize and import it on public account. This plan is incomparably better than the former. Instead of losing on the sale of its specie or bills, the public would gain a considerable profit on the commodities imported. The loan would go much further this way towards supplying the expenses of the war, and a large stock of valuable commodities useful to the army and to the country would be introduced. This would affect the prices of things in general and assist the currency. But the arts of monopolizers would prevent its having so extensive and durable an influence as it ought to have. . . .

This is a plan not altogether to be rejected. With prudent management it might enable us to carry on the war two or three years (which perhaps is as long as it may last) but if we should expect more from it, the restoration of the currency, we should be disappointed.

The only plan that can preserve the currency is one that will make it the *immediate* interest of the monied men to cooperate with government in its support. This country is in the same predicament in which France was previous to the famous Mississippi scheme projected by Mr. Law. Its paper money like ours had dwindled to nothing, and no efforts of the government could revive it because the people had lost all confidence in its ability. Mr. Law, who had much more penetration than integrity, readily perceived that no plan could succeed which did not unite the interest and credit of rich individuals with those of the state; and upon this he framed the idea of his project, which so far agreed in principle with the bank of England. The foundation was good but the superstructure too vast. The proprietors aimed at unlimited wealth and the government itself expected too much, which was the cause of the ultimate miscarriage of the scheme and of all the mischiefs that befell the Kingdom in consequence.

It will be our wisdom to select what is good in this plan and in any others that have gone before us, avoiding their defects and excesses. Something on a similar principle in America will alone accomplish the restoration of paper credit, and establish a permanent fund for the future exigencies of government.

1. Article 1st The plan I would propose is that of an American bank instituted by authority of Congress for ten years under the denomination of The Bank of The United States.
2. A foreign loan makes a necessary part of the plan; but this I am persuaded we can obtain if we pursue the proper measures. I shall suppose it to amount to 2000000 £ Sterling. This loan to be thrown into the Bank as a part of its stock.
3. A subscription to be opened for 200.000.000 of dollars and the subscribers erected into a company called the company of the Bank of the United States. . . .
7. All the money issued from the bank to be of the same denomination and on the same terms.
8. The Bank to furnish Congress with an annual loan of two millions sterling if they have occasion for it at 4 percent interest.
9. The whole, or such part of the stock as is judged necessary, to be employed in commerce, in the manner and on the terms which shall be agreed upon from time to time between the Company and a Board of Trade to be appointed by Congress.
10. The Bank to issue occasionally by permission of Congress such sums as may be thought safe and expedient in private loans on good securities at 6 percent interest.
11. The government to share one half of the whole stock and profits of the Bank.
12. The Bank to be managed by the trustees of the company under the inspection of the Board of Trade, who may have recourse to the company books whenever they think proper, to examine the state of its affairs. The same is done in England and in other countries where banks are established, and is a privilege which the Government has a right to demand for its own security. It is the more necessary in this case from the commercial nature of the bank. . . .

The national debt on this plan will stand thus at the end of three years.

| | |
|---|---:|
| Foreign loan | 2.000.000 |
| Domestic loan at 2 Millions per annum | 6.000.000 |
| Interest at 4 per Cent | 320.000 |
| | 8.320.000 |
| Half the value of the Bank | 7.900.000 |
| Balance against the United States | £ 420.000 |

We may therefore by means of this establishment carry on the war three years and only incur a debt of 420.000 £ over and above the Guarantee of the subscription money, which however is not to be paid 'till the end of ten years.

I have said in one place that abstract calculations in questions of finance are not to be relied on, and as the complex operations of trade are involved in the present plan, I am myself diffident of those flattering results which it presents at every step. I am aware how apt the imagination is to be heated in projects of this nature and to overlook the fallacies which often lurk in first principles. But when I consider on the other hand, that this scheme stands on the firm footing of public and private faith, that it links the interests of the state in an intimate connection with those of the rich individuals belonging to it, that it turns the wealth and influence of both into a commercial channel for mutual benefit, which must afford advantages not to be estimated, that there is a defect of circulating medium which this plan supplies by a sort of creative power converting what is so produced into a real and efficacious instrument of Trade; I say, when I consider these things and many more that might be added, I cannot forbear feeling a degree of confidence in the plan, and at least hoping that it is capable of being improved into something that will give relief to our finances. . . .

I give one half the whole property of the bank to The United States because it is not only just but desirable to both parties. The United States contribute a great part of the stock; their authority is essential to the existence of the Bank; their credit is pledged for its support. The plan would ultimately fail if the terms were too favorable to the company and too hard upon Government. It might be encumbered with a debt which it could never pay and be obliged to take refuge in a bankruptcy. The share which the state has in the profits will induce it to grant more ample privileges, without which the trade of the company might often be under restrictions injurious to its success.

It is not perhaps absolutely necessary that the sum subscribed should be so considerable as I have stated it, though the larger the better: It is only necessary it should be considerable enough to engage a sufficient number of the principal monied men in the scheme. But Congress must take care to proportion the advantages they give and receive.

It may be objected that this plan will be prejudicial to trade by making the Government a party with a trading company, which may be a temptation to arrogate exclusive privileges and thereby fetter that spirit of enterprise and competition on which the prosperity of commerce depends. But Congress may satisfy the jealousies on this head by a solemn resolution not to grant exclusive privileges, which alone can make the objection valid. Large trading companies must be beneficial to the commerce of a nation when they are not invested with these, because they furnish a capital with which the most extensive enterprises may be undertaken. There is no doubt the establishment proposed would be very serviceable at this juncture merely in a commercial view; for private adventurers are not a match for the numerous obstacles resulting from the present posture of affairs.

The present plan is the product of some reading on the subjects of commerce and finance and of occasional reflections on our particular situation, but a want of leisure has prevented its being examined in so many lights, and digested so maturely as its importance requires. If the outlines are thought worthy of attention and any difficulties occur which demand explanation, or if the plan be approved and the further thoughts of the writer are desired, a letter directed to James Montague Esqr. lodged in the Post Office at Morris Town will be a safe channel of any communications you may think proper to make and an immediate answer will be given. Though the Writer has reasons which make him unwilling to be known, if a personal conference with him should be thought material, he will endeavor to comply.

You will consider this as a hasty production and excuse the incorrectness with which it abounds.

I am Sir very respectfully    Your most Obedt &    humble serv

# CHAPTER TWO

# To James Duane
# (September 3, 1780)

*I sit down to give you my ideas of the defects of our present system and the changes necessary to save us from ruin.*

IN THIS LETTER to James Duane, a member of Congress from New York, Hamilton sought to save his adopted country from ruin by giving policy recommendations. Many of the arguments laid out here Hamilton reiterated in the call for a constitutional convention, in the *Federalist*, and in defense of several controversial policy recommendations he made early in the Washington administration.

Hamilton perceived that the main problem with the war effort was Congress's lack of de facto power. The states jealously guarded their own prerogatives while Congress proved too "timid and indecisive" to effectively wield the limited powers it expressly possessed. Hamilton argued that Congress could exert far more power than it hitherto had because "undefined powers are discretionary powers, limited only by the object for which they were given—in the present case, the independence and freedom of America." Congress, in other words, was already "vested with full power to preserve the republic from harm" and had already declared war and independence, made treaties with foreign powers, and issued money, acts of complete sovereignty the legitimacy of which "were never disputed, and ought to have been a standard for the whole conducts of Administration." Yet Congress continued to act indecisively when it came to actually prosecuting the war.

The Articles of Confederation had not yet been ratified but, Hamilton told Duane, they needed to be altered because the proposed frame of government was "neither fit for war, nor peace." Most appallingly, should any policy disagreement arise between Congress and any of the individual states, the latter would prevail, rendering the "union feeble and precarious." "The confederation," Hamilton complained, gave the state legislatures the "power of the purse too entirely," and "that power, which holds the purse strings absolutely, must rule."

Instead of a national military that would form "an essential cement of the union," the Articles gave the states "too much influence in the affairs of the army." The framers feared a national military would prove "dangerous to liberty" but Hamilton believed that the nation ran "much greater risk of having a weak and disunited federal government, than one which will be able to usurp upon the rights of the people." Without substantive reform, Hamilton argued, the states would soon "cut each other's throats." Some states, Hamilton warned, were already bickering about borders and reluctant to contribute to the war effort.

Ironically, Congress also caused problems by meddling "too much with details of every sort." Instead of serving as a "deliberative corps," as it should have, it attempted "to play the executive." It was impossible for a large group like Congress, which was "constantly fluctuating," to "ever act with sufficient decision, or with system." The use of boards instead of individual executive officers was just as bad because the best men had few motives to serve on a board. "Offices of real trust and importance," by contrast, would be readily taken up by individuals with "ambition." Such persons would take care of the details of administration without diminishing Congress's power. Hamilton here presaged the role of cabinet officers in the future government under the Constitution.

Much was riding on Congress, Hamilton noted, especially the fate of the army, which had devolved into "a mob . . . without clothing, without pay, without provision, without morals, without discipline."

The state supply requisition system then in place, Hamilton warned, was creating a "ruinous extremity of want" that could lead to a dissolution of the army.

"To extricate our affairs from their present deplorable situation," Hamilton proposed several remedies. First, Congress must exercise "powers competent to the public exigencies," either by assuming they had already been granted, as already suggested, or "by calling immediately a convention of all the states with full authority to conclude finally upon a general confederation." The former was preferable but unlikely, while the latter, a convention of the states to reform American government, had to be done "the sooner, the better" because the nation's disorders were too violent to admit of delay.

Hamilton here had made the first call by any American leader for a constitutional convention. But he would have to wait almost seven years before others would agree with him and make the call. He wanted the convention to cede "unoccupied lands" claimed by states outside their borders to the national government for purposes of revenue, and the states began to do this under the Confederation before the Philadelphia convention in 1787.[1]

In particular, the convention should grant Congress virtually complete sovereignty and allow it to exercise a long list of powers, including the power to establish banks and to raise "perpetual revenues, productive and easy of collection." Hamilton's long list bears a striking resemblance to Article I, Section 8, of the U.S. Constitution promulgated seven years later (see note 2 to this chapter).

Congress should also fill important offices, including those of secretary for foreign affairs, "President of war," and "Financier," with "men of the first abilities, property and character."

Next, Hamilton considered four methods of financing the war: a foreign loan, heavy taxes paid in money, taxes paid in kind, and "a bank founded on public and private credit." The need for a foreign loan was obviously unavoidable, Hamilton argued, blaming Congress for not taking the proper measures "in earnest early enough, to procure a loan abroad." Heavy pecuniary taxes, paid in paper money, were also necessary but could not "over burthen the people" because paper money was rapidly becoming worthless. For that reason, a tax in kind, in the form of products needed by the army—such as horses and hogs, corn and wheat—was necessary. Hamilton noted that in-kind taxation was "done in all those countries which are not commercial, in Russia, Prussia, Denmark Sweden &c." and sketched a detailed plan to collect such a tax in America as efficiently as possible. He knew that in-kind taxation was inherently inefficient but noted that "we cannot proceed without it."

As in his previous letter (chapter 1), Hamilton then broached the topic of a bank "founded on the joint basis of public and private credit." To work, Hamilton argued, such a bank had "to engage the monied interest," by which he meant it had to induce wealthy men to invest in its stock in exchange for a proportionate amount of the institution's profits. He cited the Bank of England and the Bank of Amsterdam as examples. What had hitherto prevented the creation of an American bank along similar lines was a want of "confidence in the government." Should Congress follow his proposals, he predicted, a bank would soon form and "give a new spring to our affairs."

Hamilton then sketched the outline of a bank that looked more like the Bank of the United States (1791–1811, discussed in chapter 10) than the Bank of North America (est. 1781), the Bank of New York (est. 1784, discussed in chapter 5), or the other early commercial banks set up during and immediately after the war. One major difference, and flaw, in this sketch was the issuance of paper money bearing interest. Hamilton would later realize that people would hoard interest-bearing notes, which therefore could not serve as a medium of exchange. He again hoped that the government would use a foreign loan to help capitalize the bank. Here, unlike in the previous letter (chapter 1), Hamilton would allow the bank to open branches in different cities and states. This became a feature of the Bank of the United States that he would recommend Congress create in 1790.

In his conclusion, Hamilton argued that mere implementation of his ideas on governmental reform and finance would be sufficient to restore confidence in government and the nation's currency. Key, he argued, was the manner in which his policies were implemented because "Men are governed by opinion" which is "as much influenced by appearances as by realities."

Hamilton's 1780 letter to Duane provides a rather accurate forecast of the major developments that would occur in the United States during the decade that followed.

Our abridgement of this 7,067-word letter runs to 3,710 words.

[Liberty Pole, New Jersey, September 3, 1780]

Dr. Sir

Agreeably to your request and my promise, I sit down to give you my ideas of the defects of our present system and the changes necessary to save us from ruin. They may perhaps be the reveries of a projector rather than the sober views of a politician. You will judge of them, and make what use you please of them.

The fundamental defect is a want of power in Congress. It is hardly worthwhile to show in what this consists as it seems to be universally acknowledged, or to point out how it has happened, as the only question is how to remedy it. It may, however, be said that it has originated from three causes—an excess of the spirit of liberty which has made the particular states show a jealousy of all power not in their own hands; and this jealousy has led them to exercise a right of judging in the last resort of the measures recommended by Congress, and of acting according to their own opinions of their propriety or necessity; a diffidence in Congress of their own powers, by which they have been timid and indecisive in their resolutions, constantly making concessions to the states till they have scarcely left themselves the shadow of power; a want of sufficient means at their disposal to answer the public exigencies and of vigor to draw forth those means, which have occasioned them to depend on the states individually to fulfill their engagements with the army, and the consequence of which has been to ruin their influence and credit with the army, to establish its dependence on each state separately rather than *on them*, that is, rather than on the whole collectively.

It may be pleaded that Congress had never any definitive powers granted them, and of course could exercise none—could do nothing more than recommend. The manner in which Congress was appointed would warrant, and the public good required, that they should have considered themselves as vested with full power *to preserve the republic from harm*. They have done many of the highest acts of sovereignty, which were always cheerfully submitted to—the declaration of independence, the declaration of war, the levying an army, creating a navy, emitting money, making alliances with foreign powers, appointing a dictator &c. &c.—all these implications of a complete sovereignty were never disputed, and ought to have been a standard for the whole conduct of Administration. . . .

But the confederation itself is defective and requires to be altered; it is neither fit for war, nor peace. The idea of an uncontrollable sovereignty in each state, over its internal police, will defeat the other powers given to Congress, and make our union feeble and precarious. . . .

The confederation gives the states individually too much influence in the affairs of the army; they should have nothing to do with it. The entire formation and disposal of our military forces ought to belong to Congress. It is an essential cement of the union; and it ought to be the policy of Congress to destroy all ideas of state attachments in the army and make it look up wholly to them. For this purpose all appointments, promotions, and provisions whatsoever ought to be made by them. It may be apprehended that this may be dangerous to liberty. But nothing appears more evident to me than that we run much greater risk of having a weak and disunited federal government, than one which will be able to usurp upon the rights of the people. Already some of the lines of the army would obey their states in opposition to Congress, notwithstanding the pains we have taken to preserve the unity of the army—if anything would hinder this it would be the personal influence of the General, a melancholy and mortifying consideration. . . .

Our own experience should satisfy us. We have felt the difficulty of drawing out the resources of the country and inducing the states to combine in equal exertions for the common cause. The ill success of our last attempt is striking. Some have done a great deal, others little or scarcely anything. The disputes about boundaries &c. testify how flattering a prospect we have of future tranquility if we do not frame in time a confederacy capable of deciding the differences and compelling the obedience of the respective members.

The confederation too gives the power of the purse too entirely to the state legislatures. It should provide perpetual funds in the disposal of Congress—by a land tax, poll tax, or the like. All imposts upon commerce ought to be laid by Congress and appropriated to their use, for without certain revenues a government can have no power; that power which holds the purse strings absolutely must rule. This seems to be a medium, which without making Congress altogether independent will tend to give reality to its authority.

Another defect in our system is want of method and energy in the administration. This has partly resulted from the other defect, but in a great degree from prejudice and the want of a proper executive. Congress have kept the power too much into their own hands and have meddled too much with details of every sort. Congress is properly a deliberative corps, and it forgets itself when it attempts to play the executive. It is impossible such a body, numerous as it is, constantly fluctuating, can ever act with sufficient decision, or with system. . . .

Lately Congress, convinced of these inconveniences, have gone into the measure of appointing boards. But this is in my opinion a bad plan. A single man in each department of the administration would be greatly preferable. It would give us a chance of more knowledge, more activity, more responsibility, and of course more zeal and attention. Boards partake of a part of the inconveniencies of larger assemblies. Their decisions are slower, their energy less, their responsibility more diffused. They will not have the same abilities and knowledge as an administration by single men. . . .

A third defect is the fluctuating constitution of our army. This has been a pregnant source of evil; all our military misfortunes, three fourths of our civil embarrassments are to be ascribed to it. . . .

The imperfect and unequal provision made for the army is a fourth defect. . . . Without a speedy change the army must dissolve; it is now a mob rather than an army, without clothing, without pay, without provision, without morals, without discipline. We begin to hate the country for its neglect of us; the country begins to hate us for our oppressions of them. Congress have long been jealous of us; we have now lost all confidence in them, and give the worst construction to all they do. Held together by the slenderest ties we are ripening for a dissolution.

The present mode of supplying the army—by state purchases—is not one of the least considerable defects of our system. It is too precarious a dependence, because the states will never be sufficiently impressed with our necessities. Each will make its own ease a primary object, the supply of the army a secondary one. . . .

These are the principal defects in the present system that now occur to me. There are many inferior ones in the organization of particular departments and many errors of administration which might be pointed out; but the task would be troublesome and tedious, and if we had once remedied those I have mentioned, the others would not be attended with much difficulty.

I shall now propose the remedies which appear to me applicable to our circumstances, and necessary to extricate our affairs from their present deplorable situation.

The first step must be to give Congress powers competent to the public exigencies. This may happen in two ways, one by resuming and exercising the discretionary powers I suppose to have been originally vested in them for the safety of the states and resting their conduct on the candor of their countrymen and the necessity of the conjuncture: the other by calling immediately a convention of all the states with full authority to conclude finally upon a general confederation, stating to them beforehand explicitly the evils arising from a want of power in Congress, and the impossibility of supporting the contest on its present footing, that the delegates may come possessed of proper sentiments as well as proper authority to give to the meeting. Their commission should include a right of vesting Congress with the whole or a proportion of the unoccupied lands, to be employed for the purpose of raising a revenue, reserving the jurisdiction to the states by whom they are granted.

The first plan, I expect will be thought too bold an expedient by the generality of Congress; and indeed their practice hitherto has so riveted the opinion of their want of power, that the success of this experiment may very well be doubted.

I see no objection to the other mode that has any weight in competition with the reasons for it. The Convention should assemble the 1st of November next, the sooner, the better; our disorders are too violent to admit of a common or lingering remedy. . . . I ask that the Convention should have a power of vesting the whole or a part of the unoccupied land in Congress because it is necessary that body should have some property as a fund for the arrangements of finance; and I know of no other kind that can be given them.

The confederation in my opinion should give Congress complete sovereignty, except as to that part of internal police, which relates to the rights of property and life among individuals and to raising money by internal taxes. It is necessary that everything belonging to this should be regulated by the state legislatures. Congress should have complete sovereignty in all that relates to war, peace, trade, finance, and to the management of foreign affairs; the right of declaring war, of raising armies, officering, paying them, directing their motions in every respect, of equipping fleets and doing the same with them, of building fortifications, arsenals, magazines &c. &c.; of making peace on such conditions as they think proper; of regulating trade, determining with what countries it shall be carried on, granting indulgencies laying prohibitions on all the articles of export or import, imposing duties, granting bounties & premiums for raising exporting, importing, and applying to their own use the product of these duties, only giving credit to the states on whom they are raised in the general account of revenues and expenses; instituting Admiralty courts &c.; of coining money, establishing banks on such terms, and with such privileges as they think proper; appropriating funds and doing whatever else relates to the operations of finance; transacting everything with foreign nations, making alliances offensive and defensive, treaties of commerce, &c. &c.[2]

The confederation should provide certain perpetual revenues productive and easy of collection, a land tax, poll tax or the like, which together with the duties on trade and the unallocated lands would give Congress a substantial existence, and a stable foundation for their schemes of finance. What more supplies were necessary should be occasionally demanded of the states, in the present mode of quotas.

The second step I would recommend is that Congress should instantly appoint the following great officers of state—A secretary for foreign affairs—a President of war—A President of Marine—A Financier—A President of trade; instead of this last a board of Trade may be preferable as the regulations of trade are slow and gradual, and require prudence and experience (more than other qualities), for which boards are very well adapted.

Congress should choose for these offices men of the first abilities, property, and character in the continent—and such as have had the best opportunities of being acquainted with the several branches. . . .

In my opinion a plan of this kind would be of inconceivable utility to our affairs; its benefits would be very speedily felt. It would give new life and energy to the operations of government. Business would be conducted with dispatch method and system. A million of abuses now existing would be corrected, and judicious plans would be formed and executed for the public good. . . .

The providing of supplies is the pivot of everything else (though a well constituted army would not in a small degree conduce to this, by giving consistency and weight to government). There are four ways all which must be united—a foreign loan, heavy pecuniary taxes, a tax in kind, a bank founded on public and private credit.

As to a foreign loan, I dare say Congress are doing everything in their power to obtain it. The most effectual way will be to tell France that without it, we must make terms with Great Britain. This must be done with plainness and firmness, but with respect and without petulance, not as a menace, but as a candid declaration of our circumstances. We need not fear to be deserted by France. . . .

Concerning the necessity of heavy pecuniary taxes I need say nothing, as it is a point in which everybody is agreed; nor is there any danger that the product of any taxes raised in this way will over burthen the people, or exceed the wants of the public. . . .

As to a tax in kind, the necessity of it results from this principle—that the money in circulation is not a sufficient representative of the productions of the country, and consequently no revenues raised from it as a medium can be a competent representative of that part of the products of the country which it is bound to contribute to the support of the public. The public therefore to obtain its due or satisfy its just demands, and its wants must call for a part of those products themselves. This is done in all those countries which are not commercial, in Russia, Prussia, Denmark Sweden &c., and is peculiarly necessary in our case. . . .

How far it may be practicable to erect a bank on the joint credit of the public and of individuals can only be certainly determined by the experiment; but it is of so much importance that the experiment ought to be fully tried. . . .

Paper credit never was long supported in any country, on a national scale, where it was not founded on the joint basis of public and private credit. An attempt to establish it on public credit alone in France under the auspices of Mr. Law had nearly ruined the kingdom; we have seen the effects of it in America, and every successive experiment proves the futility of the attempt. Our new money is depreciating almost as fast as the old, though it has in some states as real funds as paper money ever had. The reason is that the monied men have not an immediate interest to uphold its credit. They may even in many ways find it their interest to undermine it. The only certain manner to obtain a permanent paper credit is to engage the monied interest immediately in it by making them contribute the whole or part of the stock and giving them the whole or part of the profits.

The invention of banks on the modern principle originated in Venice. There the public and a company of monied men are mutually concerned. The Bank of England unites public authority and faith with private credit; and hence we see what a vast fabric of paper credit is raised on a visionary basis. Had it not been for this, England would never have found sufficient funds to carry on her wars; but with the help of this she has done and is doing wonders. The bank of Amsterdam is on a similar foundation.

And why can we not have an American bank? Are our monied men less enlightened to their own interest or less enterprising in the pursuit? I believe the fault is in our government, which does not exert itself to engage them in such a scheme. It is true the individuals in America are not very rich, but this would not prevent their instituting a bank; it would only prevent its being done with such ample funds as in other countries. Have they not sufficient confidence in the government and in the issue of the cause? Let the Government endeavor to inspire that confidence by adopting the measures I have recommended or others equivalent to them. Let it exert itself to procure a solid confederation, to establish a good plan of executive administration, to form a permanent military force, to obtain at all events a foreign loan.

If these things were in a train of vigorous execution, it would give a new spring to our affairs; government would recover its respectability and individuals would renounce their diffidence. . . .

The first step to establishing the bank will be to engage a number of monied men of influence to relish the project and make it a business. The subscribers to that lately established are the fittest persons that can be found; and their plan may be interwoven.

The outlines of my plan would be to open subscriptions in all the states for the stock, which we will suppose to be one million of pounds. Real property of every kind, as well as specie should be deemed good stock, but at least a fourth part of the subscription should be in specie or plate. There should be one great company in three divisions in Virginia, Philadelphia, and at Boston or two at Philadelphia and Boston. The bank should have a right to issue bank notes bearing two per Cent interest for the whole of their stock; but not to exceed it. These notes may be payable every three months or oftener, and the faith of government must be pledged for the support of the bank. It must therefore have a right from time to time to inspect its operations, and must appoint inspectors for the purpose.

The advantages of the bank may consist in this, in the profits of the contracts made with government, which should bear interest to be annually paid in specie, in the loan of money at interest say six per Cent, in purchasing lives by annuities as practiced in England &c. The benefit resulting to the company is evident from the consideration, that they may employ in circulation a great deal more money than they have specie in stock, on the credit of the real property which they will have in other use; this money will be employed either in fulfilling their contracts with the public by which also they will gain a profit, or in loans at an advantageous interest or in annuities. . . .

If Government can obtain a foreign loan, it should lend to the bank on easy terms to extend its influence and facilitate a compliance with its engagements. If government could engage the states to raise a sum of money in specie to be deposited in bank in the same manner, it would be of the greatest consequence. If government could prevail on the enthusiasm of the people to make a contribution in plate for the same purpose, it would be a master stroke. Things of this kind sometimes succeed in popular contests; and if undertaken with address; I should not despair of its success; but I should not be sanguine.

The bank may be instituted for a term of years by way of trial and the particular privilege of coining money be for a term still shorter. . . .

A bank of this kind even in its commencement would answer the most valuable purposes to government and to the proprietors; in its progress the advantages will exceed calculation. It will promote commerce by furnishing a more extensive medium which we greatly want in our circumstances. I mean a more extensive valuable medium. We have an enormous nominal one at this time; but it is only a name. . . .

If a Convention is called, the minds of all the states and the people ought to be prepared to receive its determinations by sensible and popular writings, which should conform to the views of Congress. There are epochs in human affairs, when *novelty* even is useful. If a general opinion prevails that the old way is bad, whether true or false, and this obstructs or relaxes the operation of the public service, a change is necessary if it be but for the sake of change. This is exactly the case now. 'Tis a universal sentiment that our present system is a bad one, and that things do not go right on this account. The measure of a Convention would revive the hopes of the people and give a new direction to their passions, which may be improved in carrying points of substantial utility. . . .

And, in future, My Dear Sir, two things let me recommend as fundamental rules for the conduct of Congress—to attach the army to them by every motive, to maintain an air of authority (not domineering) in all their measures with the states. The manner in which a thing is done has more influence than is commonly imagined. Men are governed by opinion; this opinion is as much influenced by appearances as by realities; if a Government appears to be confident of its own powers, it is the surest way to inspire the same confidence in others; if it is diffident, it may be certain there will be a still greater diffidence in others, and that its authority will not only be distrusted, controverted, but contemned. . . .

You will perceive My Dear Sir this letter is hastily written and with a confidential freedom, not as to a member of Congress, whose feelings may be sore at the prevailing clamors; but as to a friend who is in a situation to remedy public disorders, who wishes for nothing so much as truth, and who is desirous of information, even from those less capable of judging than himself. I have not even time to correct and copy, and only enough to add that I am very truly and affectionately D Sir    Your most Obed ser

A. Hamilton
Liberty Pole

Sept. 3d 1780

# CHAPTER THREE

# To Robert Morris
# (April 30, 1781)

*Most commercial nations have found it necessary*
*to institute banks, and they have proved to be the happiest*
*engines that ever were invented for advancing trade.*

IN THIS LETTER to Philadelphia merchant Robert Morris, Hamilton correctly claimed (as in the previous letter to James Duane, chapter 2) to be "among the first who were convinced, that an administration by single men was essential to the proper management" of the nation's affairs. That was because the American people, as well as the nation's European allies, had lost confidence in America's "public councils" as then constituted. Congress apparently agreed, because it had recently decided to ask Morris to become its Superintendent of Finance. Morris, Hamilton believed, was precisely the right man for the job. Independence, Hamilton told Morris, rested more on "introducing order into our finances—by restoring public credit" than on "gaining battles." Finance—public credit—was the key to winning the war.

Hamilton therefore hoped that Congress and Morris could come to a mutually satisfactory agreement regarding Morris's nomination as Superintendent of Finance. Expecting that "all difficulties" would be removed and that Morris would be appointed, Hamilton proffered the great merchant his policy advice while simultaneously admitting that he was not "an able financier" for want of sufficient time and suitable "materials to make accurate calculations." Hamilton nevertheless hoped that Morris would find something useful in his admittedly "crude and defective" plan.

"The first step," Hamilton argued, was to estimate and then compare the government's "capacity for revenue" with its necessary civil and military expenditures. Two methods for estimating potential maximum government revenues occurred to Hamilton: international comparisons and extrapolation from the states that had been "most earnest in taxation." After applying both methods, Hamilton concluded that "between six and seven Millions of dollars is the proper revenue of these states," or, in other words, the taxable capacity of the United States.

Next, Hamilton tackled the problem of government expenditures. He thought $2.5 million sufficient for the civil list (governors, judges, legislators for all the states) and $8 million enough to keep an army of 20,000 in the field. If annual expenses were about $11 million and potential tax revenues were roughly $7 million, there would be a deficit of around $4 million that would have to be financed from loans, foreign and/or domestic.

Credit from abroad, Hamilton predicted, would not meet the nation's needs. The governments of France, Spain, and the Dutch Republic were themselves too extended to meet America's financial needs. Wealthy European investors had plenty of money to buy American securities but sought only profit and hence could not be induced to invest in America under present conditions. Wealthy Americans were too few to fund the deficit by themselves and, like the European investors, suffered a "want of confidence" in American governments. They were better off investing "in traffic [commerce] than by merely lending it on interest."

To overcome all of these difficulties, Hamilton argued, Morris had to move quickly to establish a "National Bank" that would offer investors higher risk-adjusted returns than available elsewhere. Delay would move public credit closer to "catastrophe."

Banks, like all other human tools, could be abused, Hamilton conceded. "But no wise statesman," he retorted, "will reject the good from an apprehension of the ill." Wisdom meant "availing ourselves of the good, and guarding as much as possible against the bad."

The national bank would bring much good, in the form of "public and private credit." Public credit was the key to having a strong government, while private credit was the spring of commerce, industry, and agriculture. Most commercial nations had formed banks, which proved time and again "to be the happiest engines that ever were invented for advancing trade." In other words, credit made economies grow.

Without the Bank of England, Hamilton suggested, Britain would not be able to "menace . . . independence." In fact, Britain owed its own independence from absolute monarchy to the Bank of England, which saved King William's administration in the dark days after the Glorious Revolution of 1688.

Hamilton next warned Morris that many Americans had grown wary of all forms of paper money because of their recent experiences with the rapid depreciation of government-issued bills of credit. Yet some form of paper money Hamilton thought essential to the smooth functioning of the economy. Without it, people would resort to inefficient modes of transacting, like barter. Cash served a role analogous to the "regular circulation of the blood" in animals. The only way to keep the economy alive, then, was to "fix the value of the currency we now have and increase it to a proper standard in a species that will have the requisite stability." That would require, Hamilton argued, a bank to redeem the paper money in specie. Paper bills of credit such as Continental currency and state issues had depreciated because the government had no funds to support them and they were "not upheld by private credit." Paper banknotes, by contrast, would be convertible to gold or silver and find support from stockholders and other wealthy men.

Hamilton then proffered a detailed plan for his national bank, accompanied by copious notes or remarks explaining the rationale behind each proposed charter article. The details of the plan cover ten pages of the Morris letter in *The Papers of Alexander Hamilton* and are omitted in the condensation that follows. In an elaboration of the ideas previously presented to an unknown recipient and Duane (see chapters 1 and 2), Hamilton's brilliant administrative mind shone brightest, developing workable, concrete ideas from first principles. He would later backtrack on some of his recommendations, particularly regarding stock subscriptions collateralized with "good landed security." Other ideas, such as making the national government and each state government "responsible for all the transactions of the bank conjointly with the private proprietors" also were not implemented.

The payment of interest on large denomination notes was likewise rejected, as was the idea of giving the bank the power to mint coins. Nevertheless, some of Hamilton's suggestions ended up in the charter of Morris's own national bank, the Bank of North America, which began operations in early 1782 as a joint stock corporation with transferable shares, as Hamilton had called for in his detailed plan. Establishment of such a bank, Hamilton confidently predicted, would clinch independence. Ergo, no man should feel any trepidation about investing in it. "All we have to fear," he argued, was not fear itself but "the want of money" leading to the disbanding of the army. Here Hamilton proved particularly prescient as the Bank of North America did help to keep the Continental armed forces together long enough to prevent any British attempt to recoup its disastrous loss at Yorktown.

"Tis evident," Hamilton argued, "they [the British] have it not in their power to subdue us by force of arms." The only thing that could defeat America was itself, by means of imbecilic government. With the help of 5,000 French troops in Rhode Island, even 15,000 American troops would be sufficient to keep the British garrisoned in "one or two capital points," which would "destroy the national expectation of success" and hence popular support for the war, which required "splendid Successes" to fill loan subscriptions. With British taxation already at its "extreme boundary" and British debts forming an "enormous mass" of funded and unfunded obligations, only "flattering events" prevented "despair." Several months before fighting at the battle of Yorktown, Hamilton sensed that the strains of a long war were wearing on the British. Britain's defeat at Yorktown did cause despair, leading to peace negotiations that would recognize U.S. independence.

"Never did a nation unite more circumstances in its favor than we do," Hamilton argued, before stressing again that "we have nothing against us but our own misconduct." The two internal foes were the complacency of a set of men who fancied "every thing in perfect Security" and the despondency of another set of men who were "alarmed by partial misfortunes, and the disordered state of our finances."

The rebelling states would be able to repay their debts, Hamilton confidently predicted, even if the war lasted three more years and even if their economies stagnated, which was highly unlikely. The population would probably at least double in thirty years, helped by "a confluence of emigrants from all parts of the world" and the "proportional progress" of commerce. In all likelihood, "it will be a matter of choice, if we are not out of debt in twenty years, without at all encumbering the people," he concluded.

Hamilton, unlike most other American leaders, saw some advantages in the national debt. "A national debt if it is not excessive will be to us a national blessing; it will be powerful cement of our union." It would also "be a spur to industry" without creating hardships. Hamilton thought Americans labored less than Europeans, and if they had to pay some taxes to service the debts that established their independence they might work harder, which he deemed a good outcome. Hamilton then apologized for writing so much and signed off.

We have condensed this 12,300-word letter to 3,746 words.

[De Peyster's Point, New York, April 30, 1781]

Sir,
I was among the first who were convinced that an administration by single men was essential to the proper management of the affairs of this country. I am persuaded now it is the only resource we have to extricate ourselves from the distresses which threaten the subversion of our cause. It is palpable that the people have lost all confidence in our public councils, and it is a fact of which, I dare say, you are as well apprised as myself that our friends in Europe are in the same disposition. . . .

With respect to ourselves, there is so universal and rooted a diffidence of the government, that if we could be assured the future measures of Congress would be dictated by the most perfect wisdom and public spirit, there would be still a necessity for a change in the forms of our administration to give a new spring and current to the passions and hopes of the people.

To me it appears evident that an executive ministry composed of men with the qualifications I have described would speedily restore the credit of government abroad and at home, would induce our allies to greater exertions in our behalf, would inspire confidence in monied men in Europe as well as in America to lend us those sums of which it may be demonstrated we stand in need from the disproportion of our national wealth to the expenses of the War.

I hope, Sir, you will not consider it as a compliment when I assure you that I heard with the greatest satisfaction of your nomination to the department of finance. . . . I flatter myself Congress will not preclude the public from your services by an obstinate refusal of reasonable conditions; and as one deeply interested in the event, I am happy in believing you will not easily be discouraged from undertaking an office by which you may render America and the world no less a service than the establishment of American independence! Tis by introducing order into our finances—by restoring public credit—not by gaining battles, that we are finally to gain our object. Tis by putting ourselves in a condition to continue the war not by temporary, violent, and unnatural efforts to bring it to a decisive issue, that we shall in reality bring it to a speedy and successful one. In the frankness of truth I believe, Sir, you are the Man best capable of performing this great work.

In expectation that all difficulties will be removed, and that you will ultimately act on terms you approve, I take the liberty to submit to you some ideas relative to the object of your department. I pretend not to be an able financier; it is a part of administration which has been least in my way, and of course has least occupied my inquires and reflections. Neither have I had leisure or materials to make accurate calculations. I have been obliged to depend on memory for important facts for want of the authorities from which they are drawn. With all these disadvantages, my plan must necessarily be crude and defective; but if it may be a basis for something more perfect, or if it contains any hints that may be of use to you, the trouble I have taken myself, or may give you, will not be misapplied. . . .

The first step towards determining what ought to be done in the finances of this country is to estimate in the best manner we can its capacity for revenue, and the proportion between what it is able to afford and what it stands in need of for the expenses of its civil and military establishments. There occur to me two ways of doing this: 1st by examining what proportion the revenues of other countries have borne to their stock of wealth, and applying the rule to ourselves with proper allowance for the difference of circumstances. 2dly by comparing the result of this rule with the product of taxes in those states which have been the most in earnest in taxation. . . .

Reasonable deductions on these accounts being made will bring the two calculations to a pretty exact agreement and make them confirm each other. But were not this the case, I should be inclined in preference to trust the first as being founded on a basis better known and better ascertained by experience. I believe however we may safely conclude from both, that between six and seven Millions of dollars is the proper revenue of these states. . . .

Having formed an estimate of our ability for revenue, the next thing to be ascertained is the annual expense of our civil and military establishments. With tolerable reasoning I should suppose two millions and an half of dollars would amply suffice for the first, including the particular administration of each state. For the second judiciously managed, eight million of dollars would be adequate, calculating for an army of 20.000 men, which are as many as we shall stand in need of or be able to raise. Eleven Million of dollars will be then the amount of the annual expenses of these states. I speak on a supposition that a system were embraced well adapted to rescuing our affairs from the chaos in which they are now involved, and which while it continues must baffle all calculation.

The difference between our revenues and expenses on the preceding scale will be from four to four and a half millions of dollars, which deficiency must of course be supplied by credit, foreign or domestic, or both.

With regard to credit abroad I think we have little chance of obtaining a sufficiency nearly to answer our purpose. . . .

As to internal loans on which after all we must chiefly depend, there are two things that operate against them to any large amount—the want of a sufficient number of men with sufficient monied capitals to lend the sums required, and the want of confidence in those who are able to lend to make them willing to part with their money. It may be added, that they can employ it to greater advantage in traffic than by merely lending it on interest.

To surmount these obstacles and give individuals ability and inclination to lend in any proportion to the wants of government, a plan must be devised which by incorporating their means together and uniting them with those of the public will on the foundation of that incorporation and Union erect a mass of credit that will supply the defect of monied capitals and answer all the purposes of cash, a plan which will offer adventurers immediate advantages analogous to those they receive by employing their money in trade, and eventually greater advantages, a plan which will give them the greatest security the nature of the case will admit for what they lend, and which will not only advance their own interest and secure the independence of their country, but in its progress have the most beneficial influence upon its future commerce and be a source of national strength and wealth.

I mean the institution of a National Bank. This I regard, in some shape or other as an expedient essential to our safety and success, unless by a happy turn of European affairs the war should speedily terminate in a manner upon which it would be unwise to reckon. There is no other that can give to government that extensive and systematic credit which the defect of our revenues makes indispensably necessary to its operations. The longer it is delayed, the more difficult it becomes. . . .

I am aware of all the objections that have been made to public banks, and that they are not without enlightened and respectable opponents. But all that has been said against them only tends to prove that, like all other good things, they are subject to abuse and when abused become pernicious. The precious metals by similar arguments may be proved to be injurious; it is certain that the mines of South America have had great influence in banishing industry from Spain and sinking it in real wealth and importance. Great power, commerce and riches, or in other words great national prosperity, may in like manner be denominated evils; for they lead to insolence, an inordinate ambition, a vicious luxury, licentiousness of morals, and all those vices which corrupt government, enslave the people, and precipitate the ruin of a nation. But no wise statesman will reject the good from an apprehension of the ill. The truth is in human affairs, there is no good, pure and unmixed; every advantage has two sides, and wisdom consists in availing ourselves of the good, and guarding as much as possible against the bad.

The tendency of a national bank is to increase public and private credit. The former gives power to the state for the protection of its rights and interests, and the latter facilitates and extends the operations of commerce among individuals. Industry is increased, commodities are multiplied, agriculture and manufactures flourish, and herein consist the true wealth and prosperity of a state.

Most commercial nations have found it necessary to institute banks, and they have proved to be the happiest engines that ever were invented for advancing trade. Venice, Genoa, Hamburg, Holland, and England are examples of their utility. They owe their riches, commerce, and the figure they have made at different periods in a great degree to this source. Great Britain is indebted for the immense efforts she has been able to make in so many illustrious and successful wars essentially to that vast fabric of credit raised on this foundation. Tis by this alone she now menaces our independence.

She has indeed abused the advantage and now stands on a precipice. Her example should both persuade and warn us. 'Tis in republics where banks are most easily established and supported, and where they are least liable to abuse. Our situation will not expose us to frequent wars, and the public will have no temptation to overstrain its credit.

In my opinion we ought not to hesitate, because we have no other resource. The long and expensive wars of King William had drained England of its specie, its commerce began to droop for want of a proper medium, its taxes were unproductive and its revenues declined. The Administration wisely had recourse to the institution of a bank and it relieved the national difficulties. We are in the same and still greater want of a sufficient medium; we have little specie; the paper we have is of small value and rapidly descending to less; we are immersed in a war for our existence as a nation, for our liberty and happiness as a people; we have no revenues nor no credit. A bank if practicable is the only thing that can give us either the one or the other.

Besides these great and cardinal motives to such an institution and the advantages we should enjoy from it in common with other nations, our situation relatively to Europe and to the West Indies would give us some peculiar advantages.

Nothing is more common than for men to pass from the abuse of a good thing to the disuse of it. Some persons disgusted by the depreciation of the money are chimerical enough to imagine it would be beneficial to abolish all paper credit, annihilate the whole of what is now in circulation, and depend altogether upon our specie both for commerce and finance. The scheme is altogether visionary and in the attempt would be fatal. We have not a competent stock of specie in this country either to answer the purposes of circulation in Trade, or to serve as a basis for revenue. . . .

With respect to revenue, could the whole of our specie be drawn into the public treasury annually, we have seen that it would be little more than one half of our annual expense. But this would be impracticable; it has never been effected in any country. Where the numeracy of a country is a sufficient representative, there is only a certain proportion of it that can be drawn out of daily circulation because without the necessary quantity of Cash, a stagnation of business would ensue. . . .

But waving the objections on this head, there would still remain a balance of four millions of dollars more than these states can furnish in revenue, which must be provided for the yearly expense of the war. How is this to be procured without a paper credit to supply the deficiency of specie and enable the monied men to lend? This question I apprehend will be of no easy solution.

In the present system of things the health of a state, particularly a commercial one, depends on a due quantity and regular circulation of Cash, as much as the health of an animal body depends upon the due quantity and regular circulation of the blood. There are indisputable indications that we have not a sufficient medium and what we have is in continual fluctuation. The only cure to our public disorders is to fix the value of the currency we now have and increase it to a proper standard in a species that will have the requisite stability.

The error of those who would explode paper money altogether originates in not making proper distinctions. Our paper was in its nature liable to depreciations because it had no funds for its support and was not upheld by private credit. . . . No paper credit can be substantial or durable which has not funds and which does not unite immediately the interest and influence of the monied men in its establishment and preservation. A credit begun on this basis will in process of time greatly exceed its funds, but this requires time and a well settled opinion in its favor. 'Tis in a National Bank alone that we can find the ingredients to constitute a wholesome, solid and beneficial paper credit.

I am aware that in the present temper of men's minds it will be no easy task to inspire a relish for a project of this kind, but much will depend on the address and personal credit of the proposer. In your hands I should not despair . . . The men of property in America are enlightened about their own interest and would easily be brought to see the advantages of a good plan. They ought not to be discouraged at what has happened heretofore when they behold the administration of our finances put into a better channel. The violations of public engagements hitherto have proceeded more from a necessity produced by ignorance and mismanagement than from levity or a disregard to the obligations of good faith.

Should the success in the first instance not be as complete as the extent of the plan requires, this should not hinder its being undertaken. It is of the nature of a bank wisely instituted and wisely administered to extend itself, and from small beginnings grow to a magnitude that could not have been foreseen. The plan I propose requires a stock of three millions of pounds lawful money, but if one half the sum could be obtained, I should entertain no doubt of its full success.

It now remains to submit my plan which I rather offer as an outline than as a finished plan. It contains however the general principles. . . .

These as has been already observed are only intended as outlines; the form of administration for the bank and all other matters may be easily determined, if the leading principles are once approved. We shall find good models in the different European banks which we can accommodate to our circumstances. Great care in particular should be employed to guard against counterfeits, and I think methods may be devised that would be effectual.

I see nothing to prevent the practicability of a plan of this kind but a distrust of the final success of the War, which may make men afraid to risk any considerable part of their fortunes in the public funds, but without being an enthusiast, I will venture to assert that with such a resource as is here proposed, the loss of our Independence is impossible. All we have to fear is that the want of money may disband the army, or so perplex and enfeeble our operations as to create in the people a general disgust and alarm, which may make them clamor for peace on any terms. But if a judicious administration of our finances assisted by a bank takes place, and the ancient security of property is restored, no convulsion is to be apprehended; our opposition will soon assume an aspect of system and vigor that will relieve and encourage the people and put an end to the hopes of the enemy. Tis evident they have it not in their power to subdue us by force of arms; in all these states they have not more than fifteen thousand effective troops; nor is it possible for them much to augment this number. The east and west Indies demand reinforcements; in all the Islands they have not at this time above five thousand men, a force not more than equal to the proper garrisoning of Jamaica alone, and which the moment they lose a maritime superiority in those seas will leave them much cause to fear for their possessions. They will probably send out fifteen hundred or two thousand men to recruit their regiments already here; but this is the utmost they can do.

Our allies have five thousand men at Rhode Island, which in the worst event that can happen will be recruited to eight to cooperate with us on a defensive plan. Should our army amount to no more than fifteen thousand men, the combined forces, though not equal to the expulsion of the enemy, will be equal to the purpose of compelling them to renounce their offensive and content themselves with maintaining one or two capital points; this is on the supposition that the public have the means of putting their troops in activity. By stopping the progress of their conquests and reducing them to an unmeaning and disgraceful defensive, we destroy the national expectation of success, from which the ministry draws their resources. It is not a vague conjecture but a fact founded on the best information that had it not been for the capture of Charles Town and the victory of Camden, the Ministry would have been in the utmost embarrassment for the supplies of this year. On the credit of those events they procured a Loan of five and twenty millions. They are in a Situation where a want of splendid Successes is ruin. They have carried taxation nearly to its extreme boundary; they have mortgaged all their funds, they have a large unfunded debt, besides the enormous mass which is funded. This must necessarily create apprehensions in their most sanguine partisans, and if these are not counteracted by flattering events from time to time, they cannot much longer continue the delusion. Indeed in this case, I suppose they must themselves despair.

The game we play is a sure game, if we play it with skill. I have calculated in the preceding observations of the most disadvantageous side. Many events may turn up in the course of the summer to make even the present campaign decisive. . . .

Never did a nation unite more circumstances in its favor than we do; we have nothing against us but our own misconduct.

There are two classes of men among us equally mistaken—one who, in spite of daily experience of accumulated distress, persist in a narrow line of policy and amidst the most threatening dangers fancy everything in perfect Security; another, who judging too much from the outside, alarmed by partial misfortunes and the disordered state of our finances without estimating the real faculties of the parties, give themselves up to an ignorant and ill-founded despondency. We want to learn to appreciate our true situation and that of the enemy. This would preserve us from a Stupid insensibility to danger on the one hand, and inspire us with a reasonable and enlightened confidence on the other. . . .

A question may arise concerning the abilities of these states to pay their debts after the establishment of their independence, and though any doubt on this head must originate in gross ignorance, it may be necessary to oppose it with more than general argument as has been done heretofore. A very summary and obvious calculation will show that there is nothing to be dreaded on this head. . . .

This calculation supposes the ability of these states for revenue to continue the same as they now are, which is a supposition both false and unfavorable. Speaking within moderate bounds our population will be doubled in thirty years; there will be a confluence of emigrants from all parts of the world; our commerce will have a proportional progress, and of course our wealth and capacity for revenue. It will be a matter of choice if we are not out of debt in twenty years without at all encumbering the people.

A national debt if it is not excessive will be to us a national blessing; it will be powerful cement of our union. It will also create a necessity for keeping up taxation to a degree which without being oppressive will be a spur to industry; remote as we are from Europe and shall be from danger, it were otherwise to be feared our popular maxims would incline us to too great parsimony and indulgence. We labor less now than any civilized nation of Europe, and a habit of labor in the people is as essential to the health and vigor of their minds and bodies as it is conducive to the welfare of the State. We ought not to Suffer our self-love to deceive us in a comparison upon these points.

I have spun out this letter to a much greater length than I intended. To develop the whole connection of my ideas on the subject and place my plan in the clearest light I have indulged myself in many observations which might have been omitted. I shall not longer intrude upon your patience than to assure you of the sincere sentiments of esteem with which I have the honor to be   Sir   Your most Obedient   and humble servant

Alx Hamilton

# CHAPTER FOUR

# The Continentalist
# (1781–1782)

*There is something noble and magnificent in the
perspective of a great Federal Republic, closely linked
in the pursuit of a common interest, tranquil and
prosperous at home, respectable abroad.*

HAMILTON CLAIMED THAT the six essays he penned under
the title *The Continentalist* in 1781 and 1782 covered "matters of
the greatest importance to these States," and it would be difficult to
dispute the claim. The essays represent his attempt to bring many
of the thoughts expressed in his private letters to national leaders
(see chapters 1–3 in this volume) to the wider audience of newspaper
readers. They are longer versions of what we call today op-eds. *The
Continentalist* deals mostly with the need to reform American government, but essays IV–VI, condensed here, also treat economic and
financial issues.

The first number in the series, which appeared in the *New York
Packet* in July 1781, argued that the nation's councils suffered because
qualified leaders were few, not all were recognized with positions of
importance, "and when they were, their influence was too commonly
borne down by the prevailing torrent of ignorance and prejudice."
That led to the blunder of not giving Congress enough power. It was
excusable to err in our policies at first but to persist in obvious mistakes
"becomes disgraceful and even criminal." "Durable liberty" requires

providing government officials with "a proper degree of authority, to make and execute the laws with vigor." Just as too much power breeds despotism, too little encourages anarchy, "and both eventually lead to the ruin of the people." Everyone knows this but nobody has yet applied it to our situation. "Ambition and local interests," Hamilton predicted at the close of the first number, "will be constantly under-mining and usurping upon" the prerogatives of the national government until its "dissolution."

In the second *Continentalist*, which was published on the heels of the first, Hamilton argued that the threat to a unitary state was despotism, but the threat to a confederated state such as America's was anarchy. In confederated governments "each member has a distinct sovereignty," and hence the capacity to wage war. They may do so too quickly, though, because each has a tendency (which economists today recognize as the free rider problem) "to believe, that the public burthens are unequally apportioned, and that itself is the victim."

The third number of *The Continentalist*, which appeared in August 1781, noted that although America was remote from Europe, it would be quickly attacked if the national government lost its authority. The dire situation of the country in mid-1781 resulted from the "impolicy and mismanagement" of America's rulers. To win on the battlefield, Americans needed to "enlarge the powers of Congress" so that it could better direct the nation's resources to where they were most needed. That might make the difference, he concluded, between Americans' being a "conquered people" or a "happy people."

The fourth installment of *The Continentalist* appeared in late August 1781, and it immediately laid out a six-point plan for augmenting the powers of Congress. First, Congress needed "the power of regulating trade" Second, it needed the power to impose a "moderate land-tax." Third, it needed the power to levy "a moderate capitation tax" on every male older than fifteen years who was not a soldier, sailor, day laborer, cottager, or pauper. Fourth, it needed the power to sell government lands now controlled by the states. Fifth, it needed the power to tax mines. Sixth, it needed to appoint all military officers.

The first three powers Hamilton believed to be "of immediate necessity," while the last three would be more important in the future. "The whole combined," he argued, "would give solidity and permanency to the union" by providing Congress with the power of direct taxation and hence the ability to restore public credit.

To prevent the government from "running in debt," Hamilton in a footnote suggested that Congress should "be obliged in all their loans to appropriate funds for the payment of principal as well as interest." This would become a cornerstone of Hamiltonian finance that he would reiterate many times in later years (see, for example, chapters 7 and 16). In fact, "the depreciation of the currency" would have been avoided, Hamilton argued, if "the practice of funding" debts with dedicated revenue streams had been implemented "four years ago."

Some observers ignorant of "our real resources and expenses," wrote Hamilton, suppose that the war can be paid for without borrowing; in fact, an annual deficit of $5 to $6 million has been carefully calculated (see the letter to Morris, chapter 3). Even "the most powerful and opulent" nations must borrow "in time of war," which is why "most of the States of Europe are deeply immersed in debt." Obviously, the United States must borrow. But private investors will only lend "on the usual security of funds properly established," something that Congress cannot do until vested with the power to tax. The appointment of Robert Morris, "a man of acknowledged abilities and integrity," as Superintendent of Finance was wise, but he can restore public credit only if the national government can secure a source of revenue. The proposed national bank will help by "uniting the influence and interest of the monied men with the resources of government," but ultimately he will need the support of "unexceptionable funds."

The fifth and sixth installments of *The Continentalist* appeared in April and July 1782, respectively, ostensibly because Hamilton had mislaid his drafts while soldiering the previous summer and fall. In the fifth, Hamilton argued that Congress should have the power to regulate commerce for revenue purposes, but also to direct it toward the proper ends. That trade could regulate itself Hamilton believed to be "one of those wild speculative paradoxes, which have grown into credit amongst us, contrary to the uniform practice and sense of the most enlightened nations."

The reason people were skeptical of state involvement with trade, Hamilton argued, "originated in the injudicious attempts made at different times to effect a regulation of prices." They were correct, and the maxim "Trade must regulate itself" was "reasonable" when it meant only that the government could not contravene the "fundamental laws" of the marketplace. Taken to the present extreme, however, the maxim is as flawed "as the practice it was first framed to discredit."

David Hume was correct when he argued that trade was self-equilibrating, and his essay did much to prevent the "many unnecessary wars" fought to try to obtain a favorable balance of trade. Nevertheless, Jean-Baptiste Colbert in France proved that some government policies could help certain industries, like woolens, that have "excited the envy and astonishment" of France's neighbors. The Dutch have likewise extended "their traffic to a degree so much beyond their natural and comparative advantages" by means of "commercial regulations . . . more rigid and numerous, than those of any other country."

If you think that the several state governments will implement beneficial trade policies, Hamilton argued, think again. Trade is inherently a national matter because what is good for the whole might not be good for a part. Moreover, trade is the most convenient source of revenue for the national government. "It is agreed," Hamilton correctly noted, "that imposts on trade, when not immoderate, or improperly laid, is one of the most eligible species of taxation" because they rarely fall on necessities and are "imperceptibly paid by the consumer." Tariffs will never become onerously high because "experience has shown that moderate duties are more productive than high ones." Constitutional checks will also prevent Congress from abusing its taxing power.

Noncommercial states need not fret either, Hamilton explained, because though consumers pay the tariffs in theory, in practice merchants often find that in tight markets they cannot pass all of the tax on to their customers. In highly competitive markets, "the duty is divided between the merchant and the consumer." "General principles," Hamilton warned, should "always . . . be advanced with caution" because they are often mitigated, if not overturned, "in an experimental analysis." Empirical data, in other words, often trumped abstract theory.

In the final installment of *The Continentalist*, published on Independence Day 1782, Hamilton further investigated the consequences of not allowing Congress to regulate trade. In addition to a lack of revenue, power, and cohesion, Hamilton predicted that for fear of losing trade to other states, "each state will be afraid to impose duties on its commerce." The resulting loss of easy taxation would encourage the consumption of foreign luxuries and the imposition of taxes on land and "the necessaries of life." We ought to tax imports with "easy duties" instead of burdening the "soil itself and its productions with heavy impositions." Moderate land and poll

taxes can be used to augment the tariffs whenever "the public necessities must be satisfied."

Likewise, there is nothing to be feared from perpetual debt and
taxes because there will never be a period "when the state would cease
to want revenues and taxes become unnecessary." We will always have
to defend ourselves from foreign incursions, be they by land or sea.

The key, as Hamilton saw it, was to make the national government neither dependent on the states nor independent of the people.
It should be allowed permanent funds sufficient to fund its regular
expenses but not so much that it need not ask the people for additional resources when it desires some new undertaking. Assessments
are not the best way of funding the government. No way is perfectly
equal, so the legislature must "hold the scales with a judicious hand
and balance one [tax] by another." Always, though, "the rich must be
made to pay for their luxuries." A permanent source of funds would
put creditors' minds at ease, allowing the national government to borrow more, and more cheaply, which would limit the need for more
taxes and "throw more money in circulation."

Hamilton concludes *The Continentalist* series by noting that "there
is something noble and magnificent in the perspective of a great
Federal Republic" but something "diminutive and contemptible in the
prospect of a number of petty states . . . jarring, jealous and perverse,
with out any determined direction." Only the former could create a
"Happy America!" He was a realist, but also an optimist.

The six *Continentalist* essays run to 11,526 words; our abridgment
of essays IV–VI totals 2,555 words.

### *The Continentalist* No. IV
Fishkill, New York, August 30, 1781

[. . .]
The preceding numbers are chiefly intended to confirm an opinion, already pretty generally received, that it is necessary to augment the powers of the confederation. The principal difficulty yet
remains, to fix the public judgment, definitively, on the points
which ought to compose that augmentation. . . .

The great defect of the confederation is that it gives the United
States no property, or in other words no revenue, nor the means
of acquiring it inherent in themselves, and independent on the

temporary pleasure of the different members; and power without revenue in political society is a name. While Congress continue altogether dependent on the occasional grants of the several States for the means of defraying the expenses of the FEDERAL GOVERNMENT, it can neither have dignity, vigor, nor *credit*. CREDIT supposes specific and permanent funds for the punctual payment of interest, with a moral certainty of a final redemption of the principal. In our situation it will probably require more, on account of the general diffidence which has been excited by the past disorder in our finances. It will perhaps be necessary, in the first instance, to appropriate funds for the redemption of the principal in a determinate period[1], as well as for the payment of interest. . . .

The most wealthy and best established nations are obliged to pledge their funds to obtain credit; and it would be the height of absurdity in us, in the midst of a revolution, to expect to have it on better terms. This credit being to be procured through Congress, the funds ought to be provided, declared, and vested in them. It is a fact, that besides the want of specific funds, a circumstance which operates powerfully against our obtaining credit abroad, is, not a distrust of our becoming independent, but of our continuing united; and with our present confederation the distrust is natural. Both foreigners and the thinking men among ourselves would have much more confidence in the duration of the union if they were to see it supported on the foundation here proposed. . . .

Indeed nations the most powerful and opulent are obliged to have recourse to loans in time of war; and hence it is that most of the States of Europe are deeply immersed in debt. France is among the number, notwithstanding her immense population, wealth, and resources. England owes the enormous sum of two hundred millions sterling. The United Provinces with all their prudence and parsimony owe a debt of the generality of fifty millions sterling, besides the particular debts of each province. Almost all the other powers are more or less in the same circumstances.

---

1. It might indeed be a good restraint upon the spirit of running in debt with which governments are to apt to be infected, to make it a condition of the grants to Congress, that they shall be obliged in all their loans to appropriate funds for the payment of principal as well as interest; and such a restriction might be serviceable to public credit.

While this teaches us how contracted and uninformed are the views of those who expect to carry on the war without running in debt, it ought to console us, with respect to the amount of that which we now owe, or may have occasion to incur, in the remainder of the war. The whole, without burthening the people may be paid off in twenty years after the conclusion of peace.

The principal part of the deficient five or six millions must be procured by loans from private persons, at home and abroad. . . .

Private men, either foreigners or natives, will not lend to a large amount but on the usual security of funds properly established. This security Congress cannot give till the several States vest them with revenue or the means of revenue for that purpose.

Congress have wisely appointed a Superintendent of their Finances, a man of acknowledged abilities and integrity, as well as of great personal credit and pecuniary influence. It was impossible that the business of finance could be ably conducted by a body of men, however well composed or well intentioned. Order in the future management of our monied concerns, a strict regard to the performance of public engagements, and of course the restoration of public credit may be reasonably and confidently expected from Mr. Morris's administration if he is furnished with materials upon which to operate—that is, if the federal government can acquire funds as the basis of his arrangements. He has very judiciously proposed a national bank, which by uniting the influence and interest of the monied men with the resources of government can alone give it that durable and extensive credit of which it stands in need. This is the best expedient he could have devised for relieving the public embarrassments, but to give success to the plan it is essential that Congress should have it in their power to support him with unexceptionable funds.

Had we begun the practice of funding four years ago, we should have avoided that depreciation of the currency which has been as pernicious to the morals as to the credit of the nation: And there is no other method than this to prevent a continuance and multiplication of the evils flowing from that prolific source.

*The New-York Packet, and the American Advertiser,* August 30, 1781

### *The Continentalist* No. V
Fishkill, New York, April 18, 1782

The vesting Congress with the power of regulating trade ought to have been a principal object of the confederation for a variety of reasons. It is as necessary for the purposes of commerce as of revenue. There are some who maintain that trade will regulate itself, and is not to be benefitted by the encouragements or restraints of government. Such persons will imagine that there is no need of a common directing power. . . .

No mode can be so convenient as a source of revenue to the United States. It is agreed that imposts on trade, when not immoderate or improperly laid, is one of the most eligible species of taxation. They fall in a great measure upon articles not of absolute necessity, and being partly transferred to the price of the commodity are so far imperceptibly paid by the consumer. It is therefore that mode which may be exercised by the federal government with least exception or disgust. Congress can easily possess all the information necessary to impose the duties with judgment, and the collection can without difficulty be made by their own officers.

They can have no temptation to abuse this power because the motive of revenue will check its own extremes. Experience has shown that moderate duties are more productive than high ones. When they are low, a nation can trade abroad on better terms—its imports and exports will be larger—the duties will be regularly paid, and arising on a greater quantity of commodities, will yield more in the aggregate than when they are so high as to operate either as a prohibition or as an inducement to evade them by illicit practices.

The maxim that the consumer pays the duty has been admitted in theory with too little reserve; frequently contradicted in practice. . . . It will, many times be found that the duty is divided between the merchant and the consumer. . . .

It is too much characteristic of our national temper to be ingenious in finding out and magnifying the minutest disadvantages, and to reject measures of evident utility, even of necessity, to avoid trivial and sometimes imaginary evils. We seem not to reflect that in human society there is scarcely any plan, however salutary to the whole and to every part, by the share each has in the common prosperity but in one way or another, and under particular circumstances, will operate more to the benefit of some parts, than of others. Unless we can overcome this narrow disposition and learn to estimate measures by their general tendency, we shall never be a great or a happy people, if we remain a people at all.

*The New-York Packet, and the American Advertiser,* April 18, 1782

## *The Continentalist* No. VI
Fishkill, New York, July 4, 1782

Let us see what will be the consequences of not authorizing the Federal Government to regulate the trade of these states. . . .

Each state will be afraid to impose duties on its commerce lest the other states, not doing the same, should enjoy greater advantages than itself by being able to afford native commodities cheaper abroad and foreign commodities cheaper at home.

A part of the evils resulting from this would be: A loss to the revenue of those moderate duties which, without being injurious to commerce, are allowed to be the most agreeable species of taxes to the people.

Articles of foreign luxury while they would contribute nothing to the income of the state, being less dear by an exemption from duties would have a more extensive consumption.

Many branches of trade hurtful to the common interest would be continued for want of proper checks and discouragements.

As revenues must be found to satisfy the public exigencies in peace and in war, too great a proportion of taxes will fall directly upon land and upon the necessaries of life, the produce of that land. . . .

As a sufficient revenue could not be raised from trade to answer the public purposes, other articles have been proposed.

A moderate land and poll tax, being of easy and inexpensive collection and leaving nothing to discretion, are the simplest and best that could be devised. . . .

But perhaps the class is more numerous than those, who not unwilling to bear their share of public burthens, are yet averse to the idea of perpetuity, as if there ever would arrive a period, when

the state would cease to want revenues and taxes become unnecessary. It is of importance to unmask this delusion and open the
eyes of the people to the truth. It is paying too great a tribute to
the idol of popularity to flatter so injurious and so visionary an
expectation. The error is too gross to be tolerated anywhere but
in the cottage of the peasant; should we meet with it in the senate house we must lament the ignorance or despise the hypocrisy
on which it is engrafted. Expense is in the present state of things
entailed upon all governments. Though if we continue united,
we shall be hereafter less exposed to wars by land than most
other countries; yet while we have powerful neighbors on either
extremity, and our frontier is embraced by savages whose alliance
they may without difficulty command, we cannot in prudence
dispense with the usual precautions for our interior security. As
a commercial people, maritime power must be a primary object
of our attention, and a navy cannot be created or maintained
without ample revenues. The nature of our popular constitutions
requires a numerous magistracy for whom competent provision
must be made; or we may be certain our affairs will always be
committed to improper hands; and experience will teach us that
no government costs so much as a bad one.

We may preach till we are tired of the theme the necessity
of disinterestedness in republics without making a single pros-
elyte. The virtuous declaimer will neither persuade himself nor
any other person to be content with a double mess of porridge,
instead of a reasonable stipend for his services. . . .

The public, for the different purposes that have been mentioned,
must always have large demands upon its constituents, and the only
question is whether these shall be satisfied by annual grants perpetually renewed—by a perpetual grant once for all or by a compound
of permanent and occasional supplies. The last is the wisest course.
The Federal Government should neither be independent nor too
much dependent. It should neither be raised above responsibility
or control, nor should it want the means of maintaining its own
weight, authority, dignity, and credit. To this end permanent funds
are indispensable, but they ought to be of such a nature and so
moderate in their amount as never to be inconvenient. . . .

It would seem as if no mode of taxation could be relished but
that worst of all modes which now prevails, by assessment . . .

but it should be remembered that it is impossible to devise any specific tax that will operate equally on the whole community. It must be the province of the legislature to hold the scales with a judicious hand and balance one by another. The rich must be made to pay for their luxuries, which is the only proper way of taxing their superior wealth.

Do we imagine that our assessments operate equally? Nothing can be more contrary to the fact. Wherever a discretionary power is lodged in any set of men over the property of their neighbors, they will abuse it. . . . Assessors will ever be a set of petty tyrants, too unskillful, if honest, to be possessed of so delicate a trust, and too seldom honest to give them the excuse of want of skill. The genius of liberty reprobates everything arbitrary or discretionary in taxation. It exacts that every man by a definite and general rule should know what proportion of his property the state demands. Whatever liberty we may boast in theory, it cannot exist in fact while assessments continue. . . .

The establishment of permanent funds would not only answer the public purposes infinitely better than temporary supplies; but it would be the most effectual way of easing the people. With this basis for procuring credit, the amount of present taxes might be greatly diminished. Large sums of money might be borrowed abroad at a low interest, and introduced into the country to defray the current expenses and pay the public debts, which would not only lessen the demand for immediate supplies, but would throw more money into circulation and furnish the people with greater means of paying the taxes. Though it be a just rule that we ought not to run in debt to avoid present expense so far as our faculties extend; yet the propriety of doing it cannot be disputed when it is apparent that these are incompetent to the public necessities. Efforts beyond our abilities can only tend to individual distress and national disappointment.

The product of the three forgoing articles [import duties and land and poll taxes] will be as little as can be required to enable Congress to pay their debts, and restore order into their finances. . . .

There is something noble and magnificent in the perspective of a great Federal Republic, closely linked in the pursuit of a common interest, tranquil and prosperous at home, respectable abroad; but there is something proportionally diminutive and contemptible in the prospect of a number of petty states, with the appearance only of union, jarring, jealous and perverse, without any determined direction, fluctuating and unhappy at home, weak and insignificant by their dissentions in the eyes of other nations. Happy America! if those, to whom thou hast entrusted the guardianship of thy infancy know how to provide for thy future repose; but miserable and undone if their negligence or ignorance permits the spirit of discord to erect her banners on the ruins of thy tranquility!

*The New-York Packet, and the American Advertiser*, July 4, 1782

# CHAPTER FIVE

# Constitution of the Bank of New York (February 23–March 15, 1784)

*The Bank shall be called by the Name and Title of the Bank of New York.*

ON NOVEMBER 25, 1783, remaining British military forces embarked permanently from New York City, marking the unofficial end of the eight-year War of Independence. Hamilton returned to New York City the same month and commenced practicing law from his residence at 57 Wall Street. In early 1784, he joined the organizers of the newly forming Bank of New York and drafted its twenty-article constitution. Shortly thereafter, the bank began operations, which have continued to the present. Now known as Bank of New York Mellon, it is one of the very oldest American corporations.

Hamilton would have a long association with the Bank of New York, as a lawyer, director, shareholder, and customer, all the while maintaining close personal contacts with its management. These connections would particularly assist when his official duties commenced as Secretary of the Treasury in September 1789. Upon inheriting an empty U.S. Treasury, one of his first acts was to apply to the bank for a loan so the new government authorized by the U.S. Constitution would have some funds to spend.

At the time that Hamilton wrote the bank's constitution, banking was novel but not unique. Philadelphia boasted the first bank in the nation, the Bank of North America, authorized by Congress toward the end of the Revolution to assist in its financing, and Boston businessmen organized the Massachusetts Bank at the same time New Yorkers were launching theirs. Banks expected to apply for a charter of incorporation granting official approval of their rights and obligations by a state legislature or Congress. This often complicated matters because governmental consent could be as much a political as an economic decision. A future Secretary of the Treasury wrote that "of all acts of government none perhaps was more delicate, none required greater discretion and caution to guard it against improper speculations than the granting of a *bank charter*. . . . It is an act of the highest legislative nature."[1]

New York State legislators in 1784 did not see any upside in incorporating a bank in New York City. It was a political decision, not based on merit, and would not be the last one in New York State. Therefore, the state legislators refused to answer the bank's formal application to incorporate (Article 19). Hamilton and the bank boldly pushed forward anyway and simply opened the doors for business without a state charter. Hamilton foresaw that it was not an impediment. This trailblazing notion of starting without a charter would be followed by other companies, and in time state legislatures understood that it would be best to stop limiting the number of corporations. But that often took decades, and in the interim bank chartering and incorporations in general remained highly politicized.

Importantly, the bank was not opened under traditional incorporation as a partnership but rather as a "joint stock company." Partnerships had the disadvantages of having to be liquidated when a partner died, each partner being personally responsible for the firm's debts, and each partner being sued individually in a lawsuit. The advantages of the joint stock company were that partners could now buy and sell equity without affecting the operations of the firm, lawsuits would be aimed at the firm and not the individual owners, and the firm and not the owners were responsible for the debt. The most a shareholder could lose was his stock investment (Article 16).

The Bank of New York would apply again in 1791, and it finally received a corporate charter from the state. The impetus came from Hamilton. Congress enacted his plan for a Bank of the United States (BUS) in February 1791 (see chapter 10). That plan allowed the BUS to open a branch in New York City, which in fact it did in 1792. New York's legislators feared that it would be ceding the business of banking in New York to the federal bank unless it chartered a bank of its own. So, roughly a month after Congress authorized the BUS, New York at last enacted a corporate charter for the Bank of New York.

Most of Hamilton's constitution for the bank is a straightforward statement of the basic capital amounts, shareholder rights, leadership structure, safeguards, and means for removal for malfeasance like embezzlement. Article 5 called not for one vote per share or one vote per shareholder, but for graduated voting rights. As he would explain in his report of a national bank (chapter 10), he thought graduated voting rights balanced the interests of majority and minority stockholders. It is also worth noting that the 1784 constitution banned international banking (Article 8) and, while not unusual for the time period, senior staff needed to post a "security for their trust" (Article 14).

By refusing to grant a charter of incorporation for seven years, New York State's government in the 1780s could hardly be viewed as enabling economic growth, although it did not actively oppose the new bank. Hamilton, already in 1784 a skilled lawyer, bypassed the state's refusal to grant a corporate charter by inserting a limited liability provision for stockholders (Article 16). He would do this again when he drew up the Articles of Association for the Merchants Bank in 1803 (see chapter 18).

In this constitution we witness Hamilton in the role of assisting entrepreneurs—in this case, would-be bankers—to achieve their goals, which included providing credit to other entrepreneurs. In addition to theorizing about the benefits of banking before the United States had any modern banks, he actually played a key role in organizing several banks. He practiced what he preached.

This document is not abridged.

## Constitution of the Bank of New York
### Article 1st.
That the Bank shall be called by the Name and Title of the Bank of New York.
–2–
That the Capital Stock consist of Five Hundred Thousand Dollars in Gold or Silver, divided into One Thousand Shares

of Five Hundred Dollars each Share and that a Majority of all the Directors may at their discretion open new Subscriptions for increasing the Capital Stock, when they shall judge it for the Interest of the Bank so to do, provided the said New Subscriptions do not exceed the Sum of Five Hundred Thousand Dollars.

–3–

That Thirteen Directors be annually chosen by a Majority of Votes, who are to have the sole Conduct and Management of the Bank. At the first General Election, the President and Cashier are to be elected by the Subscribers to the Bank, but for ever afterwards the Thirteen Directors are to choose a President from among themselves; and the Cashier as well as every other Person employed in the Bank is to be appointed and paid by them and be under their immediate control.

–4th–

That the first Election be on the 15th. day of March 1784; that the next General Election for thirteen Directors shall be on the Second Monday in May 1785; and so continue Yearly and every Year, but in case of any Vacancy in the Direction by Death, Resignation or otherwise, public notice shall be given within one Week after such an Event, that the Vacancy may be filled; the Election to be within fourteen days after such notice.

5th.

That every Holder of one or more Shares to the Number of Four, shall have One Vote for each Share—A Subscriber of Six Shares shall have Five Votes, Eight Shares, Six Votes, and Ten Shares, Seven Votes, and One Vote for every Five Shares above Ten.

–6th–

That no Stockholder after the first Election shall be entitled to Vote, unless such person has possessed the Stock three months previous to the day fixed for an election of Directors or any other General purpose; And if any Stockholder (who shall have been a Resident in this State at least Twelve months immediately preceding such Election) should be absent, he shall be entitled to Vote by Proxy properly appointed; but in no other case shall any Vote be admitted by Proxy.

–7th–

That no Person shall be eligible to serve in the Office of Director unless he be a Stockholder.

–8th–

That the Board of Directors determine the manner of doing business and the Rules and Forms to be pursued, appoint and employ the various Clerks and Servants, which they may find necessary, and dispose of the Money and credit of the Bank for the interest and benefit of the Proprietors; but they are not to employ the money or Credit of the Bank in the drawing or negotiating of any Foreign Bill or Bills of Exchange, or advance a Loan to any Foreign Power whatever.

–9th–

That if at any time it shall be the opinion of a Majority of the Directors that any of their Body are guilty of neglect of Duty or any Mal Practice whereby the Interest of the Bank is or may be affected, such majority of the Directors with or without the consent of the President, may advertise for a general Meeting of the Stockholders to lay before them a Complaint of such neglect of Duty or breach of Trust, and if it appears to the Stockholders to be well founded such Director or Directors may be removed by a majority of Votes.

–10th–

That if any of the Directors shall convert any of the Money or Property of the Bank to his own particular use, or be guilty of fraud or Embezzlement, he shall forfeit his whole share of Stock to the Company and be expelled the Direction by a Majority of all the Directors and thereby rendered incapable of ever serving again in that Office.

–11th–

That no President or Director shall receive any other Emolument for his attendance on the Duties of his Office than such as shall be fixed and agreed to by a majority of Votes at a General Election.

–12th–

That there shall be a Meeting of the Directors Quarterly for the purpose of regulating the affairs of the Bank and not less than Seven shall constitute a Board, who may adjourn from time to time; and the President if necessary may call a Meeting of the Directors at any intermediate time; At every Meeting of the Directors all Questions are to be decided by a majority of Votes.

–13th–

That the President or a Majority of the Directors shall have Power to call a General Meeting of the Stockholders by an Advertisement in the public Papers whenever it appears to them there is urgent occasion.

14th.

That the Cashier and every principal Clerk do give a Security for their Trust to such an Amount as a Majority of all the Directors shall require.

–15th–

That all Notes issued by the Bank, shall be Signed by the President for the Time being, or any Director who may be fixed upon by the Board for that Purpose, and Counter Signed by the Cashier, or in his absence by a Clerk to be appointed by the Directors.

–16th.–

That no Stockholder shall be accountable to any Individual or the Public for Money lodged in the Bank for a greater Sum than the amount of his Stock.

–17th.–

That such a Dividend on the Profits of the Bank as a Majority of all the Directors shall determine to make, shall be declared at least fourteen days previous to the General Election in May 1785; and that all Subsequent Dividends shall be made half yearly.

–18th.–

That all Shares shall be transferable, such Transfer to be made by the Proprietor or Proprietors or his her or their lawful Attorney in Books kept at the Bank for that purpose, which Books shall be always kept open at the usual Office Hours except on particular days previous to the declaring a Dividend of which due Notice shall be given.

–19th–

That the President and Directors shall Petition the Legislature to incorporate the Subscribers or Stockholders under the Name and Title of the President Directors and Company of the Bank of New York, and to pass Laws for inflicting the most exemplary punishment on those who may commit Fraud or Embezzlement; and also to punish the Counterfeiters of Bank Notes and Checks in the like exemplary manner, with such other Clauses in the Act as they shall judge necessary and proper for the Security of the Stockholders and the Public.

–20th–

That the Constitution shall be fairly transcribed upon Parchment and remain at the Bank; the President and Directors when chosen, and prior to the opening of the Bank, shall severally Sign and Seal the same, and take an Oath or Affirmation before a Magistrate, that he will to the best of his Knowledge and abilities conduct the business of the Bank for the Interest and benefit of the Proprietors and agreeable to the true intent and meaning of the Constitution which Oath or Affirmation shall also be taken by every future Director when chosen, and before he enters upon the execution of his Trust.

# CHAPTER SIX

# To Thomas Willing (September 13, 1789)

*To the acceptance of this arduous trust, I have been not a little encouraged by the hope that my inviolable attachment to the principles which form the basis of public credit is so well and so generally understood as to insure me the confidence of those who have it most in their power to afford me support.*

WHEN HAMILTON WAS appointed Secretary of the Treasury on Friday, September 11, 1789, he inherited no formal financial system, no central bank, and no funds with which to run the new nation. The Treasury was empty.

There were only three banks in existence to turn to for possible loans—one each in New York, Philadelphia, and Boston. This letter, written two days later, on a Sunday, to Thomas Willing of the Bank of North America (BNA) in Philadelphia, underscores that one of Hamilton's very first moves was to secure bank loans to succor the fledgling federal government. He refers to a $20,000 loan from the Bank of New York (BoNY), funds that Hamilton deployed on the same day to the Secretary of War, and to BoNY's agreement to lend another $30,000.

The BNA had been created by Congress late in the Revolutionary War at Robert Morris's behest and with aid from the French, the foreign loan Hamilton had deemed so necessary in his 1780 and 1781 letters to national leaders (see chapters 1–3). That institution, which opened at the start of 1782, immediately lent the money to the Continental Congress. Hamilton reminds Willing of this as he attempts to persuade Willing once again to come to the aid of the national government.

To help ensure that Willing would agree, Hamilton states in the last sentence that he will always "promote the interest" of the BNA. Many today would be aghast at that statement, the promise of a government official to promote the interests of a specific private sector firm. But a consideration of the context is imperative. Hamilton desperately needed the funds to launch the new, tiny, untested, and in some quarters detested government to ensure that the government would survive and the country prosper.

The letter was effective. The BNA joined the BoNY in advancing funds to the Treasury. Few Americans today realize that our mighty federal government was launched with loans from private sector bankers. This reliance of the Treasury on private bankers, both American and foreign, would continue for several years. The need for such loans diminished with the creation of the national bank, the Bank of the United States, at the end of 1791, and as rising prosperity swelled imports, customs and tonnage duties, and Treasury revenues.

This letter is not abridged.

Treasury Department New York September 13th. 1789.

Sir,
You will probably have learned ere this reaches you, my appointment to the Office of Secretary of the Treasury. To the acceptance of this arduous trust, I have been not a little encouraged by the hope that my inviolable attachment to the principles which form the basis of public credit is so well and so generally understood as to insure me the confidence of those who have it most in their power to afford me support. This persuasion, and a knowledge of the disposition which has upon all occasions marked the conduct of your institution towards the Union, have led me to flatter myself that I may confidently calculate upon the aid of the Bank of North America as one of the principal means by which I may be enabled to fulfill the public expectations.

With this impression I freely have recourse to you for your assistance in a present exigency. A sum of Eighty thousand Dollars is immediately wanted. The Bank of New York have lately advanced Twenty thousand for another purpose; and have agreed to advance a further sum of Thirty thousand. There remains Fifty to be provided, the Loan of which I trust will not be inconvenient to you.

As the time presses and delay might ensue in adjusting the terms of the requested Loan by letter, I have Mr. Duer, my Assistant who will have the honor of delivering you this, to make a journey to Philadelphia in order that details may be expeditiously settled. To him I beg leave to refer you, and need only add that whatever arrangements he may concert with your Bank shall be strictly observed on my part.

Permit me to add Sir, that in the conduct of the business of my Department it will always give me pleasure to promote the interest of the Institution over which you preside.

With perfect esteem,   I have the honor to be,   Sir,   Your obt. & hble servant,

Alexr. Hamilton
Secretary of the Treasury
Thomas Willing Esqr.
President of the Bank of North America

# CHAPTER SEVEN

# Report Relative to a Provision for the Support of Public Credit (January 9, 1790)

*This reflection derives additional strength from the nature of the debt of the United States. It was the price of liberty.*

THIS, THE FIRST of Hamilton's great state papers, was a response to a House resolution passed in September 1789 seeking Hamilton's views as Treasury Secretary as to making "an adequate provision for the support of the Public Credit." In other words, Congress wanted Hamilton to devise a plan to repay the nation's debts because it was "a matter of high importance to the honor and prosperity" of the new nation.

As in his other state papers, Hamilton included a great deal of didactic material designed to lay out first principles, including the inevitability of government borrowing for "exigencies" such as a "foreign war." Even the wealthiest of nations found it expedient to borrow "in times of public danger," so a nation like America, endowed with "little monied capital," certainly must be expected to borrow in such emergencies.

The key issue, then, was not how to avoid borrowing but rather how to "borrow upon *good terms*." In order to so, the government needed to establish its credit. Conversely, bad or poor credit would result in "*borrowing* and *buying dear*" and ultimately higher taxes.

How, then, best to establish and maintain public credit, Hamilton asked. The solution was simply and promptly to pay all contractual obligations. Conversely, every broken promise would be "in different degrees hurtful to public credit." To mitigate the damage, the government should minimize defaults and "make reparation" whenever possible. It should also negotiate any contract amendments in good faith.

In addition to the self-interest reason for paying off its creditors—lower future borrowing costs—nations also had a "moral obligation" to do so. This especially applied to the case of the United States, because of the nature of the debt: "it was the price of liberty." Honor was an important eighteenth-century concept, and Hamilton took that notion and applied it to both the state and Continental Congress debts piled up during the War of Independence. It was the nation's collective responsibility, and it must be honored. These six words, "it was the price of liberty," stand out from the other 17,000 words of the document as a powerful argument for assumption.[1]

Now that the war had ended and "the embarrassments" of the weak Articles of Confederation had been replaced by the new Constitution, government could "retrieve the national credit, by doing justice to the creditors of the nation." Hamilton's evidence for the embarrassments' being ended was the recent rise in the value of public securities.

Establishing public credit would obviously help holders of government securities, but also all other Americans. Hamilton brought in evidence that in other "countries in which the national debt is properly funded . . . it answers the purposes of money." In other words, securities pass in business transactions just as specie does. That means that interest rates decrease and real estate is restored "to its due value." It also means that trade grows with the access to more capital, which benefits farmers and manufacturers by giving "greater means for enterprise."

For all those good effects to occur, though, the public debt must be well funded to acquire "an *adequate* and *stable* value." To fund a debt means to pledge specific revenues to the payment of the interest on it and possibly also to its ultimate redemption. Viewed from the opposite vantage point, an unfunded debt would exacerbate the current shortage of money because it would be traded like "a mere commodity, and a precarious one," so "all the money applied to it is so much diverted from the more useful channels of circulation."

A properly funded debt would aid landowners by raising real estate prices, an important consideration given that real estate at the time was "a serious calamity." The decrease of 25 to 50 percent and more was due to "the scarcity of money." The effect of funding might take some time, but given that securities prices were rising on expectations of improvement, it looked to be an expeditious change for the better.

So how could the debt be funded? The foreign debt, all agreed, should be paid on the agreed-upon existing terms. Public opinion, however, differed regarding the domestic debt, as some held that "a discrimination ought . . . to be made between original holders of the public securities, and present possessors, by purchase." It was unfair, some alleged, to pay twenty shillings in the pound to somebody who had paid only three or four shillings in the pound while the poor seller, who must have been very necessitous, parted with his property at a loss.[2]

"After the most mature reflection," Hamilton rejected discrimination, arguing that it would be "as highly injurious, even to the original holders of public securities" as it would be "ruinous to public credit." Discrimination was "a breach of contract," and it violated "the rights of a fair purchaser." The contracts had stipulated that the government would pay principal and interest "to the first holder, or his *assignee*." In other words, the government's IOUs were deliberately made negotiable so that the original holder could sell them at the current market price if s/he saw fit.

After all, Hamilton noted, buyers of government IOUs offered relief to sellers, who were distressed because the government had reneged on its solemn promises. "The buyer had no agency" in the sellers' distress, "and therefore ought not to suffer." Buyers did not even take "undue advantage" because they paid what everyone agreed the securities were worth—i.e., the market price. In so doing, buyers purchased "the risks of reimbursement" for a "fair equivalent" and then waited for "a revolution in government" to render repayment possible.

Those who sold out of necessity have no complaint of the buyer, but rather of "the government solely." It was the government's failure to honor its debt contracts, not any action of the buyer, that caused securities values to fall to small fractions of par. And of course many sold "either through want of confidence in an eventual provision, or from the allurements of some profitable speculation." Discovering why individuals sold, or whether they were not better off for having sold, was impossible to ascertain. Others sold only to repurchase other securities later. How should such cases be handled? Even the proposers of discrimination would be disgusted by the absurdities and "inequitable consequences" that would follow if discrimination were attempted, Hamilton argued.

Discrimination would hurt both securities prices and negotiability or "security of transfer" in the future, rendering the debt a much less valuable economic tool and future government borrowing much more expensive. It would also be unconstitutional, because Article VI clearly states that "all debts contracted" before adoption of the Constitution "shall be as valid against the United States under it, as under the confederation."[3]

Next, Hamilton proposed that the federal government assume responsibility for the debts of the state governments. Such an assumption, Hamilton argued, "would . . . contribute, in an eminent degree, to an orderly, stable and satisfactory arrangement of the national finances." After all, the total tax bill will be no higher regardless of which government makes the interest and principal payments. So the real question was whether the federal government could make those payments "more conveniently and effectually." Hamilton believed that it could.

Assumption would reduce "competition for resources" between the federal and state governments. It would also prevent "the most productive objects of revenue" from being taxed twice (by both federal and state governments) or "beyond what they could properly bear." At the same time, other sources of taxation might end up being taxed too little if left to the several states.

Moreover, tying the creditors together will ensure that they had the same interest, and hence "they will unite in the support of the fiscal arrangements of the government." That "will insure to the revenue laws a more ready and more satisfactory execution." In other words, there will be less smuggling than in a more complex system where creditors must also look to the state governments for payment.

In addition, state creditors without an assumption would be worse off than federal creditors because tariffs, "a principal branch of revenue is exclusively vested in the union." Further, states might not tax as much as they needed to because the existence of competitive states with lower taxes would cause citizens of high-tax states to move to them. State creditors would therefore be unhappy, which would hurt the credit of the United States, partly because it would be unjust if "one class of the public creditors should be more favored than the other."

Hamilton acknowledged that assumption of state debts might cause friction between the state and federal governments and that equitably reconciling and settling the accounts of the state and national governments to equalize the costs of the War of Independence would take time and "will require all the moderation and wisdom of the government." All that needed to be done at the moment, Hamilton contended, was to include those state debts in the final settlement agreement.

Not satisfied to let the matter rest with that, Hamilton then described a process for rendering "a final adjustment of accounts." The gist of the scheme was that no state would end up owing the federal government anything, and some could look forward to payments from the new federal government. Hamilton justified this by noting that in defending themselves each state helped to defend the entire nation, so they should be credited with those expenses. "The defense of each part is that of the whole; and unless all the expenditures are brought into a common mass, the tendency must be, to add, to the calamities suffered, by being the most exposed to the ravages of war, an increase of burthens." This suggestion marks the first "bailout" in our nation's history as the states' debt slates would be wiped clean.

Hamilton next tackled the question of how to handle arrearages of interest—that is, missed interest payments. Some wanted to give preference to repayment of principal, but Hamilton did not believe that opinion was well founded. He saw both interest and principal as being on equal terms.

The national debt, Hamilton explained, came from two sources: loans of money and "services performed and articles supplied." Suppliers of the former decided to keep their money at interest rather than be repaid in Continental currency, which during the war rapidly depreciated in value given the difficulties of the Patriot cause. Suppliers of the latter should have been paid in cash at the time their goods and services were obtained, but instead they received an IOU for the principal and, later, the promise of 6 percent interest for an indefinite period.

Given this history, Hamilton argued, the national debt should be considered "an annuity at the rate of six per cent. per annum, redeemable at the pleasure of the government." Security holders "have no right to demand the principal" so long as the government keeps up its interest payments as promised. Unpaid interest, by contrast, is due immediately. Even if the government does not have the resources to pay at present, that does not extinguish the creditors' right to immediate payment of past due interest. So the government must give a fair equivalent, or "reasonable interest"—i.e., "the market rate." The government had not been paying interest on the debt. Hamilton said these arrears of interest should be capitalized and honored just like the principal. Congress did not entirely accept Hamilton's recommendation; it decided to pay a lower rate on arrears of interest than on the principal of the debt.

Hamilton next tabulated the amount of debt that needed to be restructured under his plan. Including arrears of interest, the U.S. government owed foreigners $11.7 million at 4 and 5 percent interest. It owed to domestic securities holders $27.4 million in principal and $13 million in arrears of interest, plus an additional estimated $2 million in Continental currency and other "unliquidated" debt. That totaled $54.1 million, plus an estimated $25 million in debts to be assumed from the several states. To begin to pay the interest on this mass of debt at 6 percent, the U.S. government, Hamilton calculated, would need to raise $4.6 million per year.

The United States might be able to raise that much, Hamilton claimed, but to do so "would require the extension of taxation to a degree, and to objects, which the true interest of the public creditors forbids." Here Hamilton is suggesting that sharp increases in taxation to pay full 6 percent interest on the national debt might provoke taxpayers' revolts, leaving creditors worse off than if they accepted modifications of their claims. So Hamilton proposed a modest reduction, or haircut in modern parlance, that public creditors would find equitable because it would provide more security and more certainty of punctual interest payments. For the plan to work, Hamilton stressed, creditors had to give their "voluntary consent" to the contract modification, and the "consent ought to be voluntary in fact, as well as in name."

The principal of the national debt, Hamilton noted, was redeemable at the government's pleasure. So if market interest rates were to fall below 6 percent, the government could pay off its 6 percent creditors by borrowing from those willing to receive something less than 6 percent for their money. Hamilton then pointed out that if his plan for funding the national debt was implemented, the rate of interest would fall "in a very short time" to about 5 percent and in "twenty years, it will sink still lower, probably to four." If that came to pass, which Hamilton attributed to "the low rate of interest in Europe" and the increased domestic money supply due to the circulation of government bonds as near money, the current public creditors would not receive 6 percent interest because the federal government would borrow at 5 percent and redeem the principal. But they might agree to an initial interest rate of less than 6 percent in return for a promise that the government would redeem only a small amount of debt each year—Hamilton recommended no more than 1 percent, which Congress changed to 2 percent—or what today is termed call protection for bond investors.

Europeans would invest in U.S. bonds at 5 percent because often they could not get more than 3 or 4 percent at home, and the United States would be considered a good risk because it is less subject "to those casualties, which are the chief causes of expense"—i.e., wars. Another American advantage was a debt-to-GDP ratio ("incumbrances, in proportion to our real means") lower than that of most European nations. Hamilton noted that Dutch investors, the smart money of the eighteenth century, were already investing in American debt. Also, before the Revolution, in several colonies money could be borrowed at 5 percent, Hamilton reminded readers. So it was not a stretch to think that interest rates would fall to that level in a thriving, independent nation.

Given the warranted expectation that the rate of interest would fall in the United States to 5 percent in five years and to 4 percent in twenty years, Hamilton suggested Congress consider a menu of six plans, details of which are left out of our abridgment, which might appeal to government creditors. They included a reduced interest rate in exchange for western lands at twenty cents per acre, predetermined maximum annual repayments of principal (i.e., call protection), life annuities with survivorship features, and a tontine plan in which participants who lived longest profited handsomely. Hamilton then laid out the rationale for each of the plans, including the twenty-cent-per-acre valuation of land. Hitherto, he explained, western lands had been sold for one dollar per acre in public securities, but the market price of public securities was "less than three shillings in the pound" or $(3/20 =)$ 15 percent of par. That made the effective price of land about fifteen cents per acre. The market had since improved somewhat to about 20 percent of par for public securities, making the effective land price twenty cents per acre.

None of the plans included in the menu that Hamilton laid out for Congress made it into legislation, but significant parts of them did. Congress enacted legislation in 1790 to restructure the entire national debt, including assumed state debts, into three U.S. government securities: a 6 percent bond, a 3 percent bond, and a 6 percent "deferred" bond, which paid no interest for ten years and 6 percent thereafter. Holders of old U.S. debt would exchange it for a package of the three new securities. The first issues of the new securities late in 1790 marked the birth of the U.S. Treasury bond market. In time, that market became the largest in the world for the securities of a single issuer, and a key element of the U.S. and world financial systems.

Hamilton next explained that the government should make interest payments quarterly. That raised the effective interest rate a little because some payments were made before the end of the year. Thus, 6 percent bonds with quarterly payments were really 6.135 percent bonds by Hamilton's computation. Quarterly interest payments on the national debt would advance one of Hamilton's goals, making the U.S. economy more monetized.

The key point of any plan, Hamilton stressed, was fiscal responsibility to "bring the expenditure of the nation to a level with its income." Naturally, appearances and perceptions were as paramount as realities. Hamilton's menu of plans offered ways of reducing the interest payments on the national debt to about 4 percent instead of 6 percent of the principal. The simplified version of those plans that Congress adopted did exactly that.

Yet some public creditors might not choose to participate in any of the plans. Any revenues received above those needed to pay interest on the funded portion of the debt ought therefore to be "divided among those creditors, if any, who may not think fit to subscribe" to any of the new loans, with up to 4 percent interest.

Hamilton next turned to the taxes needed to fund the foreign debt and the domestic debt at 4 percent and pay the annual expenses of government, which he estimated at $0.6 million. He proposed paying the foreign debt with new loans acquired abroad to prevent a "drain of cash, at the present juncture." The rest could be funded from a tariff or tax on imports along with new taxes "on wines, spirits, including those distilled within the United States, teas and coffee." Importantly, Hamilton wanted the latter set as high as practicable but not too high, lest smuggling occur and actually reduce government revenue.

Hamilton favored luxury taxes on items like alcohol and caffeine, arguing that they would "bear high duties" more easily than other goods because people knew they were "foreign luxuries" and even "pernicious" when overused. That was especially the case with "ardent spirits" when they came to market too cheap. It was to be little feared, however, that taxing such goods would so greatly reduce their consumption as to hurt government revenues. That is because "luxuries of every kind lay the strongest hold on the attachments of mankind, which, especially when confirmed by habit, are not easily alienated from them." Hamilton the economist here describes what a modern economist would term a low elasticity of demand for luxuries and alcoholic beverages: taxes can raise their prices a lot while reducing consumption only a little, thereby raising a lot of revenue.

In the next section (its details abridged here), Hamilton proposed duties (per gallon or pound) on almost two dozen imported wines, spirits, teas, and coffee, paying careful attention to differences in quality and alcohol content. That was followed by excise taxes on domestically distilled spirits, again by proof or alcohol content, and an annual tax on the capacity of stills at sixty cents per gallon. To ensure that lawmakers paid sufficient attention to important details, Hamilton took the liberty of appending draft legislation and then explained its virtues, foremost of which were checks against "abuses of authority" by government revenue collectors. Collection would be rendered easier and cheaper, Hamilton explained, if import merchants largely policed themselves, out of their own self-interest, and saw the government as a partner in the endeavor.

The duties should produce $1.7 million which, added to the existing duties and tonnage, would "complete the sum required." However, Hamilton noted, "in so unexplored a field there must be a considerable degree of uncertainty in the data. . . . That there may be no possibility of disappointment to the public creditors," therefore, Hamilton wanted to establish "an auxiliary resource for the first year, in which the interest will become payable." That would be 1791, so Hamilton here meant that his revenue measures would produce a budget surplus in 1790 that could be drawn on in 1791. He may also have been referring to an institution he was about to mention in the report, a national bank.

Although Hamilton believed that "the proper funding" of the national debt would "render it a national blessing," he was not of the view that "public debts are public benefits" because it invited "prodigality" and was "liable to dangerous abuse." So Hamilton wanted to see it established "as a fundament maxim, in the system of public credit of the United States, that the creation of debt should always be accompanied with the means of extinguishment." Such a policy would render "public credit immortal." Hamilton had hit upon this idea a decade earlier in a footnote to his *Continentalist IV* essay, and he would reiterate it in his final Public Credit Report in January 1795. If a nation was to borrow, it must have the means to pay it back.

The profits of the post office, up to $1 million annually, Hamilton proposed applying to a "sinking fund" that the government could use to purchase its own bonds in the market when it saw fit. The fund would be administered by commissioners consisting of the Vice President of the United States, the Speaker of the House, the Chief Justice of the Supreme Court, the Attorney General, and the Secretary of the Treasury. Congress would accept this recommendation, but substituted the Secretary of State for the Speaker of the House.

The commissioners of the sinking fund should be authorized to borrow up to $12 million to repay the foreign debt, to make good any shortfalls in the government's other revenues, and to purchase public debt in the market "while it continues below its true value." Hamilton wanted "to raise the value of the stock"—that is, the government bonds—"to its true standard as fast as possible," so that well-heeled foreign investors would not to be able to buy it on the cheap. Then their purchases of U.S. debt would transfer more foreign capital to the United States, a major goal of Hamilton's program because "their money laid out in this country, upon our agriculture, commerce and manufactures, will produce much more to us, than the income they receive from it."

Sinking fund operations would, Secretary Hamilton said, be executed "through the medium of a national bank." Hamilton would present his bank plan eleven months later, in the Bank Report of December 1790 (see chapter 10). It would call for a Bank of the United States, an institution he had first envisioned more than a decade earlier in his first writings on finance.

Hamilton concluded by providing drafts of resolutions regarding funding and assumption that he hoped both houses of Congress would pass. He noted that he "omitted details, as well to avoid fatiguing the attention of the House, as because more time would have been desirable even to digest the general principles of the plan." He included the details, omitted here, in ten appendices to this first Public Credit Report.

We have abridged the report's 16,313 words to 9,994 words.

Treasury Department, January 9, 1790.
Communicated on January 14, 1790

To the Speaker of the House of Representatives
The Secretary of the Treasury, in obedience to the resolution of the House of Representatives, of the twenty-first day of September last, has during the recess of Congress applied himself to the consideration of a proper plan for the support of the Public Credit, with all the attention which was due to the authority of the House and to the magnitude of the object.

In the discharge of this duty, he has felt in no small degree the anxieties which naturally flow from a just estimate of the difficulty of the task, from a well-founded diffidence of his own qualifications for executing it with success, and from a deep and solemn conviction of the momentous nature of the truth contained in the resolution under which his investigations have been conducted, "That an *adequate* provision for the support of the Public Credit, is a matter of high importance to the honor and prosperity of the United States."

With an ardent desire that his well-meant endeavors may be conducive to the real advantage of the nation, and with the utmost deference to the superior judgment of the House, he now respectfully submits the result of his enquiries and reflections to their indulgent construction.

In the opinion of the Secretary, the wisdom of the House in giving their explicit sanction to the proposition which has been stated cannot but be applauded by all who will seriously consider and trace through their obvious consequences, these plain and undeniable truths.

That exigencies are to be expected to occur in the affairs of nations in which there will be a necessity for borrowing.

That loans in times of public danger, especially from foreign war, are found an indispensable resource even to the wealthiest of them.

And that in a country which, like this, is possessed of little active wealth, or in other words little monied capital, the necessity for that resource must in such emergencies be proportionally urgent.

And as on the one hand, the necessity for borrowing in particular emergencies cannot be doubted, so on the other, it is equally evident that to be able to borrow upon *good terms* it is essential that the credit of a nation should be well established.

For when the credit of a country is in any degree questionable, it never fails to give an extravagant premium in one shape or another upon all the loans it has occasion to make. Nor does the evil end here; the same disadvantage must be sustained upon whatever is to be bought on terms of future payment.

From this constant necessity of *borrowing* and *buying dear*, it is easy to conceive how immensely the expenses of a nation in a course of time will be augmented by an unsound state of the public credit.

To attempt to enumerate the complicated variety of mischiefs in the whole system of the social economy which proceed from a neglect of the maxims that uphold public credit, and justify the solicitude manifested by the House on this point, would be an improper intrusion on their time and patience.

In so strong a light nevertheless do they appear to the Secretary, that on their due observance at the present critical juncture materially depends, in his judgment, the individual and aggregate prosperity of the citizens of the United States, their relief from the embarrassments they now experience, their character as a People, the cause of good government.

If the maintenance of public credit, then, be truly so important, the next enquiry which suggests itself is by what means it is to be effected? The ready answer to which question is by good faith, by a punctual performance of contracts. States, like individuals, who observe their engagements are respected and trusted: while the reverse is the fate of those who pursue an opposite conduct.

Every breach of the public engagements, whether from choice or necessity, is in different degrees hurtful to public credit. When such a necessity does truly exist, the evils of it are only to be palliated by a scrupulous attention on the part of the government to carry the violation no farther than the necessity absolutely requires, and to manifest, if the nature of the case admits of it, a sincere disposition to make reparation whenever circumstances shall permit. But with every possible mitigation, credit must suffer and numerous mischiefs ensue. It is therefore highly important, when an appearance of necessity seems to press upon the public councils, that they should examine well its reality, and be perfectly assured that there is no method of escaping from it before they yield to its suggestions. For though it cannot safely be affirmed that occasions have never existed, or may not exist, in which violations of the public faith in this respect are inevitable; yet there is great reason to believe that they exist far less frequently than precedents indicate; and are oftenest either pretended through levity, or want of firmness, or supposed through want of knowledge. Expedients might often have been devised to effect consistently with good faith what has been done in contravention of it. Those who are most commonly creditors of a nation, are, generally speaking, enlightened men; and there are signal examples to warrant a conclusion that when a candid and fair appeal is made to them, they will understand their true interest too well to refuse their concurrence in such modifications of their claims as any real necessity may demand.

While the observance of that good faith which is the basis of public credit is recommended by the strongest inducements of political expediency, it is enforced by considerations of still greater authority. There are arguments for it which rest on the immutable principles of moral obligation. And in proportion as the mind is disposed to contemplate, in the order of Providence, an intimate connection between public virtue and public happiness, will be its repugnancy to a violation of those principles.

This reflection derives additional strength from the nature of the debt of the United States. It was the price of liberty. The faith of America has been repeatedly pledged for it, and with solemnities that give peculiar force to the obligation. There is indeed reason to regret that it has not hitherto been kept; that the necessities of the war, conspiring with inexperience in the subjects of finance, produced direct infractions; and that the subsequent period has been a continued scene of negative violation or non-compliance. But a diminution of this regret arises from the reflection that the last seven years have exhibited an earnest and uniform effort on the part of the government of the union to retrieve the national credit, by doing justice to the creditors of the nation; and that the embarrassments of a defective constitution, which defeated this laudable effort, have ceased.

From this evidence of a favorable disposition given by the former government, the institution of a new one clothed with powers competent to calling forth the resources of the community has excited correspondent expectations. A general belief accordingly prevails, that the credit of the United States will quickly be established on the firm foundation of an effectual provision for the existing debt. The influence which this has had at home is witnessed by the rapid increase that has taken place in the market value of the public securities. From January to November, they rose thirty-three and a third per cent, and from that period to this time they have risen fifty per cent more. And the intelligence from abroad announces effects proportionally favorable to our national credit and consequence.

It cannot but merit particular attention that among ourselves the most enlightened friends of good government are those whose expectations are the highest.

To justify and preserve their confidence; to promote the increasing respectability of the American name; to answer the calls of justice; to restore landed property to its due value; to furnish new resources both to agriculture and commerce; to cement more closely the union of the states; to add to their security against foreign attack; to establish public order on the basis of an upright and liberal policy. These are the great and invaluable ends to be secured by a proper and adequate provision at the present period for the support of public credit.

To this provision we are invited, not only by the general considerations which have been noticed, but by others of a more particular nature. It will procure to every class of the community some important advantages, and remove some no less important disadvantages.

The advantage to the public creditors from the increased value of that part of their property which constitutes the public debt needs no explanation.

But there is a consequence of this, less obvious though not less true, in which every other citizen is interested. It is a well known fact that in countries in which the national debt is properly funded and an object of established confidence, it answers most of the purposes of money. Transfers of stock or public debt are there equivalent to payments in specie; or in other words, stock in the principal transactions of business passes current as specie. The same thing would in all probability happen here under the like circumstances.

The benefits of this are various and obvious.

First. Trade is extended by it because there is a larger capital to carry it on, and the merchant can at the same time afford to trade for smaller profits, as his stock which, when unemployed brings him in an interest from the government, serves him also as money when he has a call for it in his commercial operations.

Secondly. Agriculture and manufactures are also promoted by it: For the like reason, that more capital can be commanded to be employed in both; and because the merchant, whose enterprise in foreign trade gives to them activity and extension, has greater means for enterprise.

Thirdly. The interest of money will be lowered by it; for this is always in a ratio to the quantity of money and to the quickness of circulation. This circumstance will enable both the public and individuals to borrow on easier and cheaper terms.

And from the combination of these effects additional aids will be furnished to labor, to industry, and to arts of every kind.

But these good effects of a public debt are only to be looked for when, by being well funded, it has acquired an *adequate* and *stable* value. Till then it has rather a contrary tendency. The fluctuation and insecurity incident to it in an unfunded state render it a mere commodity, and a precarious one. As such, being only an object of occasional and particular speculation, all the money applied to it is so much diverted from the more useful channels of circulation for which the thing itself affords no substitute: So that, in fact, one serious inconvenience of an unfunded debt is that it contributes to the scarcity of money.

This distinction which has been little if at all attended to is of the greatest moment. It involves a question immediately interesting to every part of the community, which is no other than this—Whether the public debt, by a provision for it on true principles, shall be rendered a *substitute* for money; or whether, by being left as it is, or by being provided for in such a manner as will wound those principles and destroy confidence, it shall be suffered to continue as it is, a pernicious drain of our cash from the channels of productive industry.

The effect which the funding of the public debt on right principles would have upon landed property is one of the circumstances attending such an arrangement which has been least adverted to, though it deserves the most particular attention. The present depreciated state of that species of property is a serious calamity. The value of cultivated lands, in most of the states has fallen since the revolution from 25 to 50 per cent. In those farthest south, the decrease is still more considerable. Indeed, if the representations continually received from that quarter may be credited, lands there will command no price which may not be deemed an almost total sacrifice.

This decrease in the value of lands ought, in a great measure to be attributed to the scarcity of money. Consequently whatever produces an augmentation of the monied capital of the country must have a proportional effect in raising that value. The beneficial tendency of a funded debt in this respect has been manifested by the most decisive experience in Great-Britain.

The proprietors of lands would not only feel the benefit of this increase in the value of their property, and of a more prompt and better sale when they had occasion to sell; but the necessity of selling would be itself greatly diminished. As the same cause would contribute to the facility of loans, there is reason to believe that such of them as are indebted would be able through that resource to satisfy their more urgent creditors.

It ought not, however, to be expected that the advantages described as likely to result from funding the public debt would be instantaneous. It might require some time to bring the value of stock to its natural level, and to attach to it that fixed confidence which is necessary to its quality as money. Yet the late rapid rise of the public securities encourages an expectation that the progress of stock to the desirable point will be much more expeditious than could have been foreseen. And as in the meantime it will be increasing in value, there is room to conclude that it will from the outset answer many of the purposes in contemplation. Particularly it seems to be probable that from creditors who are not themselves necessitous, it will early meet with a ready reception in payment of debts at its current price.

Having now taken a concise view of the inducements to a proper provision for the public debt, the next enquiry which presents itself is, what ought to be the nature of such a provision? This requires some preliminary discussions.

It is agreed on all hands that that part of the debt which has been contracted abroad and is denominated the foreign debt ought to be provided for according to the precise terms of the contracts relating to it. The discussions which can arise, therefore, will have reference essentially to the domestic part of it, or to that which has been contracted at home. It is to be regretted, that there is not the same unanimity of sentiment on this part as on the other.

The Secretary has too much deference for the opinions of every part of the community not to have observed one which has, more than once, made its appearance in the public prints and which is occasionally to be met with in conversation. It involves this question, whether a discrimination ought not to be made between original holders of the public securities and present possessors by purchase. Those who advocate a discrimination are for making a full provision for the securities of the former at their nominal value, but contend, that the latter ought to receive no more than the cost to them and the interest: And the idea is sometimes suggested of making good the difference to the primitive possessor.

In favor of this scheme, it is alleged that it would be unreasonable to pay twenty shillings in the pound to one who had not given more for it than three or four. And it is added that it would be hard to aggravate the misfortune of the first owner, who probably through necessity parted with his property at so great a loss, by obliging him to contribute to the profit of the person who had speculated on his distresses.

The Secretary, after the most mature reflection on the force of this argument, is induced to reject the doctrine it contains as equally unjust and impolitic, as highly injurious even to the original holders of public securities, as ruinous to public credit.

It is inconsistent with justice, because in the first place it is a breach of contract, in violation of the rights of a fair purchaser.

The nature of the contract in its origin is, that the public will pay the sum expressed in the security to the first holder or his *assignee*. The *intent* in making the security assignable is that the proprietor may be able to make use of his property by selling it for as much as it *may be worth in the market*, and that the buyer may be *safe* in the purchase. . . .

The impolicy of a discrimination results from two consider-ations; one, that it proceeds upon a principle destructive of that *quality* of the public debt or the stock of the nation which is essen-tial to its capacity for answering the purposes of money—that is the *security* of *transfer*; the other, that as well on this account, as because it includes a breach of faith, it renders property in the funds less valuable; consequently induces lenders to demand a higher premium for what they lend, and produces every other inconvenience of a bad state of public credit.

It will be perceived at first sight that the transferable quality of stock is essential to its operation as money, and that this depends on the idea of complete security to the transferee, and a firm persuasion that no distinction can in any circumstances be made between him and the original proprietor.

The precedent of an invasion of this fundamental principle would of course tend to deprive the community of an advan-tage, with which no temporary saving could bear the least comparison. . . .

For this diminution of the value of stock, every person who should be about to lend to the government would demand a compensation; and would add to the actual difference between the nominal and the market value, and equivalent for the chance of greater decrease, which in a precarious state of public credit is always to be taken into the account.

Every compensation of this sort, it is evident, would be an absolute loss to the government. . . .

It is equally unnecessary to add anything to what has been already said to demonstrate the fatal influence which the principle of discrimination would have on the public credit.

But there is still a point in view in which it will appear per-haps even more exceptionable, than in either of the former.

It would be repugnant to an express provision of the Constitution of the United States. This provision is that "all debts contracted and engagements entered into before the adoption of that Constitution shall be as valid against the United States under it, as under the confederation." which amounts to a constitutional ratification of the contracts respecting the debt in the state in which they existed under the confederation. And resorting to that standard, there can be no doubt, that the rights of assignees and original holders must be considered as equal. . . .

The Secretary concluding that a discrimination, between the different classes of creditors of the United States cannot with propriety be *made*, proceeds to examine whether a difference ought to be permitted to *remain* between them and another description of public creditors—Those of the states individually.

The Secretary, after mature reflection on this point, entertains a full conviction that an assumption of the debts of the particular states by the union, and a like provision for them as for those of the union, will be a measure of sound policy and substantial justice.

It would, in the opinion of the Secretary, contribute in an eminent degree to an orderly, stable and satisfactory arrangement of the national finances.

Admitting, as ought to be the case, that a provision must be made in some way or other for the entire debt, it will follow that no greater revenues will be required whether that provision be made wholly by the United States, or partly by them, and partly by the states separately.

The principal question then must be whether such a provision cannot be more conveniently and effectually made by one general plan issuing from one authority than by different plans originating in different authorities.

In the first case there can be no competition for resources; in the last, there must be such a competition. The consequences of this without the greatest caution on both sides might be interfering regulations, and thence collision and confusion. Particular branches of industry might also be oppressed by it. The most productive objects of revenue are not numerous. Either these must be wholly engrossed by one side, which might lessen the efficacy of the provisions by the other; or both must have recourse to the same objects in different modes, which might occasion an accumulation upon them beyond what they could properly bear. . . .

If all the public creditors receive their dues from one source, distributed with an equal hand, their interest will be the same. And having the same interests, they will unite in the support of the fiscal arrangements of the government: As these, too, can be made with more convenience where there is no competition: These circumstances combined will insure to the revenue laws a more ready and more satisfactory execution.

If on the contrary there are distinct provisions, there will be distinct interests drawing different ways. That union and concert of views among the creditors, which in every government is of great importance to their security and to that of public credit, will not only not exist, but will be likely to give place to mutual jealousy and opposition. And from this cause, the operation of the systems which may be adopted both by the particular states and by the union with relation to their respective debts will be in danger of being counteracted.

There are several reasons which render it probable that the situation of the state creditors would be worse than that of the creditors of the union if there be not a national assumption of the state debts. Of these it will be sufficient to mention two; one, that a principal branch of revenue is exclusively vested in the union; the other, that a state must always be checked in the imposition of taxes on articles of consumption from the want of power to extend the same regulation to the other states, and from the tendency of partial duties to injure its industry and commerce. Should the state creditors stand upon a less eligible footing than the others, it is unnatural to expect they would see with pleasure a provision for them. The influence which their dissatisfaction might have could not but operate injuriously, both for the creditors and the credit of the United States.

Hence, it is even the interest of the creditors of the union that those of the individual states should be comprehended in a general provision. Any attempt to secure to the former either exclusive or peculiar advantages would materially hazard their interests.

Neither would it be just that one class of the public creditors should be more favored than the other. The objects for which both descriptions of the debt were contracted are in the main the same. Indeed, a great part of the particular debts of the States has arisen from assumptions by them on account of the union. And it is most equitable that there should be the same measure of retribution for all.

There is an objection, however, to an assumption of the state debts which deserves particular notice. It may be supposed that it would increase the difficulty of an equitable settlement between them and the United States. . . .

To equalize the contributions of the states, let each be then charged with its proportion of the aggregate of those balances according to some equitable ratio to be devised for that purpose.

If the contributions should be found disproportionate, the result of this adjustment would be that some states would be creditors, some debtors to the union.

Should this be the case, as it will be attended with less inconvenience for the United States to have to pay balances to, than to receive them from the particular states, it may perhaps, be practicable to effect the former by a second process, in the nature of a transfer of the amount of the debts of debtor states, to the credit of creditor states, observing the ratio by which the first apportionment shall have been made. This, whilst it would destroy the balances due from the former, would increase those due to the latter. These to be provided for by the United States at a reasonable interest, but not to be transferable. . . .

The whole of this arrangement to be under the superintendence of commissioners, vested with equitable discretion, and final authority. . . .

The general principle of it seems to be equitable, for it appears difficult to conceive a good reason why the expenses for the particular defense of a part in a common war should not be a common charge, as well as those incurred professedly for the general defense. The defense of each part is that of the whole; and unless all the expenditures are brought into a common mass, the tendency must be to add to the calamities suffered by being the most exposed to the ravages of war, an increase of burthens."[4]

The only discussion of a preliminary kind which remains relates to the distinctions of the debt into principal and interest. It is well known that the arrears of the latter bear a large proportion to the amount of the former. The immediate payment of these arrears is evidently impracticable, and a question arises, what ought to be done with them?

There is good reason to conclude, that the impressions of many are more favorable to the claim of the principal than to that of the interest; at least so far as to produce an opinion that an inferior provision might suffice for the latter.

But to the Secretary this opinion does not appear to be well founded. His investigations of the subject have led him to a conclusion that the arrears of interest have pretensions at least equal to the principal.

The liquidated debt, traced to its origin, falls under two principal discriminations. One relating to loans; the other to services performed and articles supplied.

The part arising from loans, was at first made payable at fixed periods which have long since elapsed, with an early option to lenders either to receive back their money at the expiration of those periods or to continue it at interest 'till the whole amount of continental bills circulating should not exceed the sum in circulation at the time of each loan. This contingency, in the sense of the contract, never happened; and the presumption is that the creditors preferred continuing their money indefinitely at interest to receiving it in a depreciated and depreciating state.

The other parts of it were chiefly for objects which ought to have been paid for at the time, that is, when the services were performed or the supplies furnished, and were not accompanied with any contract for interest. . . .

If this view of the subject be a just one, the capital of the debt of the United States may be considered in the light of an annuity at the rate of six per cent. per annum, redeemable at the pleasure of the government by payment of the principal. For it seems to be a clear position that when a public contracts a debt payable with interest, without any precise time being stipulated or understood for payment of the capital, that time is a matter of pure discretion with the government, which is at liberty to consult its own convenience respecting it, taking care to pay the interest with punctuality.

Wherefore, as long as the United States should pay the interest of their debt as it accrued, their creditors would have no right to demand the principal.

But with regard to the arrears of interest the case is different. These are now due, and those to whom they are due have a right to claim immediate payment. To say that it would be impracticable to comply would not vary the nature of the right. Nor can this idea of impracticability be honorably carried further than to justify the proposition of a new contract upon the basis of a commutation of that right for an equivalent. This equivalent too ought to be a real and fair one. And what other fair equivalent can be imagined for the detention of money but a reasonable interest? Or what can be the standard of that interest, but the market rate, or the rate which the government pays in ordinary cases?

From this view of the matter, which appears to be the accurate and true one, it will follow, that the arrears of interest are entitled to an equal provision with the principal of the debt.

The result of the foregoing discussions is this—That there ought to be no discrimination between the original holders of the debt and present possessors by purchase—That it is expedient there should be an assumption of the state debts by the Union, and that the arrears of interest should be provided for on an equal footing with the principal.

The next enquiry, in order, towards determining the nature of a proper provision, respects the quantum of the debt and the present rates of interest.

The debt of the union is distinguishable into foreign and domestic.

|  | Dollars. | Cents. |
|---|---|---|
| The foreign debt . . . amounts to principal bearing an interest of four, and partly an interest of five per cent. | 10,070,307 | |
| Arrears of interest to the last of December, 1789, | 1,640,071 | 62 |
| Making together, dollars | 11,710,378 | 62 |
| The domestic debt may be sub-divided into liquidated and unliquidated; principal and interest. | | |
| The principal of the liquidated part . . . amounts to bearing an interest of six per cent. | 27,383,917 | 74 |
| The arrears of interest . . . to the end of 1790, amount to | 13,030,168 | 20 |
| Making together, dollars | 40,414,085 | 94 |

This includes all that has been paid in indents (except what has come into the treasury of the United States) which, in the opinion of the Secretary, can be considered in no other light than as interest due.

The unliquidated part of the domestic debt, which consists chiefly of the continental bills of credit, is not ascertained, but may be estimated at 2,000,000 dollars.

These several sums constitute the whole of the debt of the United States, amounting together to 54,124,464 dollars, and 56 cents.

That of the individual states is not equally well ascertained. . . . The Secretary, however, presumes, that the total amount may be safely stated at 25 millions of dollars, principal and interest. The present rate of interest of the state debts is in general the same with that of the domestic debt of the union.

On the supposition that the arrears of interest ought to be provided for on the same terms with the principal, the annual amount of the interest, which at the existing rates would be payable on the entire mass of the public debt, would be,

|  | *Dollars.* | *Cents.* |
|---|---|---|
| On the foreign debt, computing the interest on the principal as it stands, and allowing four per cent on the arrears of interest, | 542,599 | 66 |
| On the domestic debt, including that of the states, | 4,044,845 | 15 |
| Making together, dollars | 4,587,444 | 81 |

The interesting problem now occurs. Is it in the power of the United States, consistently with those prudential considerations which ought not to be overlooked, to make a provision equal to the purpose of funding the whole debt at the rates of interest which it now bears, in addition to the sum which will be necessary for the current service of the government?

The Secretary will not say that such provision would exceed the abilities of the country; but he is clearly of opinion that to make it would require the extension of taxation to a degree, and to objects, which the true interest of the public creditors forbids. It is therefore to be hoped, and even to be expected, that they will cheerfully concur in such modifications of their claims, on fair and equitable principles, as will facilitate to the government an arrangement substantial, durable, and satisfactory to the community. The importance of the last characteristic will strike every discerning mind. No plan, however flattering in appearance, to which it did not belong could be truly entitled to confidence.

It will not be forgotten that exigencies may ere long, arise which would call for resources greatly beyond what is now deemed sufficient for the current service; and that, should the faculties of the country be exhausted or even *strained* to provide for the public debt, there could be less reliance on the sacredness of the provision.

But while the Secretary yields to the force of these considerations, he does not lose sight of those fundamental principles of good faith which dictate that every practicable exertion ought to be made scrupulously to fulfill the engagements of the government; that no change in the rights of its creditors ought to be attempted without their voluntary consent; and that this consent ought to be voluntary in fact as well as in name. Consequently, that every proposal of a change ought to be in the shape of an appeal to their reason and to their interest, not to their necessities. To this end it is requisite that a fair equivalent should be offered for what may be asked to be given up, and unquestionable security for the remainder. Without this, an alteration consistently with the credit and honor of the nation would be impracticable.

It remains to see, what can be proposed in conformity to these views.

It has been remarked that the capital of the debt of the union is to be viewed in the light of an annuity at the rate of six per cent. per annum, redeemable at the pleasure of the government by payment of the principal. And it will not be required, that the arrears of interest should be considered in a more favorable light. The same character, in general, may be applied to the debts of the individual states.

This view of the subject admits that the United States would have it in their power to avail themselves of any fall in the market rate of interest for reducing that of the debt.

This property of the debt is favorable to the public; unfavorable to the creditor. And may facilitate an arrangement for the reduction of interest upon the basis of a fair equivalent.

Probabilities are always a rational ground of contract. The Secretary conceives that there is good reason to believe, if effectual measures are taken to establish public credit, that the government rate of interest in the United States will in a very short time fall at least as low as five per cent. and that in a period not exceeding twenty years, it will sink still lower, probably to four.

There are two principal causes which will be likely to produce this effect; one, the low rate of interest in Europe; the other, the increase of the monied capital of the nation by the funding of the public debt.

From three to four per cent. is deemed good interest in several parts of Europe. Even less is deemed so in some places. And it is on the decline; the increasing plenty of money continually tending to lower it. It is presumable that no country will be able to borrow of foreigners upon better terms than the United States, because none can, perhaps, afford so good security. Our situation exposes us less than that of any other nation to those casualties which are the chief causes of expense; our encumbrances in proportion to our real means are less, though these cannot immediately be brought so readily into action, and our progress in resources from the early state of the country, and the immense tracts of unsettled territory must necessarily exceed that of any other. The advantages of this situation have already engaged the attention of the European moneylenders, particularly among the Dutch. And as they become better understood, they will have the greater influence. Hence as large a proportion of the cash of Europe as may be wanted will be, in a certain sense, in our market for the use of government. And this will naturally have the effect of a reduction of the rate of interest, not indeed to the level of the places which send their money to market, but to something much nearer to it than our present rate.

The influence which the funding of the debt is calculated to have in lowering interest has been already remarked and explained. It is hardly possible that it should not be materially affected by such an increase of the monied capital of the nation as would result from the proper funding of seventy millions of dollars. But the probability of a decrease in the rate of interest acquires confirmation from facts which existed prior to the revolution. It is well known that in some of the states money might with facility be borrowed on good security at five per cent. and not infrequently even at less.

The most enlightened of the public creditors will be most sensible of the justness of this view of the subject, and of the propriety of the use which will be made of it.

The Secretary in pursuance of it will assume, as a probability, sufficiently great to be a ground of calculation, both on the part of the government and of its creditors—That the interest of money in the United States will in five years fall to five per cent., and in twenty to four. The probability in the mind of the Secretary is rather that the fall may be more rapid and more considerable; but he prefers a mean as most likely to engage the assent of the creditors, and more equitable in itself because it is predicated on probabilities, which may err on one side as well as on the other.

Premising these things, the Secretary submits to the House the expediency of proposing a loan to the full amount of the debt, as well of the particular states as of the union. . . .

It will have appeared that in all the proposed loans the Secretary has contemplated the putting the interest upon the same footing with the principal: *That* on the debt of the United States, he would have computed to the last of the present year: *That* on the debt of the particular states, to the last of the year 1791; the reason for which distinction will be seen hereafter.

In order to keep up a due circulation of money, it will be expedient that the interest of the debt should be paid quarter-yearly. This regulation will at the same time conduce to the advantage of the public creditors, giving them in fact, by the anticipation of payment, a higher rate of interest, which may with propriety be taken into the estimate of the compensation to be made to them. Six per cent. per annum paid in this mode will truly be worth six dollars and one hundred and thirty-five thousandth parts of a dollar computing the market interest at the same rate.

The Secretary thinks it advisable to hold out various propositions, all of them compatible with the public interest, because it is in his opinion of the greatest consequence that the debt should, with the consent of the creditors, be remolded into such a shape as will bring the expenditure of the nation to a level with its income. 'Till this shall be accomplished, the finances of the United States will never wear a proper countenance. Arrears of interest, continually accruing, will be as continual a monument either of inability or of ill faith; and will not cease to have an evil influence on public credit. In nothing are appearances of greater moment than in whatever regards credit. Opinion is the soul of it, and this is affected by appearances as well as realities. By offering an option to the creditors between a number of plans, the change meditated will be more likely to be accomplished. Different tempers will be governed by different views of the subject.

But while the Secretary would endeavor to effect a change in the form of the debt by new loans, in order to render it more susceptible of an adequate provision, he would not think it proper to aim at procuring the concurrence of the creditors by operating upon their necessities.

Hence, whatever surplus of revenue might remain after satisfying the interest of the new loans and the demand for the current service ought to be divided among those creditors, if any, who may not think fit to subscribe to them. But for this purpose, under the circumstance of depending propositions, a temporary appropriation will be most advisable, and the sum must be limited to four per cent., as the revenues will only be calculated to produce in that proportion to the entire debt.

The Secretary confides for the success of the propositions to be made, on the goodness of the reasons upon which they rest; on the fairness of the equivalent to be offered in each case; on the discernment of the creditors of their true interest; and on their disposition to facilitate the arrangements of the government and to render them satisfactory to the community.

The remaining part of the task to be performed is, to take a view of the means of providing for the debt according to the modification of it which is proposed.

On this point the Secretary premises, that, in his opinion, the funds to be established ought, for the present to be confined to the existing debt of the United States; as well, because a progressive augmentation of the revenue will be most convenient, as because the consent of the state creditors is necessary to the assumption contemplated; and though the obtaining of that consent may be inferred with great assurance from their obvious interest to give it; yet 'till it shall be obtained, an actual provision for the debt would be premature. Taxes could not with propriety be laid for an object which depended on such a contingency.

All that ought now to be done respecting it, is to put the matter in an effectual train for a future provision. For which purpose, the Secretary will in the course of this report submit such propositions, as appear to him advisable.

The Secretary now proceeds to a consideration of the necessary funds.

It has been stated that the debt of the United States consists of

|  | Dollars. | Cents. |
|---|---|---|
| The foreign debt, amounting, with arrears of interest, to | 11,710,378 | 62 |
| And the domestic debt amounting, with like arrears, computed to the end of the year 1790, to | 42,414,085 | 94 |
| Making together, Dollars | 54,124,464 | 56 |

The interest on the domestic debt is computed to the end of this year, because the details of carrying any plan into execution will exhaust the year.

|  | Dollars. | Cents. |
|---|---|---|
| The annual interest of the foreign debt has been stated at | 542,599 | 66 |
| And the interest on the domestic debt at four per cent. would amount to | 1,696,563 | 43 |
| Making together, dollars, | 2,239,163 | 09 |

Thus to pay the interest of the foreign debt, and to pay four per cent on the whole of the domestic debt, principal and interest, forming a new capital,

| will require a yearly income of | 2,239,163 dollars, 9 cents. |
|---|---|

The sum which in the opinion of the Secretary ought now to be provided in addition to what the current service will require. . . .

With regard to the installments of the foreign debt, these in the opinion of the Secretary ought to be paid by new loans abroad. Could funds be conveniently spared from other exigencies for paying them, the United States could ill bear the drain of cash, at the present juncture, which the measure would be likely to occasion.

But to the sum which has been stated for payment of the interest must be added a provision for the current service. This the Secretary estimates at six hundred thousand dollars; making, with the amount of the interest, two millions, eight hundred and thirty-nine thousand, one hundred and sixty-three dollars, and nine cents.

This sum may in the opinion of the Secretary be obtained from the present duties on imports and tonnage, with the additions which, without any possible disadvantage either to trade, or agriculture, may be made on wines, spirits, including those distilled within the United States, teas and coffee.

The Secretary conceives that it will be sound policy to carry the duties upon articles of this kind as high as will be consistent with the practicability of a safe collection. This will lessen the necessity both of having recourse to direct taxation, and of accumulating duties where they would be more inconvenient to trade, and upon objects which are more to be regarded as necessaries of life.

That the articles which have been enumerated will, better than most others, bear high duties can hardly be a question. They are all of them, in reality—luxuries—the greatest part of them foreign luxuries; some of them, in the excess in which they are used, pernicious luxuries. And there is, perhaps, none of them which is not consumed in so great abundance, as may justly denominate it a source of national extravagance and impoverishment. The consumption of ardent spirits particularly, no doubt very much on account of their cheapness, is carried to an extreme which is truly to be regretted, as well in regard to the health and the morals as to the economy of the community.

Should the increase of duties tend to a decrease of the consumption of those articles, the effect would be in every respect desirable. The saving which it would occasion would leave individuals more at their ease, and promote a more favorable balance of trade. As far as this decrease might be applicable to distilled spirits, it would encourage the substitution of cider and malt liquors, benefit agriculture, and open a new and productive source of revenue.

It is not, however, probable that this decrease would be in a degree which would frustrate the expected benefit to the revenue from raising the duties. Experience has shown that luxuries of every kind lay the strongest hold on the attachments of mankind, which, especially when confirmed by habit, are not easily alienated from them.

The same fact affords a security to the merchant that he is not likely to be prejudiced by considerable duties on such articles. They will usually command a proportional price. The chief things in this view to be attended to are that the terms of payment be so regulated as not to require inconvenient advances, and that the mode of collection be secure.

To other reasons which plead for carrying the duties upon the articles which have been mentioned to as great an extent as they will bear may be added these; that they are of a nature, from their extensive consumption, to be very productive, and are amongst the most difficult objects of illicit introduction. . . .

The proper appropriation of the funds provided and to be provided seems next to offer itself to consideration.

On this head, the Secretary would propose that the duties on distilled spirits should be applied in the first instance to the payment of the interest of the foreign debt.

That, reserving out of the residue of those duties an annual sum of six hundred thousand dollars for the current service of the United States; the surplus together with the product of the other duties, be applied to the payment of the interest on the new loan by an appropriation co-extensive with the duration of the debt.

And that, if any part of the debt should remain unsubscribed, the excess of the revenue be divided among the creditors of the unsubscribed part, by a temporary disposition, with a limitation, however, to four per cent.

It will hardly have been unnoticed that the Secretary had been thus far silent on the subject of the post-office. The reason is that he has had in view the application of the revenue arising from that source to the purposes of a sinking fund. The post-master-general gives it as his opinion that the immediate product of it, upon a proper arrangement, would probably be not less than one hundred thousand dollars. And from its nature, with good management, it must be a growing, and will be likely to become a considerable fund. The post-master-general is now engaged in preparing a plan which will be the foundation of a proposition for a new arrangement of the establishment. This, and some other points relative to the subject referred to the Secretary, he begs leave to reserve for a future report.

Persuaded as the Secretary is, that the proper funding of the present debt, will render it a national blessing: Yet he is so far from acceding to the position, in the latitude in which it is sometimes laid down, that "public debts are public benefits," a position inviting to prodigality, and liable to dangerous abuse,—that he ardently wishes to see it incorporated as a fundamental maxim, in the system of public credit of the United States that the creation of debt should always be accompanied with the means of extinguishment. This he regards as the true secret for rendering public credit immortal. And he presumes that it is difficult to conceive a situation in which there may not be an adherence to the maxim. At least he feels an unfeigned solicitude, that this may be attempted by the United States, and that they may commence their measures for the establishment of credit with the observance of it.

Under this impression, the Secretary proposes that the net product of the post-office to a sum not exceeding one million of dollars be vested in commissioners, to consist of the Vice-President of the United States or President of the Senate, the Speaker of the House of Representatives, the Chief Justice, Secretary of the Treasury and Attorney-General of the United States, for the time being in trust, to be applied by them, or any three of them to the discharge of the existing public debt, either by purchases of stock in the market, or by payments on account of the principal, as shall appear to them most advisable in conformity to the public engagements; to continue so vested until the whole of the debt shall be discharged.

As an additional expedient for effecting a reduction of the debt, and for other purposes which will be mentioned, the Secretary

would further propose that the same commissioners be authorized with the approbation of the President of the United States
to borrow, on their credit, a sum not exceeding twelve millions
of dollars, to be applied,

First. To the payment of the interest and installments of the
foreign debt to the end of the present year, which will require
3,491,923 dollars, and 46 cents.

Secondly. To the payment of any deficiency which may happen
in the product of the funds provided for paying the interest of
the domestic debt.

Thirdly. To the effecting a change in the form of such part of
the foreign debt, as bears an interest of five per cent. It is conceived that for this purpose a new loan at a lower interest may be
combined with other expedients. The remainder of this part of
the debt, after paying the installments which will accrue in the
course of 1790, will be 3,888,888 dollars, and 81 cents.

Fourthly. To the purchase of the public debt at the price it shall
bear in the market while it continues below its true value. This
measure which would be, in the opinion of the Secretary, highly
dishonorable to the government if it were to precede a provision
for funding the debt, would become altogether unexceptionable
after that had been made. Its effect would be in favor of the public
creditors, as it would tend to raise the value of stock. And all the
difference between its true value and the actual price would be so
much clear gain to the public. The payment of foreign interest on
the capital to be borrowed for this purpose, should that be a necessary consequence, would not, in the judgment of the Secretary,
be a good objection to the measure. The saving by the operation
would be itself a sufficient indemnity; and the employment of
that capital in a country situated like this would much more than
compensate for it. Besides, if the government does not undertake
this operation, the same inconvenience which the objection in
question supposes would happen in another way with a circumstance of aggravation. As long, at least, as the debt shall continue
below its proper value, it will be an object of speculation to foreigners, who will not only receive the interest upon what they
purchase, and remit it abroad as in the case of the loan, but will
reap the additional profit of the difference in value. By the government's entering into competition with them, it will not only

reap a part of this profit itself, but will contract the extent and lessen the extra profit of foreign purchases. That competition will accelerate the rise of stock; and whatever greater rate this obliges foreigners to pay for what they purchase, is so much clear saving to the nation. In the opinion of the Secretary, and contrary to an idea which is not without patrons, it ought to be the policy of the government to raise the value of stock to its true standard as fast as possible. When it arrives to that point, foreign speculations (which, till then, must be deemed pernicious, further than as they serve to bring it to that point) will become beneficial. Their money laid out in this country upon our agriculture, commerce and manufactures will produce much more to us than the income they will receive from it.

The Secretary contemplates the application of this money through the medium of a national bank, for which, with the permission of the House, he will submit a plan in the course of the session.

The Secretary now proceeds in the last place to offer to the consideration of the House his ideas of the steps which ought at the present session to be taken towards the assumption of the state debts.

These are briefly, that concurrent resolutions of the two Houses, with the approbation of the President, be entered into, declaring in substance,

That the United States do assume, and will at the first session in the year 1791, provide on the same terms with the present debt of the United States for all such part of the debts of the respective states, or any of them as shall, prior to the first day of January in the said year 1791, be subscribed towards a loan to the United States upon the principles of either of the plans which shall have been adopted by them for obtaining a re-loan of their present debt.

Provided that the provision to be made as aforesaid shall be suspended, with respect to the debt of any state which may have exchanged the securities of the United States for others issued by itself, until the whole of the said securities shall, either be re-exchanged, or surrendered to the United States.

And provided also, that the interest upon the debt assumed be computed to the end of the year 1791; and that the interest to be paid by the United States commence on the first day of January, 1792.

That the amount of the debt of each state so assumed and provided for be charged to such state in account with the United States, upon the same principles upon which it shall be lent to the United States.

That subscriptions be opened for receiving loans of the said debts at the same times and places, and under the like regulations as shall have been prescribed in relation to the debt of the United States.

The Secretary has now completed the objects which he proposed to himself to comprise in the present report. He has for the most part omitted details, as well to avoid fatiguing the attention of the House as because more time would have been desirable even to digest the general principles of the plan. If these should be found right, the particular modifications will readily suggest themselves in the progress of the work.

The Secretary in the views which have directed his pursuit of the subject, has been influenced, in the first place, by the consideration that his duty from the very terms of the resolution of the House obliged him to propose what appeared to him an adequate provision for the support of the public credit, adapted at the same time to the real circumstances of the United States; and in the next, by the reflection that measures which will not bear the test of future unbiased examination can neither be productive of individual reputation nor (which is of much greater consequence) public honor, or advantage.

Deeply impressed, as the Secretary is, with a full and deliberate conviction that the establishment of public credit upon the basis of a satisfactory provision for the public debt is, under the present circumstances of this country, the true desideratum towards relief from individual and national embarrassments; that without it, these embarrassments will be likely to press still more severely upon the community—He cannot but indulge an anxious wish, that an effectual plan for that purpose may during the present session be the result of the united wisdom of the legislature.

He is fully convinced that it is of the greatest importance that no further delay should attend the making of the requisite provision; not only, because it will give a better impression of the good faith of the country, and will bring earlier relief to the creditors; both which circumstances are of great moment to public credit: but because the advantages to the community from raising stock as speedily as possible to its natural value will be incomparably greater than any that can result from its continuance below that standard. No profit which could be derived from purchases in the market on account of the government to any practicable extent would be an equivalent for the loss which would be sustained by the purchases of foreigners at a low value. Not to repeat, that governmental purchases to be honorable ought to be preceded by a provision. Delay by disseminating doubt would sink the price of stock; and as the temptation to foreign speculations from the lowness of the price would be too great to be neglected, millions would probably be lost to the United States.

All which is humbly submitted.
Alexander Hamilton, *Secretary of the Treasury.*

# CHAPTER EIGHT

# To Wilhem and Jan Willink, Nicholaas and Jacob Van Staphorst, and Nicholas Hubbard (August 28, 1790)

*It cannot escape your observation, not only that the faith of our Government is fully pledged by the laws . . . for the performance of the conditions of the Loans which shall be made in consequence of them, but that there is an actual appropriation of unexceptionable funds for payment of the Interest.*

ON ENTERING THE office of Secretary of the Treasury, Hamilton had to deal not only with the messy condition of an unserviced domestic debt and its arrears left over from the War of Independence, but also with the foreign debt. During the war, the Continental Congress had borrowed extensively from abroad, principally from King Louis XVI of France. In part, however, the French loans had come not directly from the king but rather from Dutch bankers, who had lent the funds to America with guarantees provided by the king.

Complicating factors for Hamilton included France's entering the first phases of its own revolution. The king was in peril and therefore wanted his money returned even if he incurred a steep loss, and America was in arrears on its obligations for these loans. American and other speculators were in Europe offering to buy up the American debt owed to the king at deeply discounted prices in hopes of making big profits if and when Hamilton's debt restructuring occurred. The last issue was particularly bothersome as it would set a precedent that the United States was not creditworthy. The implication of poor credit would hurt Hamilton's future ability to borrow both domestically and abroad. It would also injure the credit of the Dutch bankers who held and had marketed other U.S. loans. Thus, the interests of both Hamilton and the Dutch bankers were aligned. They wanted to avoid any machinations by third parties that might harm American public credit.

In a previous letter to Hamilton, dated January 25, 1790, the Dutch bankers—the firm of Willink, Van Staphorst, and Hubbard—had raised concerns about these problems, referring to themselves as "the natural guardians of the Honor and credit of the united States in their Financial concerns [on the continent of Europe]."[1] Their solution was to offer a new loan by tapping into "the present plenty of Money [in Amsterdam]."[2] In this letter, Hamilton agrees to the terms of the loan, provides the legal basis on which he is authorized to borrow on behalf of the United States, and designates half of the funds to repay the French king. This template would continue for several years into the future, with Hamilton borrowing from the Dutch bankers to repay the French and also to invest on behalf of the federal government in his newly created Bank of the United States.

By the time of this letter, Hamilton had been in office almost a year. There was reason for optimism. His state-debt assumption plan had been enacted, and the economy was responding with a renewed burst of energy. Congress had authorized Hamilton to borrow on behalf of the nation. He had definite plans for restructuring both the foreign and domestic debts and restoring the credit of the United States.

Hamilton ends the letter with a boast that America would honor its financial commitments, with laws in place pledging to repay principal and interest. The Dutch could expect "absolute reliance" on "pecuniary dispositions, *once made.*" Therefore, Hamilton allowed himself to envision a future in which new loans could he made to the United States government on even better terms. On this score Hamilton would prove to be right for most of the next two and a quarter centuries as U.S. government debt became a prime asset for investors in both domestic and international capital markets.

This letter is not abridged.

Treasury Department
August 28th 1790

Gentlemen

Since the date of my last letter to you, the Legislature of the United States have passed two Acts, that is to say, on the fourth and twelfth of the present month; by which, among other things, they empower the President to cause to be borrowed on account of the United States Fourteen Millions of Dollars; The execution of which power has been by him committed to me: as will appear by a copy of each of those acts and of the President's commission or warrant to me herewith transmitted, authenticated in due form.

In consequence of these proceedings I am now in condition to determine on the provisional Loan announced in your letter of the 25th day of January last; and after due consideration I have concluded to accept and ratify it. For this purpose I send a power which I doubt not you will find competent, executed under my hand and the seal of the Treasury.

While I pursue, by this acceptance, what appears to me to be the interest of the United States, I am pleased with the opportunity of doing a thing which will be agreeable to you. At the same time, your own judgment will suggest to you, that in dismissing all scruple about the manner in which the business has been undertaken, I give you a proof of my confidence that no inconvenience will result from the precedent. The qualifications annexed by you to the undertaking show that you were fully sensible of its delicacy, and satisfy me that I need not press upon you the inadmissibility of anything of a like nature in future; however cogent the motives to it. The situation of the United States, hereafter, will not, I trust, expose their friends to such disagreeable dilemmas as they have been accustomed to in times past.

You will perceive that my authority to you goes as well to the making a new loan, as to the confirmation of that which you have undertaken. The design of this is not to double or increase the loan, but to enable you to give such a form to the business as circumstances may require. Your engagements, of course, must not extend beyond the sum of three Millions of Florins.

You will observe also that by the first act the time of reimbursement of the loans to be made in virtue of it is not to exceed fifteen years. That which is mentioned in your letter will somewhat, though but little, exceed this limit. I presume you can easily arrange the installments so as to come within it. I shall be glad it may be so modified if the state of the business will permit. But as the last act has no such limitation of time, I do not mean that the difference should be an obstacle.

I should also wish for particular reasons that the business may be so regulated as to give it the form of two loans; one, for two millions under the first Act, and the other, for one million under the second. But neither about this am I so solicitous, as to be willing that it should constitute an embarrassment. And it can only be proper if the time of reimbursement can be made to correspond with the first act.

I destine a million and a half of this sum as a payment to France under the direction of Mr. Short, our Chargé des affaires at that Court, whose order for the purpose you will be pleased to follow. Of this, however, I rely on your prudence that nothing will be said till you receive his instructions to remit or pay.

It cannot escape your observation, not only that the faith of our Government is fully pledged by the laws, of which I send you copies, for the performance of the conditions of the Loans which shall be made in consequence of them, but that there is an actual appropriation of unexceptionable funds for payment of the Interest. This, if properly considered, ought materially to influence the terms upon which the future loans shall be made. The nature of our present Government is such, that absolute reliance may be placed on its pecuniary dispositions, *once made.*

I have the honor to be with great consideration and esteem, Gentlemen, Your obedt. Servt.

Alex Hamilton
Secretary of the Treasy

# CHAPTER NINE

# First Report on the Further Provision Necessary for Establishing Public Credit (December 13, 1790)

*The object which appears to be most immediately essential to the further support of public credit . . . is the establishment of proper and sufficient funds for paying the interest which will begin to accrue . . . on the amount of the debts of the several States assumed by the United States.*

CONGRESS'S ADOPTION OF Hamilton's recommendation to assume the debts of the states in the summer of 1790 meant that the federal government would need more revenues to pay the interest on the assumed debt, which would commence in the first quarter of 1792. It therefore ordered Hamilton to prepare and report on what further provisions were needed to make these payments and establish public credit.

In this report, Hamilton estimates that an additional $827,000 of revenue annually would be needed to meet the mandated debt payments. To secure that revenue, he recommends increases in the duties already laid on imports of distilled spirits and a duty on spirits distilled in the United States—in short, taxes on foreign and domestic whiskey.

Hamilton reminds Congress that relying on the vigilance of official tax collectors to collect public revenues is better than the method, then common, of asking those taxed to comply and relying on their integrity even though they have an interest in avoiding tax payments. The latter system does not accord "with the bias of human nature," as it punishes the honest and rewarded the dishonest.

Hamilton further states that he prefers taxes on consumption to taxes on houses and land—i.e., property taxes. The latter were mainstays of state and local finance, and there might be clashes in the federal system if the federal government were to tax them also. Still, federal property taxes could be held in reserve in case of emergencies.

The alternative to domestic excise taxes such as the whiskey tax would be to increase the duties levied on imports. Hamilton was reluctant to increase these duties because it would increase the taxes merchants were already paying, which constituted most of federal government's revenues. Higher duties could discourage the merchants from cooperation with the government and compliance with the tax laws.

Further, Hamilton wanted to diversify the federal tax base. Customs duties were "too liable to the vicissitudes of the continuance, or interruption of foreign intercourse." He implied without saying so that a war might interrupt imports and reduce revenues from customs duties, so it would be a good idea to have some domestic revenues.

Hamilton closes this report by saying that the institution of a national bank is "a necessary auxiliary" to the support of public credit and "an indispensable engine in the administrations of the finances." He would submit his plan for a Bank of the United States in a separate report to Congress the next day (see chapter 10).

We have condensed this report from 3,882 words to 2,052 words.

Treasury Department
December 13th. 1790
[Communicated on December 13, 1790]

[To the Speaker of the House of Representatives]
In obedience to the order of the House of Representatives, of the ninth day of August last, requiring the Secretary of the Treasury to prepare and report, on this day, such further provision as may, in his opinion, be necessary for establishing the public credit

The said Secretary
Respectfully reports

That the object which appears to be most immediately essential to the further support of public credit, in pursuance of the plan adopted during the last session of Congress, is the establishment of proper and sufficient funds for paying the interest which will begin to accrue, after the year one thousand seven hundred and ninety one, on the amount of the debts of the several States assumed by the United States; having regard at the same time to the probable or estimated deficiency in those already established as they respect the original debt of the Union.

In order to this, it is necessary, in the first place, to take a view of the sums requisite for those purposes.

| | | |
|---|---|---:|
| The amount which has been assumed of the State Debts is | Dollars | 21,500,000 |
| The sum of annual interest upon that amount, which according to the terms of the proposed loan will begin to accrue after the year one thousand seven hundred and ninety one, is | Dollars | Cents 788,333.33 |
| The estimated deficiency in the funds already established, as they respect the original debt of the United States, is | | 38,291.40 |
| Making together | Dollars. | 826,624.73 |

For procuring which sum, the reiterated reflections of the Secretary have suggested nothing so eligible and unexceptionable, in his judgment, as a further duty on foreign distilled spirits and a duty on spirits distilled within the United States to be collected in the mode delineated in the plan of a bill, which forms a part of his report to the house of Representatives of the ninth day of January last. . . .

The product of these several duties (which correspond in their rates with those proposed in the report above referred to, of the ninth of January last) may upon as good grounds as the nature of the case will admit, prior to an experiment, be computed at Eight hundred and seventy seven thousand and five hundred Dollars; the particulars of which computation are contained in the statement which accompanies this report.

This computed product exceeds the sum which has been stated as necessary to be provided by fifty thousand eight hundred and seventy five Dollars, and twenty seven Cents; an excess, which if it should be realized by the actual product, may be beneficially applied, towards increasing the sinking fund. . . .

The Secretary, however, begs leave to remark that there appear to him two leading principles; one or the other of which must necessarily characterize whatever plan may be adopted. One of them makes the *security* of the *revenue* to depend chiefly on the *vigilance* of the *public officers*; the other rests it essentially on the *integrity* of the *individuals* interested to avoid the payment of it.

The first is the basis of the plan submitted by the Secretary; the last has pervaded most, if not all the systems which have been hitherto practiced upon in different parts of the United States. The oaths of the dealers have been almost the only security for their compliance with the laws.

It cannot be too much lamented that these have been found an inadequate dependence. But experience has on every trial manifested them to be such. Taxes or duties relying for their collection on that security wholly, or almost wholly, are uniformly unproductive: And they cannot fail to be unequal as long as men continue to be discriminated by unequal portions of rectitude. The most conscientious will pay most; the least conscientious, least.

The impulse of interest, always sufficiently strong, acts with peculiar force in matters of this kind, in respect to which a loose mode of thinking is too apt to prevail. The want of a habit of appreciating properly the nature of the public rights renders that impulse in such cases too frequently an overmatch for the sense of obligation: And the evasions which are perceived or suspected to be practiced by some, prompt others to imitation, by the powerful motive of self-defense. They infer that they must follow the example, or be unable to maintain an advantageous competition in the business; an alternative very perplexing to all but men of exact probity who are thereby rendered in a great measure victims to a principle of legislation which does not sufficiently accord with the bias of human nature. And thus the laws become sources of discouragement and loss to honest industry, and of profit and advantage to perjury and fraud. It is a truth that cannot be kept too constantly in view that all revenue laws which are so constructed, as to involve a lax and defective execution are instruments of oppression to the most meritorious part of those on whom they immediately operate, and of additional burdens, on the community at large. . . .

Duties of the kind proposed are not novel in the United States; as has been intimated in another place. They have existed to a considerable extent under several of the State Governments, particularly in Massachusetts, Connecticut and Pennsylvania. In Connecticut, a State exemplary for its attachment to popular principles, not only all ardent spirits, but foreign articles of consumption generally have been the subjects of an excise, or inland duty.

If the supposition that duties of this kind are attended with greater expense in the collection than taxes on land should seem an argument for preferring the latter, it may be observed that the fact ought not too readily to be taken for granted. . . .

Among other substantial reasons which recommend, as a provision for the public Debt, duties upon articles of consumption in preference to taxes on houses and lands is this: It is very desirable, if practicable, to reserve the latter fund for objects and occasions which will more immediately interest the sensibility of the whole community, and more directly affect the public safety. It will be a consolatory reflection that so capital a resource remains untouched by that provision which, while it will have a very material influence, in favor of public credit, will be also conducive to the tranquility of the public mind in respect to external danger, and will really operate as a powerful guarantee of peace. In proportion as the estimation of our resources is exalted in the eyes of foreign nations, the respect for us must increase; and this must beget a proportional caution neither to insult nor injure us with levity. While on the contrary, the appearance of exhausted resources (which would perhaps be a consequence of mortgaging the revenue to be derived from land for the interest of the public debt) might tend to invite both insult and injury by inspiring an opinion that our efforts to resent or repel them were little to be dreaded.

It may not be unworthy of reflection that while the idea of residuary resources, in so striking a particular, cannot fail to have many beneficial consequences; the suspension of taxes on real estate can as little fail to be pleasing to the mass of the community; and it may reasonably be presumed that so provident a forbearance on the part of the Government will ensure a more cheerful acquiescence on that of the class of the community immediately to be affected whenever experience and the exigency of conjunctures shall dictate a resort to that species of revenue.

But in order to be at liberty to pursue this salutary course, it is indispensable that an efficacious use should be made of those articles of consumption which are the most proper and the most productive; to which class distilled spirits very evidently belong: And a prudent energy will be requisite, as well in relation to the mode of collection, as to the quantum of the duty.

It need scarcely be observed, that the duties on the great mass of imported articles have reached a point which it would not be expedient to exceed. There is, at least, satisfactory evidence that they cannot be extended further without contravening the sense of the body of the Merchants; and though it is not to be admitted, as a general rule, that this circumstance ought to conclude against the expediency of a public measure; yet, when due regard is had to the disposition which that enlightened class of citizens has manifested towards the National Government, to the alacrity with which they have hitherto seconded its operations, to the accommodating temper with which they look forward to those additional impositions on the objects of Trade which are to commence with the ensuing year, and to the greatness of the innovation which in this particular has already taken place in the former state of things: there will be perceived to exist the most solid reasons against lightly passing the bounds which coincide with their impressions of what is reasonable and proper. It would be, in every view, inauspicious to give occasion for a supposition that trade alone is destined to feel the immediate weight of the hand of government in every new emergency of the Treasury.

However true, as a general position, that the consumer pays the duty; yet it will not follow, that trade may not be essentially distressed and injured by carrying duties on importation to a height which is disproportioned to the mercantile capital of a country. . . .

The inconveniencies of exceeding the proper limit in this respect, which will be felt everywhere, will fall with particular severity on those places which have not the advantage of public banks; and which abound least in pecuniary resources. Appearances do not justify such an estimate of the extent of the mercantile capital of the United States as to encourage to material accumulations on the already considerable, rates of the duties on the mass of foreign importation. . . .

It is presumed, too, that a still further augmentation would have an influence, the reverse of favorable to the public credit. . . .

A diversification of the nature of the funds is desirable on other accounts. It is clear that less dependence can be placed on one species of funds, and that too liable to the vicissitudes of the continuance or interruption of foreign intercourse, than upon a variety of different funds formed by the union of internal with external objects.

The inference, from these various and important considerations seems to be that to attempt to extract wholly from duties on imported articles the sum necessary to a complete provision for the public debt would probably be both deceptive and pernicious, incompatible with the interests not less of revenue than of commerce: That resources of a different kind must of necessity be explored: And that the selection of the most fit objects is the only thing which ought to occupy inquiry.

Besides the establishment of supplementary funds, it is requisite to the support of the public credit that those established should stand upon a footing which will give all reasonable assurance of their effectual collection.

Among the articles enumerated in the act making *further provision for the payment of the debt of the United States*, there are two, Wines and Teas, in regard to which some other regulations than have yet been adopted, seem necessary for the security of the revenue and desirable for the accommodation of the merchant.

*With these views, it is submitted,* that the term for the payment of the duties on wines be enlarged as it respects Madeira wines to eighteen months, and as it respects other wines, to nine months; and that they be collected on a plan similar to that proposed in relation to imported distilled spirits. . . .

To these more direct expedients for the support of public credit, the institution of a National Bank presents itself as a necessary auxiliary. This the Secretary regards as an indispensable engine in the administration of the finances. To present this important object in a more distinct and more comprehensive light, he has concluded to make it the subject of a separate report, which he begs leave herewith to submit No. II.

All which is humbly submitted
Alexander Hamilton
Secretary of the Treasury

# CHAPTER TEN

# Second Report on the Further Provision Necessary for Establishing Public Credit (Report on a National Bank, December 14, 1790)

*A National Bank is an Institution of primary impor-*
*tance to the prosperous administration of the Finances,*
*and would be of the greatest utility in the operations*
*connected with the support of the Public Credit.*

TOWARD THE END of his January 9, 1790, Public Credit Report (chapter 7), Hamilton told Congress that he would soon come back to it with a proposal for a national bank. Perhaps he did not anticipate that the debates concerning discrimination between original lenders to the government and current holders of its debt securities, and especially his controversial proposal to assume the debts of the states into the national debt, would occupy Congress for the next six months. When Congress finally enacted the gist of Hamilton's proposals for restructuring the national debt in July and August, it requested that he make further proposals for measures he would deem necessary to support public credit. By December he was ready to do that with two new reports. The first (see chapter 9) dealt with additional tax measures. The second, and far the more important, dealt with creating a national bank.

Hamilton had a vision and an understanding of the role of finance in the workings of an economy. Sound public and private credit strengthened government and promoted economic growth. Funding the national debt and promoting banking and a national bank were therefore complementary measures. Hamilton wanted to take advantage of the synergy of funding and banking. He embodied that synergy in his bank proposal. Shares in his proposed Bank of the United States (BUS) could be paid for mostly with government bonds and not specie (gold or silver). And those bonds were the very same ones that Congress had authorized when it adopted Hamilton's debt restructuring proposals. The new bonds began to appear in the fall of 1790 as public creditors exchanged old debt for new funded debt. Making the new debt tenderable for shares in the BUS would support bond prices at higher levels as individuals bought them to pay for Bank stock. That would accomplish two of Hamilton's objectives—raising the market value of public debt and making public debt serve as a means of capitalizing the Bank.

Next, the BUS would issue paper banknotes (currency) convertible into specie. BUS currency would then become a major component of the nation's money supply. In this fashion, the banking and funding systems would work together to produce growth.

In the United States today there are nearly six thousand banks, and therefore it might be difficult to imagine that in 1790 there were only three—the Bank of North America in Philadelphia, the Massachusetts Bank in Boston, and the Bank of New York. Two of the three had corporate charters from their respective states, but the Bank of New York as of late 1790 had been rebuffed by the state legislature after applying more than once for a charter. Shortly after Congress approved the BUS, New York relented and granted the Bank of New York a charter; the BUS would likely open a branch in New York, and rather than cede the ground of corporate banking to the federally chartered BUS, the legislature wanted to have a bank of its own. Hamilton wanted his BUS to prod the states into chartering more banks, and New York's action indicated his strategy was beginning to work.

Banks in the America of 1790 were novel, controversial, and misunderstood. The granting of a bank charter became a matter of serious debate in the state legislatures. Hamilton's Bank Report therefore became a groundbreaking document. Never before in America had such a lengthy treatise outlining the basic functions of modern banks and national banks been published. The charter outlined in the report became the basis for future charters of many U.S. banks and, with its authorization of a nationwide system of branch banks, had an even stronger influence on the development of the banking system in Canada.

Hamilton's early ideas on banking had been set forth almost a decade before in his letter to Robert Morris (see chapter 3). Hamilton's most succinct letter with respect to the utility of a national bank—more or less a summary of the Bank Report—was addressed to George Washington and dated March 27, 1791.[1] With hindsight we can see that in the decade of the 1780s Hamilton had developed his notions with respect to banking and economy. By 1791, with congressional enactment of his proposal for a national bank and the president's assent, his ideas were becoming a reality. In retrospect, Hamilton proved himself well ahead of his time.

The report opened with "a conviction . . . That a National Bank is an Institution of primary importance to the prosperous administration of the Finances, and would be of the greatest utility in the operations connected with the support of the Public Credit."

The Secretary then pointed to the success of European banking. Hamilton stressed that all the great powers of Europe possessed public banks and were indebted to them for successful trade and commerce. Hamilton's implication was clear: if young America wanted eventually to join the ranks of the elite powers, it too must create a banking infrastructure.

Next, Hamilton laid out the perceived advantages of a bank. The first would be "the augmentation of the active or productive capital of a country." Hamilton meant that the bank would perform the traditional function of bringing savers of capital and users of capital together. In short, the bank would be the heart of the monetary and financial system. Second, the bank would be a "greater facility to the Government in obtaining the pecuniary aids, especially in sudden emergencies." Why? Because its capital would be centralized and therefore readily available should the government apply for loans. This implied a potential "intimate connection of interest between the government and the Bank of a Nation." Third, the bank would ease the tax collection process.

Hamilton's report also addressed the arguments raised by the opponents of a national bank: that it would promote usury, it would prevent other types of lending, it would encourage overtrading and speculative ventures, it would aid and abet fraudulent traders with fictitious credit, and it would deplete specie from the country. Anticipating the intense debate later, Hamilton devoted almost twice as much space in the report to countering arguments against the bank as he did in discussing its advantages. He did not deny that problems might arise, but he contended that the advantages of banks and banking much more than offset them.

Once he had adequately countered the charges, Hamilton asked two questions: Was there an institution currently available to fulfill the role, and if the answer was negative, what form should a new bank take? The Bank of North America was the only institution worth upgrading, if only because it had a relationship with the government that dated back to the War of Independence. But he rejected the possibility for a number of reasons, including that the Bank of North America had a Pennsylvania charter that was limited to fourteen years, a capital base of only $2 million, directors who were nonrotating, and a lack of limitations on indebtedness. Hamilton suggested that either the Bank of North America alter its charter or an entirely new bank be organized.

The remainder of the report was devoted to a description of the proposed national bank. The bank would be chartered for twenty years, during which time the Congress would agree not to establish another national bank. This was done to make investment in the bank's stock attractive to investors. The bank's capital would be $10 million: $8 million from private sources and $2 million from the government. The government would not raise the $2 million directly in capital, but would borrow the $2 million from the bank and repay the sum in ten annual installments. The bank would have the right to issue notes or currency up to $10 million. The government would pledge that the bank's notes would be unique in that they were valid for payments to the United States. In short, the notes would be suitable for payment of taxes, a feature that would provide the national bank with an advantage over its state bank competitors.

The national bank would confer many benefits on the government, including a ready source of loans, a principal depository for federal monies that were transferable from city to city without charge, easier tax collections, and a clearing agent for payments on the national debt as well as government salaries. The Secretary of the Treasury would be empowered to inspect the state of the bank, although not more than once a week. The bill also imposed on the bank certain restrictions on loans to individual states and foreigners unless previously authorized by Congress, as well as a cap of 6 percent on the rate of interest that could be charged for loans and discounts. The government, as the largest stockholder, would share in the profits but have no direct participation in the management. In Hamilton's view, independent managers would prevent abuse by politicians and the government. The Secretary was adamant regarding rotating directors as a preventive measure against a small cadre of individuals' controlling the institution. Only a U.S. citizen could hold the post of director, and the directors were authorized to elect a president. Additionally, foreigners owning stock would not be allowed to vote in bank elections. Although Hamilton personally thought that the bank should not immediately establish branches because he anticipated administrative problems, the charter he wrote for it included the possibility that these might be opened. Hamilton also proposed limits on the amount of the bank's business that could be collateralized by land because of volatility in real estate prices.

Some historians conclude that the model for Hamilton's plan was the greatest banking force of the day, the Bank of England. In 1790, Tench Coxe, Hamilton's assistant at Treasury, sent him a note with a pamphlet he had written in 1786 which highlighted the English institution: "The Bank of England is better worth our attention, than any which has ever existed."[2] The parallels in the report between the two institutions are most easily visible in the clauses about restrictions on liabilities, the prohibition of trade in commodities, and the forbidding of financial aid to the state without the approval of the legislature. It should be noted, however, that the institution differed from its English predecessor in several significant ways: (1) Hamilton suggested a minimum specie requirement, whereas the Bank of England had none; (2) Hamilton directed that shareholders' votes be related to the size of their investment, whereas at the Bank of England each shareholder had only one vote regardless of the number of shares owned; (3) the U.S. government was to be a part owner of the bank, whereas the Bank of England was entirely owned by private investors; and (4) the bank was authorized to open branches around the United States, whereas the Bank of England would not open branches in that country until the 1820s.

Hamilton had recommended creation of a Bank of the United States as early as 1780 (see chapter 1), and when Congress enacted a more mature plan for such a bank in early 1791, it seemed he at last had gotten his way. Not quite. Opponents of the BUS immediately raised the issue of whether such a measure was constitutional. Hamilton had to fight that one last battle before the BUS could become a reality (see chapter 12).

We have abridged the Bank Report from 15,107 words to 8,959 words.

Treasury Department
December 13th, 1790
[Communicated on December 14, 1790]

[To the Speaker of the House of Representatives]
In obedience to the order of the House of Representatives of the ninth day of August last, requiring the Secretary of the Treasury to prepare and report on this day such further provision as may in his opinion be necessary for establishing the public Credit

The said Secretary further respectfully reports

That from a conviction that a National Bank is an Institution of primary importance to the prosperous administration of the Finances, and would be of the greatest utility in the operations connected with the support of the Public Credit, his attention has been drawn to devising the plan of such an institution upon a scale which will entitle it to the confidence, and be likely to render it equal to the exigencies of the Public.

Previously to entering upon the detail of this plan, he entreats the indulgence of the House, towards some preliminary reflections naturally arising out of the subject, which he hopes will be deemed neither useless nor out of place. Public opinion being the ultimate arbiter of every measure of Government, it can scarcely appear improper in deference to that, to accompany the origination of any new proposition with explanations which the superior information of those to whom it is immediately addressed would render superfluous.

It is a fact well understood, that public Banks have found admission and patronage among the principal and most enlightened commercial nations. They have successively obtained in

Italy, Germany, Holland, England and France, as well as in the United States. And it is a circumstance which cannot but have considerable weight in a candid estimate of their tendency that after an experience of centuries, there exists not a question about their utility in the countries in which they have been so long established. Theorists and men of business unite in the acknowledgment of it.

Trade and industry, wherever they have been tried, have been indebted to them for important aid. And Government has been repeatedly under the greatest obligations to them in dangerous and distressing emergencies. That of the United States, as well in some of the most critical conjunctures of the late war as since the peace, has received assistance from those established among us with which it could not have dispensed.

With this two-fold evidence before us, it might be expected that there would be a perfect union of opinions in their favor. Yet doubts have been entertained; jealousies and prejudices have circulated: and though the experiment is every day dissipating them within the spheres in which effects are best known; yet there are still persons by whom they have not been entirely renounced. To give a full and accurate view of the subject would be to make a Treatise of a report; but there are certain aspects in which it may be cursorily exhibited which may perhaps conduce to a just impression of its merits. These will involve a comparison of the advantages with the disadvantages, real or supposed, of such institutions.

The following are among the principal advantages of a Bank.

First. The augmentation of the active or productive capital of a country. Gold and Silver, when they are employed merely as the instruments of exchange and alienation, have been not improperly denominated dead Stock; but when deposited in Banks to become the basis of a paper circulation, which takes their character and place as the signs or representatives of value, they then acquire life, or, in other words, an active and productive quality. This idea, which appears rather subtle and abstract in a general form, may be made obvious and palpable by entering into a few particulars. It is evident, for instance, that the money which a merchant keeps in his chest, waiting for a favorable opportunity to employ it produces nothing 'till that opportunity arrives. But if instead of locking it up in this manner, he either deposits it in a Bank or invests it in the Stock of a Bank, it yields a profit during the interval in which he partakes, or not, according to the choice he may have made of being a depositor or a proprietor; and when any advantageous speculation offers, in order to be able to embrace it he has only to withdraw his money, if a depositor, or if a proprietor to obtain a loan from the Bank, or to dispose of his Stock; an alternative seldom or never attended with difficulty, when the affairs of the institution are in a prosperous train. His money thus deposited or invested is a fund, upon which himself and others can borrow to a much larger amount. It is a well established fact, that Banks in good credit can circulate a far greater sum than the actual quantum of their capital in Gold & Silver. The extent of the possible excess seems indeterminate, though it has been conjecturally stated at the proportions of two and three to one. This faculty is produced in various ways. First: A great proportion of the notes which are issued and pass current as Cash are indefinitely suspended in circulation, from the confidence which each holder has that he can at any moment turn them into gold and silver. Secondly, Every loan which a Bank makes is in its first shape a credit given to the borrower on its books, the amount of which it stands ready to pay, either in its own notes or in gold or silver, at his option. But in a great number of cases no actual payment is made in either. The Borrower frequently by a check or order transfers his credit to some other person, to whom he has a payment to make; who in his turn is as often content with a similar credit because he is satisfied, that he can, whenever he pleases, either convert it into cash or pass it to some other hand, as an equivalent for it. And in this manner the credit keeps circulating, performing in every stage the office of money, till it is extinguished by a discount with some person who has a payment to make to the Bank to an equal or greater amount. Thus large sums are lent and paid, frequently through a variety of hands, without the intervention of a single piece of coin. Thirdly, There is always a large quantity of gold and silver in the repositories of the Bank, besides its own Stock, which is placed there with a view partly to its safe keeping and partly to the accommodation of an institution which is itself a source of general accommodation. These deposits are of immense consequence in the operations of a Bank. Though liable to be redrawn at any moment, experience proves that the money so much oftener changes proprietors than place, and that what is drawn out is generally so speedily replaced as to authorize the counting upon the sums deposited as an *effective fund*; which, concurring with the Stock of the Bank, enables it to extend its loans and to answer all the demands for coin, whether in consequence of those loans or arising from the occasional return of its notes.

These different circumstances explain the manner in which the ability of a bank to circulate a greater sum than its actual capital in coin is acquired. This however must be gradual; and must be preceded by a firm establishment of confidence; a confidence which may be bestowed on the most rational grounds, since the excess in question will always be bottomed on good security of one kind or another. This every well conducted Bank carefully requires before it will consent to advance either its money or its credit; and where there is an auxiliary capital (as will be the case in the plan hereafter submitted) which, together with the capital in coin, define the boundary that shall not be exceeded by the engagements of the Bank, the security may consistently with all the maxims of a reasonable circumspection be regarded as complete.

The same circumstances illustrate the truth of the position that it is one of the properties of Banks to increase the active capital of a country. This in other words is the sum of them. The money of one individual, while he is waiting for an opportunity to employ it, by being either deposited in the Bank for safe keeping or invested in its Stock, is in a condition to administer to the wants of others without being put out of his own reach when occasion presents. This yields an extra profit arising from what is paid for the use of his money by others when he could not himself make use of it; and keeps the money itself in a state of incessant activity. In the almost infinite vicissitudes and competitions of mercantile enterprise, there never can be danger of an intermission of demand or that the money will remain for a moment idle in the vaults of the Bank. This additional employment given to money and the faculty of a bank to lend and circulate a greater sum than the amount of its stock in coin are to all the purposes of trade and industry an absolute increase of capital. Purchases and undertakings in general can be carried on by any given sum of bank paper or credit as effectually as by an equal sum of gold and silver. And thus by contributing to enlarge the mass of industrious and commercial enterprise, banks become nurseries of national wealth: a consequence as satisfactorily verified by experience as it is clearly deducible in theory.

Secondly. Greater facility to the Government in obtaining pecuniary aids, especially in sudden emergencies. This is another and an undisputed advantage of public banks: one which as already remarked, has been realized in signal instances among ourselves. The reason is obvious: The capitals of a great number of individuals are by this operation collected to a point, and placed under one direction. The mass formed by this union is in a certain sense magnified by the credit attached to it: And while this mass is always ready and can at once be put in motion in aid of the Government, the interest of the bank to afford that aid, independent of regard to the public safety and welfare, is a sure pledge for its disposition to go as far in its compliances as can in prudence be desired. There is in the nature of things, as will be more particularly noticed in another place, an intimate connection of interest between the government and the Bank of a Nation.

Thirdly. The facilitating of the payment of taxes. This advantage is produced in two ways. Those who are in a situation to have access to the Bank can have the assistance of loans to answer with punctuality the public calls upon them. . . . The other way, in which the effect here contemplated is produced, and in which the benefit is general, is the increasing of the quantity of circulating medium and the quickening of circulation. . . . Even where the circulation of the bank paper is not general, it must still have the same effect, though in a less degree. For whatever furnishes additional supplies to the channels of circulation in one quarter, naturally contributes to keep the streams fuller elsewhere. This last view of the subject serves both to illustrate the position that Banks tend to facilitate the payment of taxes; and to exemplify their utility to business of every kind in which money is an agent.

It would be to intrude too much on the patience of the House to prolong the details of the advantages of Banks; especially as all those which might still be particularized are readily to be inferred as consequences from those which have been enumerated.

Their disadvantages, real or supposed, are now to be reviewed. The most serious of the charges which have been brought against them are—

That they serve to increase usury:

That they tend to prevent other kinds of lending:

That they furnish temptations to overtrading:

That they afford aid to ignorant adventurers who disturb the natural and beneficial course of trade:

That they give to bankrupt and fraudulent traders a fictitious credit which enables them to maintain false appearances and to extend their impositions: And lastly

That they have a tendency to banish gold and silver from the country.

There is great reason to believe that on a close and candid survey, it will be discovered that these charges are either destitute of foundation or that, as far as the evils they suggest have been found to exist, they have proceeded from other, or partial, or temporary causes, are not inherent in the nature and permanent tendency of such institutions; or are more than counterbalanced by opposite advantages. This survey shall be had in the order in which the charges have been stated.

The first of them is that Banks serve to increase usury.

It is a truth which ought not to be denied that the method of conducting business which is essential to bank operations has among us, in particular instances, given occasion to usurious transactions. The punctuality in payments which they necessarily exact has sometimes obliged those who have adventured beyond both their capital and their *credit* to procure money at any price, and consequently to resort to usurers for aid.

But experience and practice gradually bring a cure to this evil. A general habit of punctuality among traders is the natural consequence of the necessity of observing it with the Bank. . . .

The Directors of a bank too, though in order to extend its business and its popularity in the infancy of an institution they may be tempted to go further in accommodations than the strict rules of prudence will warrant, grow more circumspect of course as its affairs become better established, and as the evils of too great facility are experimentally demonstrated. They become more attentive to the situation and conduct of those with whom

they deal; they observe more narrowly their operations and pursuits; they economize the credit they give to those of suspicious
solidity; they refuse it to those whose career is more manifestly
hazardous. In a word, in the course of practice from the very
nature of things the *interest* will make it the *policy* of a Bank
to succor the wary and industrious; to discredit the rash and
unthrifty; to discountenance both usurious lenders and usurious
borrowers.

There is a leading view in which the tendency of banks will be
seen to be to abridge rather than to promote usury. This relates
to their property of increasing the quantity and quickening the
circulation of money. If it be evident that usury will prevail or
diminish according to the proportion which the demand for
borrowing bears to the quantity of money at market to be lent;
whatever has the property just mentioned, whether it be in the
shape of paper or of coin, by contributing to render the supply
more equal to the demand must tend to counteract the progress
of usury.

But bank-lending, it is pretended, is an impediment to other
kinds of lending, which by confining the resource of borrowing
to a particular class, leaves the rest of the community more destitute and therefore more exposed to the extortions of usurers. . . ..

The fact on which this charge rests is not to be admitted without several qualifications, particularly in reference to the state of
things in this country. . . .

These considerations serve in a material degree to narrow the
foundation of the objection, as to the point of fact. But there is a
more satisfactory answer to it. The effect supposed, as far as it has
existence, is temporary. The reverse of it takes place in the general
and permanent operation of the thing.

The capital of every public bank will of course be restricted
within a certain defined limit. It is the province of legislative prudence so to adjust this limit, that while it will not be too contracted for the demand which the course of business may create
and for the security which the public ought to have for the solidity of the paper which may be issued by the bank, it will still be
within the compass of the pecuniary resources of the community;
so that there may be an easy practicability of completing the subscriptions to it. . . .

The Bank furnishes an extraordinary supply for borrowers within its immediate sphere. A larger supply consequently remains for borrowers elsewhere. In proportion as the circulation of the Bank is extended, there is an augmentation of the aggregate mass of money, for answering the aggregate mass of demand. Hence a greater facility in obtaining it for every purpose.

It ought not to escape without a remark that as far as the citizens of other countries become adventurers in the Bank, there is a positive increase of the gold and silver of the Country. . . .

That Banks furnish temptations to overtrading is the third of the enumerated objections. This must mean that by affording additional aids to mercantile enterprise, they induce the merchant sometimes to adventure beyond the prudent or salutary point. But the very statement of the thing shows that the subject of the charge is an occasional ill incident to a general good. Credit of every kind (as a species of which only can bank lending have the effect supposed) must be in different degrees chargeable with the same inconvenience. It is even applicable to gold and silver when they abound in circulation. But would it be wise on this account to decry the precious metals, to root out credit; or to proscribe the means of that enterprise which is the main spring of trade and a principal source of national wealth because it now and then runs into excesses, of which overtrading is one?

If the abuses of a beneficial thing are to determine its condemnation, there is scarcely a source of public prosperity which will not speedily be closed. In every case, the evil is to be compared with the good; and in the present case such a comparison will issue in this, that the new and increased energies derived to commercial enterprise from the aid of banks are a source of general profit and advantage which greatly outweigh the partial ills of the overtrading of a few individuals at particular times, or of numbers in particular conjunctures.

The fourth and fifth charges may be considered together. These relate to the aid which is sometimes afforded by banks to unskillful adventurers and fraudulent traders. These charges also have some degree of foundation, though far less than has been pretended; and they add to the instances of partial ills connected with more extensive and overbalancing benefits.

The practice of giving fictitious credit to improper persons is one of those evils which experience guided by interest speedily corrects. The bank itself is in so much jeopardy of being a sufferer by it that it has the strongest of all inducements to be on its guard. It may not only be injured immediately by the delinquencies of the persons to whom such credit is given; but eventually, by the incapacities of others, whom their impositions or failures may have ruined.

Nor is there much danger of a bank's being betrayed into this error from want of information. The Directors, themselves, being for the most part selected from the class of Traders are to be expected to possess individually an accurate knowledge of the characters and situations of those who come within that description. . . . Hence it not infrequently happens that Banks are the first to discover the unsoundness of such characters, and by withholding credit to announce to the public that they are not entitled to it.

If banks, in spite of every precaution, are sometimes betrayed into giving a false credit to the persons described, they more frequently enable honest and industrious men of small or perhaps of no capital to undertake and prosecute business with advantage to themselves and to the community; and assist merchants of both capital and credit who meet with fortuitous and unforeseen shocks, which might without such helps prove fatal to them and to others; to make head against their misfortunes and finally to retrieve their affairs: Circumstances, which form no inconsiderable encomium on the utility of Banks.

But the last and heaviest charge is still to be examined. This is that Banks tend to banish the gold and silver of the Country.

The force of this objection rests upon their being an engine of paper credit, which by furnishing a substitute for the metals is supposed to promote their exportation. It is an objection, which if it has any foundation lies not against Banks, peculiarly, but against every species of paper credit.

The most common answer given to it is that the thing supposed is of little, or no consequence; that it is immaterial what serves the purpose of money, whether paper or gold and silver; that the effect of both upon industry is the same; and that the intrinsic wealth of a nation is to be measured not by the abundance of the precious metals contained in it, but by the quantity of the productions of its labor and industry.

This answer is not destitute of solidity, though not entirely satisfactory. It is certain that the vivification of industry by a full circulation with the aid of a proper and well regulated paper credit, may more than compensate for the loss of a part of the gold and silver of a Nation; if the consequence of avoiding that loss should be a scanty or defective circulation.

But the positive and permanent increase or decrease of the precious metals in a Country can hardly ever be a matter of indifference. As the commodity taken in lieu of every other, it is a species of the most effective wealth; and as the money of the world, it is of great concern to the state that it possess a sufficiency of it to face any demands which the protection of its external interests may create. . . .

The objection seems to admit of another and a more conclusive answer which controverts the fact itself. A nation that has no mines of its own must derive the precious metals from others, generally speaking in exchange for the products of its labor and industry. The quantity it will possess will therefore, in the ordinary course of things be regulated by the favorable or unfavorable balance of its trade; that is, by the proportion between its abilities to supply foreigners, and its wants of them; between the amount of its exportations and that of its importations. Hence the state of its agriculture and manufactures, the quantity and *quality* of its labor and industry must, in the main, influence and determine the increase or decrease of its gold and silver.

If this be true, the inference seems to be that well constituted Banks favor the increase of the precious metals. It has been shown that they augment in different ways the active capital of the country. This it is which generates employment; which animates and expands labor and industry. Every addition which is made to it, by contributing to put in motion a greater quantity of both, tends to create a greater quantity of the products of both: And, by furnishing more materials for exportation, conduces to a favorable balance of trade and consequently to the introduction and increase of gold and silver. . . .

These several views of the subject appear sufficient to impress a full conviction of the utility of Banks, and to demonstrate that they are of great importance not only in relation to the administration of the finances, but in the general system of the political economy.

The judgment of many concerning them has no doubt been perplexed by the misinterpretation of appearances which were to be ascribed to other causes. The general devastation of personal property occasioned by the late war naturally produced, on the one hand, a great demand for money, and on the other a great deficiency of it to answer the demand. Some injudicious laws which grew out of the public distresses, by impairing confidence and causing a part of the inadequate sum in the country to be locked up, aggravated the evil. . . .

These evils have either ceased, or been greatly mitigated. Their more complete extinction may be looked for from that additional security to property which the constitution of the United States happily gives (a circumstance of prodigious moment in the scale both of public and private prosperity), from the attraction of foreign capital, under the auspices of that security, to be employed upon objects & in enterprises, for which the state of this country opens a wide and inviting field, from the consistency and stability which the public debt is fast acquiring, as well in the public opinion at home and abroad as in fact; from the augmentation of capital which that circumstance and the quarter yearly payment of interest will afford; and from the more copious circulation which will be likely to be created by a well constituted National Bank.

The establishment of Banks in this country seems to be recommended by reasons of a peculiar nature. Previously to the revolution circulation was in a great measure carried on by paper emitted by the several local governments. In Pennsylvania alone the quantity of it was near a million and a half of dollars. This auxiliary may be said to be now at an end. And it is generally supposed that there has been for some time past a deficiency of circulating medium. . . .

The appearances alluded to are, greater prevalence of direct barter in the more interior districts of the country, which however has been for some time past gradually lessening; and greater difficulty generally in the advantageous alienation of improved real estate; which also has of late diminished, but is still seriously felt in different parts of the Union. The difficulty of getting money, which has been a general complaint, is not added to the number; because it is the complaint of all times, and one in which imagination must ever have too great scope to permit an appeal to it.

If the supposition of such a deficiency be in any degree founded, and some aid to circulation be desirable, it remains to inquire what ought to be the nature of that aid.

The emitting of paper money by the authority of Government is wisely prohibited to the individual States by the National Constitution. And the spirit of that prohibition ought not to be disregarded by the Government of the United States. Though paper emissions under a general authority might have some advantages not applicable, and be free from some disadvantages which are applicable to the like emissions by the States separately; yet they are of a nature so liable to abuse, and it may even be affirmed so certain of being abused, that the wisdom of the Government will be shown in never trusting itself with the use of so seducing and dangerous an expedient. In times of tranquility it might have no ill consequence: it might even perhaps be managed in a way to be productive of good; but in great and trying emergencies there is almost a moral certainty of its becoming mischievous. The stamping of paper is an operation so much easier than the laying of taxes that a government, in the practice of paper emissions would rarely fail in any such emergency to indulge itself too far in the employment of that resource, to avoid as much as possible one less auspicious to present popularity. If it should not even be carried so far as to be rendered an absolute bubble, it would at least be likely to be extended to a degree which would occasion an inflated and artificial state of things incompatible with the regular and prosperous course of the political economy.

Among other material differences between a paper currency issued by the mere authority of Government, and one issued by a Bank payable in coin, is this—That in the first case, there is no standard to which an appeal can be made as to the quantity which will only satisfy, or which will surcharge the circulation; in the last, that standard results from the demand. If more should be issued, than is necessary, it will return upon the bank. Its emissions, as elsewhere intimated, must always be in a compound ratio to the fund and to the demand: Whence it is evident that there is a limitation in the nature of the thing: While the discretion of the government is the only measure of the extent of the emissions, by its own authority.

This consideration further illustrates the danger of emissions of that sort, and the preference which is due to Bank paper.

The payment of the interest of the public debt at thirteen different places is a weighty reason, peculiar to our immediate situation, for desiring a Bank circulation. Without a paper in general currency, equivalent to gold and silver, a considerable proportion of the specie of the country must always be suspended from circulation and left to accumulate preparatory to each day of payment; and as often as one approaches there must in several cases be an actual transportation of the metals at both expense and risk from their natural and proper reservoirs to distant places. This necessity will be felt very injuriously to the trade of some of the States; and will embarrass not a little the operations of the Treasury in those States. It will also obstruct those negotiations, between different parts of the Union by the instrumentality of Treasury bills, which have already afforded valuable accommodations to Trade in general.

Assuming it then as a consequence from what has been said that a national bank is a desirable institution; two inquiries emerge. Is there no such institution already in being which has a claim to that character, and which supersedes the propriety or necessity of another? If there be none, what are the principles upon which one ought to be established?

There are at present three banks in the United States. That of North America, established in the city of Philadelphia; that of New York, established in the city of New York; that of Massachusetts, established in the city of Boston. Of these three, the first is the only one which has at any time had a direct relation to the Government of the United States.

The Bank of North America originated in a resolution of Congress of the 26th of May 1781, founded upon a proposition of the Superintendant of finance, which was afterwards carried into execution by an ordinance of the 31st of December following, entitled, "An Ordinance to incorporate the Subscribers to the Bank of North America."

The aid afforded to the United States by this institution during the remaining period of the war was of essential consequence, and its conduct towards them since the peace has not weakened its title to their patronage and favor. So far its pretensions to the character in question are respectable; but there are circumstances which militate against them, and considerations which indicate the propriety of an establishment on different principles.

The Directors of this Bank, on behalf of their constituents, have since *accepted* and *acted* under a new charter from the State of Pennsylvania, materially variant from their original one; and which so narrows the foundation of the institution as to render it an incompetent basis for the extensive purposes of a National Bank. . . .

A further consideration in favor of a change is the improper rule, by which the right of voting for Directors is regulated in the plan upon which the Bank of North America was originally constituted, namely a vote for each share, and the want of a rule in the last charter, unless the silence of it on that point may signify that every Stockholder is to have an equal and a single vote, which would be a rule in a different extreme not less erroneous. It is of importance that a rule should be established on this head, as it is one of those things which ought not to be left to discretion; and it is consequently of equal importance that the rule should be a proper one.

A vote for each share renders a combination between a few principal Stockholders to monopolize the power and benefits of the Bank too easy. An equal vote to each Stockholder, however great or small his interest in the institution, allows not that degree of weight to large stockholders which it is reasonable they should have, and which perhaps their security and that of the bank require. A prudent mean is to be preferred. A conviction of this has produced a by-law of the corporation of the bank of North America, which evidently aims at such a mean. But a reflection arises here that a like majority with that which enacted this law may at any moment repeal it. . . .

If the objections which have been stated to the constitution of the Bank of North America are admitted to be well founded, they will nevertheless not derogate from the merit of the main design, or of the services which that bank has rendered, or of the benefits which it has produced. The creation of such an institution at the time it took place was a measure dictated by wisdom. Its utility has been amply evinced by its fruits. American Independence owes much to it. . . .

The order of the subject leads next to an inquiry into the principles upon which a national Bank ought to be organized.

The situation of the United States naturally inspires a wish that the form of the institution could admit of a plurality of branches. But various considerations discourage from pursuing this idea. The complexity of such a plan would be apt to inspire doubts, which might deter from adventuring in it. And the practicability of a safe and orderly administration, though not to be abandoned as desperate, cannot be made so manifest in perspective as to promise the removal of those doubts, or to justify the Government in adopting the idea as an original experiment. The most that would seem advisable on this point is to insert a provision which may lead to it hereafter, if experience shall more clearly demonstrate its utility and satisfy those who may have the Direction that it may be adopted with safety. It is certain that it would have some advantages both peculiar and important. Besides more general accommodation, it would lessen the danger of a run upon the bank.

The argument against it is that each branch must be under a distinct, though subordinate direction, to which a considerable latitude of discretion must of necessity be entrusted. And as the property of the whole institution would be liable for the engagements of each part, that and its credit would be at stake upon the prudence of the Directors of every part. The mismanagement of either branch might hazard serious disorder in the whole.

Another wish dictated by the particular situation of the country is that the Bank could be so constituted as to be made an immediate instrument of loans to the proprietors of land; but this wish also yields to the difficulty of accomplishing it. Land is alone an unfit fund for a bank circulation. . . .

Considerations of public advantage suggest a further wish, which is that the Bank could be established upon principles that would cause the profits of it to redound to the immediate benefit of the State. This is contemplated by many who speak of a National Bank, but the idea seems liable to insuperable objections. To attach full confidence to an institution of this nature, it appears to be an essential ingredient in its structure that it shall be under a *private* not a *public* Direction, under the guidance of *individual interest*, not of *public policy*, which would be supposed to be, and in certain emergencies under a feeble or too sanguine administration would really be, liable to being too much influenced by *public necessity*. The suspicion of this would most probably be a canker that would continually corrode the vitals of the credit of the Bank, and would be most likely to prove fatal in those situations in which the public good would require that they should be most sound and vigorous. It would indeed be little less than a miracle, should the credit of the Bank be at the disposal of the Government, if in a long series of time there was not experienced a calamitous abuse of it. It is true that it would be the real interest of the Government not to abuse it; its genuine policy to husband and cherish it with the most guarded circumspection as an inestimable treasure. But what Government ever uniformly consulted its true interest in opposition to the temptations of momentary exigencies? What nation was ever blessed with a constant succession of upright and wise Administrators?

The keen, steady, and, as it were, magnetic sense of their own interest as proprietors in the Directors of a Bank pointing invariably to its true pole, the prosperity of the institution is the only security that can always be relied upon for a careful and prudent administration. It is therefore the only basis on which an enlightened, unqualified and permanent confidence can be expected to be erected and maintained. . . .

As far as may concern the aid of the Bank within the proper limits, a good government has nothing more to wish for than it will always possess, though the management be in the hands of private individuals. As the institution, if rightly constituted, must depend for its renovation from time to time on the pleasure of the Government, it will not be likely to feel a disposition to render itself by its conduct unworthy of public patronage. The Government, too, in the administration of its finances has it in its power to reciprocate benefits to the Bank of not less importance than those which the bank affords to the Government, and which besides are never unattended with an immediate and adequate compensation. Independent of these more particular considerations, the natural weight and influence of a good Government will always go far towards procuring a compliance with its desires; and as the Directors will usually be composed of some of the most discreet, respectable and well informed citizens, it can hardly ever be difficult to make them sensible of the force of the inducements which ought to stimulate their exertions.

It will not follow from what has been said that the State may not be the holder of a part of the Stock of a Bank, and consequently share in the profits of it. It will only follow that it ought not to desire any participation in the Direction of it, and therefore ought not to own the whole or a principal part of the Stock; for if the mass of the property should belong to the public, and if the direction of it should be in private hands, this would be to commit the interests of the State to persons not interested, or not enough interested, in their proper management.

There is one thing, however, which the Government owes to itself and to the community; at least to all that part of it who are not Stockholders; which is to reserve to itself a right of ascertaining as often as may be necessary the state of the Bank, excluding however all pretension to control. . . . And its propriety stands upon the clearest reasons. If the paper of a Bank is to be permitted to insinuate itself into all the revenues and receipts of a country; if it is even to be tolerated as the substitute for gold and silver in all the transactions of business, it becomes in either view a national concern of the first magnitude. As such the ordinary rules of prudence require that the Government should possess the means of ascertaining, whenever it thinks fit, that so delicate a trust is executed with fidelity and care. A right of this nature is not only desirable as it respects the Government; but it ought to be equally so to all those concerned in the institution as an additional title to public and private confidence; and as a thing which can only be formidable to practices that imply mismanagement. The presumption must always be that the characters who would be entrusted with the exercise of this right on behalf of the Government will not be deficient in the discretion which it may require. . . .

Abandoning, therefore, ideas which however agreeable or desirable, are neither practicable nor safe, the following plan for the constitution of a National Bank is respectfully submitted to the consideration of the House.

I. The capital Stock of the Bank shall not exceed ten Millions of Dollars, divided into Twenty five thousand shares, each share being four hundred Dollars; to raise which sum, subscriptions shall be opened on the first Monday of April next, and shall continue open, until the whole shall be subscribed. Bodies politic as well as individuals may subscribe.

II. The amount of each share shall be payable, one fourth in gold and silver coin, and three fourths in that part of the public debt, which according to the loan proposed by the Act making provision for the debt of the United States, shall bear an accruing interest at the time of payment of six per centum per annum.

III. The respective sums subscribed shall be payable in four equal parts, as well specie as debt, in succession, and at the distance of six calendar months from each other; the first payment to be made at the time of subscription. . . .

IV. The Subscribers to the Bank and their successors shall be incorporated, and shall so continue until the final redemption of that part of its stock which shall consist of the public debt.

V. The capacity of the corporation to hold real and personal estate shall be limited to fifteen millions of Dollars, including the amount of its capital, or original stock. The lands and tenements which it shall be permitted to hold shall be only such as shall be requisite for the immediate accommodation of the institution; and such as shall have been bona fide mortgaged to it by way of security, or conveyed to it in satisfaction of debts previously contracted in the usual course of its dealings, or purchased at sales upon judgments which shall have been obtained for such debts.

VI. The totality of the debts of the company, whether by bond, bill, note, or other contract, (credits for deposits excepted) shall never exceed the amount of its capital stock. In case of excess, the Directors under whose administration it shall happen shall be liable for it in their private or separate capacities. Those who may have dissented may excuse themselves from this responsibility by immediately giving notice of the fact and their dissent to the President of the United States, and to the Stockholders at a general meeting to be called by the President of the Bank at their request.

VII. The Company may sell or demise its lands and tenements, or may sell the whole, or any part of the public Debt, whereof its Stock shall consist; but shall *trade* in nothing except bills of exchange, gold and silver bullion, or in the sale of goods pledged for money lent: nor shall take more than at the rate of six per centum per annum upon its loans or discounts.

VIII. No loan shall be made by the bank for the use or on account of the Government of the United States, or of either of them, to an amount exceeding fifty thousand Dollars, or of any foreign prince or State; unless previously authorized by a law of the United States.

IX. The Stock of the Bank shall be transferable according to such rules as shall be instituted by the Company in that behalf.

X. The affairs of the Bank shall be under the management of Twenty five Directors, one of whom shall be the President. And there shall be on the first Monday of January, in each year, a choice of Directors, by plurality of suffrages of the Stockholders, to serve for a year. The Directors at their first meeting, after each election, shall choose one of their number as President.

XI. The number of votes to which each Stockholder shall be entitled shall be according to the number of shares he shall hold in the proportions following, that is to say, for one share and not more than two shares one vote; for every two shares, above two and not exceeding ten, one vote; for every four shares above ten and not exceeding thirty, one vote; for every six shares above thirty and not exceeding sixty, one vote; for every eight shares above sixty and not exceeding one hundred, one vote; and for every ten shares above one hundred, one vote; but no person, co-partnership, or body politic, shall be entitled to a greater number than thirty votes . . .

XII. Not more than three fourths of the Directors in office, exclusive of the President, shall be eligible for the next succeeding year. But the Director who shall be President at the time of an election may always be reelected.

XIII. None but a Stockholder being a citizen of the United States shall be eligible as a Director.

XIV. Any number of Stockholders not less than sixty, who together shall be proprietors of two hundred shares, or upwards, shall have power at any time to call a general meeting of the Stockholders, for purposes relative to the Institution; giving at least six weeks notice in two public gazettes of the place where the Bank is kept, and specifying in such notice the object of the meeting.

XV. In case of the death, resignation, absence from the United States or removal of a Director by the Stockholders, his place may be filled by a new choice for the remainder of the year.

XVI. No Director shall be entitled to any emolument unless the same shall have been allowed by the Stockholders at a General meeting. The Stockholders shall make such compensation to the President for his extraordinary attendance at the Bank as shall appear to them reasonable.

XVII. Not less than seven Directors shall constitute a Board for the transaction of business.

XVIII. Every Cashier, or Treasurer, before he enters on the duties of his office shall be required to give bond, with two or more sureties, to the satisfaction of the Directors, in a sum not less than twenty thousand Dollars, with condition for his good behavior.

XIX. Half yearly dividends shall be made of so much of the profits of the Bank as shall appear to the Directors advisable. . . .

XX. The bills and notes of the Bank originally made payable, or which shall have become payable on demand, in gold and silver coin, shall be receivable in all payments to the United States.

XXI. The Officer at the head of the Treasury Department of the United States shall be furnished from time to time, as often as he may require, not exceeding once a week, with statements of the amount of the capital Stock of the Bank and of the debts due to the same; of the monies deposited therein; of the notes in circulation, and of the Cash in hand; and shall have a right to inspect such general account in the books of the bank as shall relate to the said statements; provided, that this shall not be construed to imply a right of inspecting this account of any private individual or individuals with the Bank.

XXII. No similar institution shall be established by any future act of the United States during the continuance of the one hereby proposed to be established.

XXIII. It shall be lawful for the Directors of the Bank to establish offices wheresoever they shall think fit, within the United States, for the purposes of discount and deposit only, and upon the same terms, and in the same manner, as shall be practiced at the Bank. . . .

XXIV. And lastly. The President of the United States shall be authorized to cause a subscription to be made to the Stock of the said Company, on behalf of the United States, to an amount not exceeding two Millions of Dollars, to be paid out of the monies which shall be borrowed . . . borrowing of the bank an equal sum, to be applied to the purposes for which the said monies shall have been procured, reimbursable in ten years by equal annual installments; or at any time sooner, or in any greater proportions, that the Government may think fit.

The reasons for the several provisions contained in the foregoing plan, have been so far anticipated, and will for the most part be so readily suggested by the nature of those provisions, that any comments which need further be made will be both few and concise.

The combination of a portion of the public Debt in the formation of the Capital is the principal thing of which an explanation is requisite. The chief object of this is to enable the creation of a capital sufficiently large to be the basis of an extensive circulation, and an adequate security for it. . . . [T]he original plan of the Bank of North America contemplated a capital of ten millions of Dollars, which is certainly not too broad a foundation for the extensive operations to which a National Bank is destined. But to collect such a sum in this country, in gold and silver, into one depository may without hesitation be pronounced impracticable. Hence the necessity of an auxiliary which the public debt at once presents.

This part of the fund will be always ready to come in aid of the specie. It will more and more command a ready sale; and can therefore expeditiously be turned into coin if an exigency of the Bank should at any time require it. This quality of prompt convertibility into coin renders it an equivalent for that necessary agent of Bank circulation; and distinguishes it from a fund in land of which the sale would generally be far less compendious and at great disadvantage. The quarter yearly receipts of interest will also be an actual addition to the specie fund during the intervals between them and the half yearly dividends of profits. . . .

The debt composing part of the capital, besides its collateral effect in enabling the Bank to extend its operations and consequently to enlarge its profits, will produce a direct annual revenue of six per centum from the Government, which will enter into the half yearly dividends received by the Stockholders.

When the present price of the public debt is considered, and the effect which its conversion into Bank Stock, incorporated with a specie fund, would in all probability have to accelerate its rise to the proper point, it will easily be discovered that the operation presents in its outset a very considerable advantage to those who may become subscribers; and from the influence, which that rise would have on the general mass of the Debt, a proportional benefit to all the public creditors, and, in a sense which has been more than once adverted to, to the community at large.

There is an important fact which exemplifies the fitness of the public Debt for a bank fund, and which may serve to remove doubts in some minds on this point. It is this, that the Bank of England in its first erection rested wholly on that foundation. The subscribers to a Loan to Government of one million two hundred thousand pounds sterling were incorporated as a Bank, of which the Debt created by the Loan and the interest upon it were the sole fund. The subsequent augmentations of its capital, which now amount to between eleven and twelve millions of pounds sterling, have been of the same nature. . . .

The interdiction of loans on account of the United States, or of any particular State, beyond the moderate sum specified, or of any foreign power, will serve as a barrier to executive encroachments; and to combinations inauspicious to the safety or contrary to the policy of the Union. . . .

The last thing, which will require any explanatory remark is the authority proposed to be given to the President to subscribe to the amount of two millions of Dollars on account of the public. The main design of this is to enlarge the specie fund of the

Bank, and to enable it to give a more early extension to its operations. Though it is proposed to borrow with one hand what is lent with the other, yet the disbursement of what is borrowed will be progressive, and Bank notes may be thrown into circulation instead of the gold and silver. Besides, there is to be an annual reimbursement of a part of the sum borrowed, which will finally operate as an actual investment of so much specie. In addition to the inducements to this measure which results from the general interest of the Government to enlarge the sphere of the utility of the Bank, there is this more particular consideration, to wit, that as far as the dividend on the Stock shall exceed the interest paid on the loan, there is a positive profit. . . .

All which is humbly submitted
Alexander Hamilton,
Secy of the Treasury

# CHAPTER ELEVEN

# Report on the Establishment of a Mint (January 28, 1791)

*The unit in the coins of the United States ought to correspond with 24 Grains and ¾ of a Grain of a pure Gold and with 371 Grains and ¼ of a Grain of pure silver, each answering to a dollar in the money of account.*

AS PART OF his overall financial plan, Hamilton needed to define the "money" of the United States—the unit of account, an agreed-upon measure used to place values on commercial and individual transactions. At the time the United States had a variegated money supply, comprised chiefly of a mixture of Spanish, English, Portuguese, and domestic coins. Adding a layer of complexity and confusion, different states had fiat paper currencies of differing values, even if they were called pounds or dollars, a natural impediment to interstate trade. Added to that mix and hampering overall commerce was a lack of actual coins in circulation. Hamilton had already taken steps to bolster the money supply by calling for the creation of the Bank of United States, which would issue banknotes and deposits convertible into specie dollar coins of the United States. But the specie dollar, the monetary base of the country, had yet to be defined. That was the subject of the Mint Report, one of Hamilton's most technical state papers.

Hamilton began his report, the final version of which he submitted to the House of Representatives in January 1791, per its request of 15 April 1790, with the observation that money was the critical lynchpin of all commercial economies because it encompassed "the general state of Debtor and Creditor; all the relations and consequences of *price*," as well as incomes, interest rates, and property values.

Creation of a mint, though complicated by "the immense disorder" in the nation's monetary affairs, was, as stated in the first draft of the report, "indispensable to the order which ought to reign in the pecuniary affairs of the government and of Individuals".[1] The United States could no longer allow the value of its primary unit of account, the Spanish milled dollar, to be determined by a "foreign sovereign." Nor could it continue to allow the same foreign coins to be rated differently "in different parts of the Union" or to suffer the use of different units of account in different states, an allusion to the continued use of Pennsylvania pounds, York shillings, and other holdovers from the colonial period. A national coinage, denominated in dollars as defined by the United States, would help to reduce such embarrassments and the "inconveniences" (i.e., transaction costs) associated with them.

Hamilton divided the report into six sections, each concerned with distinct issues.

1. *The U.S. unit of account.* All of the former colonies, now states, emitted local pounds less valuable than the British pound sterling. All of them had ratings for the Spanish dollar that were fixed by "invariable usage." There were multiple exchange rates in each state, between local pounds and British pounds, local pounds and Spanish dollars, and Spanish dollars and British pounds. The Spanish dollar, while common because of a trade surplus with the West Indies and Spanish America, held constant despite fluctuations in its silver content because it was "permitted to circulate by tale . . . very much as a mere money of convenience." The United States should fix the value of the U.S. dollar as a specific amount of silver and not rely on the Spanish dollar, which circa 1761 contained 374 grains of fine silver on average but now contains just 368 grains. The latter standard (one dollar = 368 grains) is what was intended in more recent contracts, and the holders of earlier contracts did not insist on being paid in older, more valuable Spanish dollars or their equivalent. The United States should fix the value of the U.S. dollar on that basis, which would be more consistent with the world ratio of gold to silver.

2. *The relative valuation of gold and silver coins.* Hamilton realized that if one of the precious metals was overvalued at a future

U.S. mint vis-à-vis the other, it would dominate the actual circulating money supply because people rationally would import the overvalued metal and export the undervalued one. Silver was difficult to find in Spain and England, for example, because they rated gold higher there than in other parts of Europe. So it was crucial to set the relative value accurately. Although difficult to achieve and maintain, a de facto bimetallic standard—i.e., the simultaneous circulation of both gold and silver coins—could increase the aggregate money supply and provide convenient denominations for both small (silver) and large (gold) payments. The proper ratio, Hamilton argued, based on both domestic and foreign ratios, was about 1:15 (gold: silver), which was less than the legal proportion in Britain (1:15.2) but more aligned with current market price. If bimetallism did not work, Hamilton's preference was for a gold definition of the dollar (gold standard) because gold's market value fluctuated less than that of silver and "less liberties have been taken with it, in the Regulations of different countries." A silver standard would encourage the circulation of bank paper money by rendering it easier to make large payments, but Hamilton thought that bank money "ought to be left to its natural course" and not artificially extended.

3. *The proper alloy composition of each.* Portugal, England, France, and Spain all professed to mix "one part alloy to 11 parts fine" in their gold coins, and the U.S. standard, set by a resolution of Congress on 8 August 1786, was to do likewise in both silver and gold coins. French and Spanish coins, however, were in reality somewhat baser than that because of an allowance made to the master of the mint to compensate for "errors and imperfections in the process." French and Spanish gold, therefore, was not 22 carat (11 parts in 12 fine). The gold coins of Germany, Holland, Sweden, Denmark, Poland, and Italy ranged from 1.25 to 1.875 carats finer than the British standard—i.e., almost 24 carat (pure gold). Silver coins also varied. In Britain, for example, the standard was 222 parts fine to 18 alloy. Alloying, Hamilton explained, was necessary to prevent excess expense during processing and "too great waste by friction or wearing" after coinage. The nature of the alloy also had to be considered. In silver coins, only copper served properly. In gold ones, a mixture of silver and copper in various ratios was used, the former to keep the final coin from becoming too reddish, and the latter to keep the final coins from turning out too white. Copper should be used with discretion, between one-third and one-half of the alloy.

4. *The fee, if any, the mint should charge for turning bullion (un-coined gold and silver) into coin.* "This forms," Hamilton noted, "one of the nicest questions in the doctrine of Money" because "the practice of different Nations is dissimilar." In England, coinage was "said to be entirely free." France, by contrast, charged 8 percent, while Holland charged about 1 percent for gold and 1.5 percent for silver. The resolution of August 1786 imposed 0.5 percent on gold and 2 percent on silver. But how should that fee be collected? Certainly not by reducing the quantity of gold and silver in the coins, which is nothing more than debasement, a degradation of the unit of account that would soon "be defeated by a rise of prices, proportioned to the diminution of the intrinsic value of the coins." In other words, the price level would rise, hurting those on fixed incomes and creditors public and private. "There is scarcely any point," Hamilton noted, "in the economy of national affairs of greater moment, than the uniform preservation of the intrinsic value of the money unit [unit of account]." The way to fund the mint, then, was to deduct the fee from the bullion brought in. People would be willing to pay the price in order to obtain national coins, which would be of "superior utility . . . for domestic purposes," especially if foreign coins were rendered "mere articles of Merchandize." Free coinage, by contrast, would, as in England, encourage speculators to melt down heavier coins only to have the government re-coin them at its own expense. (Such an operation would leave speculators with more coins than they started with, a clear profit.) In Britain there was a time delay between a deposit of bullion and receipt of coin equivalent to about 0.5 percent in lost interest, which did not cause untoward consequences, so Hamilton suggested that the mint start with that, for both gold and silver, as "an experiment." The 0.5 percent fee would probably be enough to fund the minting of gold coins, but it might not be sufficient to fund the minting of silver coins. So "some additional provision"—i.e., funding from the government—might "be found necessary."

5. *The value of the dollar, the denomination of coins, and the devices thereon.* Hamilton concluded, the U.S. dollar—i.e., the unit of account—should be defined as 24.75 grains of pure gold, or 27 grains of gold at the mint standard 22 carats (one-twelfth alloy), and 371.25 grains of pure silver, or 405 grains of silver at the mint standard 22 carats. Furthermore, decimal subdivisions (an earlier recommendation

of Jefferson, which Hamilton seconded) should be employed because nothing else was as "simple or convenient." Coins denominated in decimals, "dimes, cents, and milles, or tenths, hundredths and thousandths," would help to speed adoption of the system, as would the use of decimals in account books. Hamilton recognized a tradeoff between the number of different denominations produced (the more denominations, the greater the convenience) and the expense of coinage. He also knew that smaller coins were more costly to produce per dollar of coin in circulation. Given those considerations, Hamilton recommended minting a gold dollar, a gold ten-dollar piece, a silver dollar, and a silver dime, along with a copper cent and half-cent. The gold dollar's main purpose was to make the bimetallic standard real by having a coin of the same denomination in both metals. The halfpenny was a great aid to the poor, Hamilton noted, because it allowed them to buy necessities "in small portions, and at a more reasonable rate." For the names of the coins, Hamilton suggested the eagle ($10), unit or dollar ($1), a tenth ($.10, instead of a disme), a cent ($.01) and a half-cent ($.005). Next, Hamilton tackled the dimensions of the coins, noting a tradeoff between thickness, surface area, appearance, and rate of wear (loss of metal content). His rule was to make coins as thick as possible without reducing their "neatness and good appearance," and he suggested specific coins to emulate, like the double guinea, the Spanish dollar, and the Spanish one-eighth and one-sixteenth coins. Copper cent coins should weigh eleven pennyweight, which would give them an intrinsic value near their face value, something that the copper coins then in circulation did not achieve. This policy, Hamilton was quick to point out, would not create a profit, but it would deter counterfeits. Next, Hamilton moved on to the devices—the images—on the coins, noting that the topic was important as the designs "may be made the vehicles of useful impressions." He argued they should be "emblematical, but without losing sight of simplicity."

6. *The rating of foreign coins in terms of the domestic unit of account.* Hamilton wanted to abolish the circulation of foreign coins in the United States by tale or rating, which was the ubiquitous practice of banks, merchants, and other economic entities of assigning each foreign coin (of full weight) a value in dollars. While the abolition was "a necessary part of the system contemplated for the national coinage," Hamilton warned that was expedient to defer it

until the mint was producing substitutes. "A graduation may therefore be found most convenient," he concluded, proposing a period of several years, aided by the Treasury's giving any foreign coins it received into the mint for recoinage.[2] Banknotes could also help to fill some of the void.

Hamilton ended the report by briefly sketching the organization of the mint. It was to be headed by a director, or general superintendent. An assay master would receive and value the metals brought to the mint. A master coiner would make the coins, and a cashier would pay them out. An auditor would keep the mint's accounts. A modest number of clerks, workmen, and a porter would also be hired to do the everyday work. The other types of officers employed by European mints appeared unnecessary to Hamilton, who always sought "greater economy." He estimated the initial annual budget of the mint at $15,000 to $20,000.

In the Mint Act a year later, Congress adopted Hamilton's bimetallic definition of the dollar unit of account and laid out the U.S. Mint along the general lines prescribed in the report, with some exceptions and in somewhat more detail. The Mint fell victim to political squabbling, however, and it was not an important force in the economy until after the California gold strikes half a century later. The bimetallic definition of the U.S. dollar unit of account, however, proved an important and stable point of reference in domestic economic transactions, allowing market participants to agree on current and future prices eventually settled by payment in bank money or rated foreign coins.

Despite Hamilton's wish for a larger money supply based on both gold and silver, the United States was essentially on a silver standard most of the time from the 1790s to the 1830s. Then a tweak of the 15:1 mint ration overvalued silver, and the country was on a gold standard most of the time from the 1830s to the 1930s, when President Franklin D. Roosevelt ended it by nationalizing Americans' gold coins, melting them to make gold ingots, and storing the ingots at the Fort Knox, Kentucky, gold depository. From that time to the present, the domestic money supply of the United States has been a fiat paper currency.

The Mint Report ran to 15,044 words; we have abridged it to 7,958 words.

[Philadelphia, January 28, 1791
Communicated on January 28, 1791]

[To the Speaker of the House of Representatives]
The Secretary of the Treasury having attentively considered
the subject referred to him by the Order of the House of
Representatives of the fifteenth day of April last, relatively to the
establishment of a Mint most respectfully submits the result of his
enquiries and reflections.

A plan for an establishment of this nature involves a great variety of considerations, intricate, nice, and important. The general
state of Debtor and Creditor; all the relations and consequences
of *price*; the essential interests of trade and industry; the value
of all property; the whole income both of the State and of individuals are liable to be sensibly influenced, beneficially or otherwise, by the judicious or injudicious regulation of this interesting
object. It is one likewise not more necessary than difficult to be
rightly adjusted; one which has frequently occupied the reflections and researches of politicians without having harmonized
their opinions on some of the most important of the principles
which enter into its discussion. Accordingly, different systems
continue to be advocated, and the systems of different Nations,
after much investigation, continue to differ from each other.

But if a right adjustment of the matter be truly of such nicety
and difficulty, a question naturally arises, whether it may not be
most advisable to leave things in this respect in the state in which
they are. Why might it be asked, since they have so long proceeded in a train which has caused no general sensation of inconvenience, should alterations be attempted the precise effect of
which cannot with certainty be calculated?

The answer to this question is not perplexing. The immense
disorder which actually reigns in so delicate and important a concern, and the still greater disorder which is every moment possible call loudly for a reform. The dollar, originally contemplated
in the money transactions of this country, by successive diminutions of its weight and fineness, has sustained a depreciation of
5 per Cent. And yet the new dollar has a Currency in all payments
in place of the Old, with scarcely any attention to the difference
between them. The operation of this in depreciating the value of

property depending upon past Contracts; and (as far as inattention to the alteration in the Coin may be supposed to leave prices stationary) of all other property is apparent. Nor can it require argument to prove that a Nation ought not to suffer the value of the property of its Citizens to fluctuate with the fluctuations of a foreign Mint, and to change with the changes in the regulations of a foreign sovereign. This, nevertheless, is the condition of one, which having no Coins of its own, adopts with implicit confidence those of other Countries.

The unequal values allowed in different parts of the Union to coins of the same intrinsic worth; the defective species of them which embarrass the circulation of some of the States; and the dissimilarity in their several Monies of account, are inconveniencies which, if not to be ascribed to the want of a National Coinage, will at least be most effectually remedied by the establishment of one; a measure that will at the same time give additional security against impositions by counterfeit as well as by base currencies.

It was with great reason, therefore, that the attention of Congress under the late confederation was repeatedly drawn to the establishment of a Mint; and it is with equal reason that the subject has been resumed now that the favorable change which has taken place in the situation of public affairs admits of its being carried into execution.

But though the difficulty of devising a proper establishment ought not to deter from undertaking so necessary a work; yet it cannot but inspire diffidence in one whose duty it is made to propose a plan for the purpose, and may perhaps be permitted to be relied upon as some excuse for any errors which may be chargeable upon it, or for any deviations from sounder principles which may have been suggested by others, or even in part acted upon by the former Government of the United States.

In order to a right judgment of what ought to be done, the following particulars require to be discussed.

1st.—What ought to be the nature of the money unit of the United States?

2ndly.—What the proportion between gold and silver; if coins of both metals are to be established?

3dly.—What the proportion and composition of alloy in each kind?

4thly.—Whether the expense of coinage shall be defrayed by the Government, or out of the material itself?

5thly.—What shall be the number, denominations, sizes, and devices of the Coins?

6thly.—Whether foreign Coins shall be permitted to be current or not; if the former, at what rate and for what period?

A prerequisite to determining with propriety what ought to be the money unit of the United States is to endeavor to form as accurate an idea, as the nature of the case will admit, of what it actually is. The pound, though of various value, is the unit in the money of account of all the States. But it is not equally easy to pronounce what is to be considered as the unit in the Coins. There being no formal regulation on the point (the resolutions of Congress of the 6th. of July 1785 and 8th. of August 1786, having never yet been carried into operation) it can only be inferred from usage or practice. The manner of adjusting foreign exchanges would seem to indicate the Dollar as best entitled to that Character. In these the old piastre of Spain; or Old Seville piece of eight *Rials* of the value of four shillings and sixpence sterling is evidently contemplated. The computed par between Great Britain and Pennsylvania will serve as an Example. According to that, One hundred pounds sterling is equal to One hundred and sixty six pounds and two thirds of a pound Pennsylvania Currency; which corresponds with the proportion between 4/6 sterling and 7/6 the current value of the dollar in that State by invariable *usage*. And as far as the information of the Secretary goes, the same comparison holds in the other States.

But this circumstance in favor of the dollar, loses much of its weight from two considerations. That species of coin has never had any settled or standard value, according to weight or fineness, but has been permitted to circulate by tale without regard to either, very much as a mere money of convenience; while gold has had a fixed price by weight and with an eye to its fineness. The greater stability of value of the Gold Coins is an argument of force for regarding the money unit as having been hitherto virtually attached to Gold rather than to silver.

Twenty four grains and ⅞ of a Grain of fine gold have corresponded with the nominal value of the dollar in the several States; without regard to the successive diminutions of its intrinsic worth.

But if the dollar should, notwithstanding, be supposed to have the best title to being considered as the present unit in the coins, it would remain to determine what kind of dollar ought to be understood, or, in other words, what precise quantity of fine silver.

The old piastre of Spain, which appears to have regulated our foreign exchanges, weighed 17 dwt. 12 grains and contained 386. grains and 15 Mites of fine silver. But this piece has been long since out of circulation. The dollars now in common currency are of recent date, and much inferior to that both in weight and fineness. The average weight of them, upon different trials in large Masses, has been found to be 17 dwt. 8 grains. . . .

A recurrence therefore to the ancient Dollar would be in the greatest number of cases an innovation *in fact*, and in all, an innovation in respect to opinion. The actual dollar in common circulation has evidently a much better claim to be regarded as the actual money unit.

The mean intrinsic value of the different kinds of known dollars has been intimated as affording the proper criterion. But when it is recollected that the more ancient and more valuable ones are not now to be met with at all in circulation, and that the mass of those generally current is composed of the newest and most inferior kinds, it will be perceived that even an equation of that nature would be a considerable innovation upon the real present state of things; which it will certainly be prudent to approach, as far as may be consistent with the permanent order, designed to be introduced.

An additional reason for considering the prevailing dollar as the standard of the present money unit rather than the ancient one, is that it will not only be conformable to the true existing proportion between the two Metals in this Country, but will be more conformable to that which obtains in the commercial world, generally. . . .

The preceding view of the subject does not indeed afford a precise or certain definition of the present unit in the coins, but it furnishes data which will serve as guides in the progress of the investigation. It ascertains at least, that the sum in the money of account of each State corresponding with the nominal value of the dollar in such state corresponds also with 24 Grains and ⅝ of a grain of fine gold, and with something between 368 and 374 Grains of fine silver.

The next enquiry towards a right determination of what ought to be the future money unit of the United States turns upon these questions. Whether it ought to be peculiarly attached to either of the Metals, in preference to the other, or not; and, if to either, to which of them?

The suggestions and proceedings hitherto have had for object the annexing of it emphatically to the silver dollar. A resolution of Congress of the 6th of July 1785 declares that the money unit of the United States shall be a Dollar; and another resolution of the 8th of August 1786, fixes that dollar at 375 Grains and 64 hundredths of a grain of fine silver. The same resolution, however, determines that there shall also be two Gold Coins, one of 246 grains and 268 parts of a grain of pure Gold equal to ten dollars, and the other of half that quantity of pure Gold equal to five dollars: and it is not explained whether either of the two species of Coins, of Gold or Silver, shall have any greater legality in payments than the other. . . .

Contrary to the ideas which have heretofore prevailed, in the suggestions concerning a Coinage for the United States, though not without much hesitation arising from a deference for those ideas, The Secretary is upon the whole strongly inclined to the Opinion that a preference ought to be given to neither of the Metals for the money unit: Perhaps if either were to be preferred, it ought to be Gold rather than silver.

The reasons are these. The inducement to such a preference is to render the unit as little variable as possible, because on this depends the steady value of all contracts, and in a certain sense of all other property. And it is truly observed that if the unit belong indiscriminately to both the Metals, it is subject to all the fluctuations that happen in the relative value which they bear to each other: But the same reason would lead to annexing it to that particular one which is itself the least liable to variation; if there be in this respect any discernible difference between the two.

Gold may perhaps in certain senses be said to have greater stability than silver: As being of superior value, less liberties have been taken with it in the Regulations of different countries. Its standard has remained more uniform, and it has in other respects undergone fewer changes: As being not so much an article of Merchandize owing to the use made of silver in the trade with the East Indies and China, it is less liable to be influenced by circumstances of Commercial demand. And if reasoning by analogy, it could be affirmed that there is a physical probability of greater proportional increase in the quantity of silver than in that of Gold, it would afford an additional reason for calculating on greater steadiness in the value of the latter.

As long as Gold, either from its intrinsic superiority as a Metal, from its greater rarity, or from the prejudices of mankind, retains so considerable a preeminence in value over silver as it has hitherto had, a natural consequence of this seems to be that its condition will be more stationary. The revolutions, therefore, which may take place in the comparative value of gold and silver will be changes in the state of the latter, rather than in that of the former.

If there should be an appearance of too much abstraction in any of these ideas, it may be remarked that the first and most simple impressions do not naturally incline to giving a preference to the inferior or least valuable of the two Metals.

It is sometimes observed that silver ought to be encouraged rather than Gold, as being more conducive to the extension of Bank circulation from the greater difficulty and inconvenience which its greater bulk, compared with its value, occasions in the Transportation of it. But Bank circulation is desirable rather as an *auxiliary to*, than as a *substitute for* that of the precious metals; and ought to be left to its natural course. Artificial expedients to extend it by opposing obstacles to the other are at least not recommended by any very obvious advantages. And in general, it is the safest rule to regulate every particular institution, or object, according to the principles which in relation to itself appear the most sound. In addition to this, it may be observed that the inconvenience of transporting either of the metals is sufficiently great to induce a preference of Bank paper whenever it can be made to answer the purpose equally well.

But upon the whole it seems to be most advisable, as has been observed, not to attach the unit exclusively to either of the Metals; because this cannot be done effectually without destroying the office and character of one of them as money, and reducing it to the situation of a mere merchandize; which, accordingly, at different times has been proposed from different and very respectable quarters; but which would probably be a greater evil than occasional variations in the unit from the fluctuations in the relative value of the metals; especially if care be taken to regulate the proportion between them with an eye to their average commercial value.

To annul the use of either of the metals as money is to abridge the quantity of circulating medium; and is liable to all the objections which arise from a comparison of the benefits of a full with the evils of a scanty circulation. . . .

Neither could the exclusion of either of them be deemed, in other respects, favorable to commerce. It is often in the course of trade as desirable to possess the kind of money, as the kind of commodities, best adapted to a foreign market. . . .

If then the unit ought not to be attached exclusively to either of the metals, the proportion which ought to subsist between them in the coins, becomes a preliminary inquiry in order to its proper adjustment. This proportion appears to be, in several views, of no inconsiderable moment.

One consequence of overvaluing either metal, in respect to the other, is the banishment of that which is undervalued. If two countries are supposed, in one of which the proportion of Gold to silver is as 1 to 16 in the other as 1 to 15, gold being worth more, silver less in one than in the other, it is manifest that in their reciprocal payments, each will select that species which it values least, to pay to the other where it is valued most. Besides this, the dealers in money will from the same cause often find a profitable traffic in an exchange of the Metals between the two Countries. And hence, it would come to pass, if other things were equal, that the greatest part of the Gold would be collected in one, and the greatest part of the silver in the other. The course of Trade might in some degree counteract the tendency of the difference in the legal proportions by the market value; but this is so far and so often influenced by the legal rates that it does not prevent their producing the effect which is inferred. Facts, too, verify the inference. In Spain and England where gold is rated higher than in other parts of Europe, there is a scarcity of silver; while it is found to abound in France and Holland, where it is rated higher in proportion to gold than in the Neighboring Nations. And it is continually flowing from Europe to China and the East Indies, owing to the comparative cheapness of it in the former, and dearness of it in the latter.

This consequence is deemed by some not very material; and there are even persons who from a fanciful predilection to Gold are willing to invite it, even by a higher price. But general utility will best be promoted by a due proportion of both metals. If gold be most convenient in large payments, silver is best adapted to the more minute and ordinary circulation.

But it is to be suspected, that there is another consequence more serious than the one which has been mentioned. This is the diminution of the total quantity of specie which a Country would naturally possess. . . .

In establishing a proportion between the Metals, there seems to be an option of one of two things.

To approach as nearly as it can be ascertained the mean or average proportion in what may be called the Commercial world, Or

To retain that which now exists in the United States: As far as these happen to coincide, they will render the course to be pursued plainer and more certain.

To ascertain the first with precision would require better materials than are possessed, or than could be obtained, without an inconvenient delay.

Sir Isaac Newton, in a representation to the Treasury of Great Britain in the year 1717, after stating the particular proportions in the different countries of Europe concludes thus—"by the course of trade and exchange between nation, and nation in all Europe, fine gold is to fine silver as 14 4/5 or 15 to 1."

But however accurate and decisive this authority may be deemed, in relation to the period to which it applies, it cannot be taken at the distance of more than seventy years as a rule for determining the existing proportion. Alterations have been since made in the regulations of their coins by several Nations; which as well as the course of trade have an influence upon the Market values. Nevertheless, there is reason to believe that the State of the matter, as represented by Sir Isaac Newton is not very remote from its actual state.

In Holland, the greatest *money* market of Europe, gold was to silver in December 1789 as 1 to 14.88; and in that of London it has been for some time past but little different, approaching perhaps something nearer 1 to 15.

It has been seen that the existing proportion between the two metals in this Country is about as 1 to 15.

It is fortunate in this respect that the innovations of the Spanish Mint have imperceptibly introduced a proportion so analogous as this is, to that which prevails among the principal commercial nations; as it greatly facilitates a proper regulation of the matter.

This proportion of 1 to 15 is recommended by the particular situation of our trade, as being very nearly that which obtains in the market of Great Britain, to which Nation our Specie is principally exported. . . .

The only question seems to be whether the value of Gold ought not to be a little lowered to bring it to a more exact level with the two markets which have been mentioned. But as the ratio of 1 to 15 is so nearly conformable to the state of those markets, and best agrees with that of our own, it will probably be found the most eligible. If the market of Spain continues to give a higher value to Gold (as it has done in time past) than that which is recommended, there may be some advantage in a middle station.

A further preliminary to the adjustment of the future money unit is to determine what shall be the proportion and composition of alloy in each species of the Coins.

The first, by the resolution of the 8th of August 1786 before referred to, is regulated at one twelfth, or in other words, at one part alloy to 11 parts fine, whether Gold or Silver, which appears to be a convenient rule; unless there should be some collateral consideration which may dictate a departure from it. Its correspondence, in regard to both metals, is a recommendation of it because a difference could answer no purpose of pecuniary or commercial utility, and uniformity is favorable to order. . . .

The principal reasons assigned for the use of alloy are the saving of expense in the refining of the metals, (which in their natural state are usually mixed with a portion of the coarser kinds) and the rendering of them harder as a security against too great waste by friction or wearing. The first reason, drawn from the original composition of the Metals, is strengthened at present by the practice of alloying their coins, which has obtained among so many Nations. The reality of the effect to which the last reason is applicable has been denied, and experience has been appealed to as proving that the more alloyed coins wear faster than the purer. The true state of this matter may be worthy of future investigation, though first appearances are in favor of alloy. In the meantime, the saving of trouble and expense are sufficient inducements to following those examples which suppose its expediency. And the same considerations lead to taking as our models those nations with whom we have most intercourse, and whose coins are most prevalent in our circulation. These are Spain, Portugal, England and France. The relation which the proposed proportion bears to their Gold Coins has been explained. In respect to their silver coins, it will not be very remote from the mean of their several standards.

The component ingredients of the alloy in each Metal will also require to be regulated. In silver, Copper is the only kind in use, and it is doubtless the only proper one. In Gold there is a mixture of silver and copper; in the English coins consisting of equal parts, in the coins of some other Countries varying from $\frac{1}{3}$ to $\frac{2}{3}$ Silver.

The reason of this union of Silver with Copper is this—the silver counteracts the Tendency of the Copper to injure the Color or Beauty of the Coin by giving it too much redness, or rather a Coppery hue; which a small quantity will produce; and the Copper prevents the too great whiteness which silver alone would confer. It is apprehended that there are considerations which may render it prudent to establish by law, that the proportion of Silver to Copper in the Gold Coins of the United States shall not be more than $\frac{1}{2}$ nor less than $\frac{1}{3}$; vesting a discretion, in some proper place, to regulate the matter within those limits, as experience in the execution may recommend.

A third point remains to be discussed, as a prerequisite to the determination of the money unit, which is whether the expense of coining shall be defrayed by the public, or out of the material itself; or, as it is sometimes stated, whether coinage shall be free or shall be subject to a duty or imposition? This forms, perhaps, one of the nicest questions in the doctrine of Money.

The practice of different Nations is dissimilar in this particular. In England coinage is said to be entirely free: the Mint price of the Metals in bullion being the same with the value of them in coin. In France, there is a duty which has been, if it is not now, Eight per Cent. In Holland, there is a difference between the Mint price and the value in the Coins, which has been computed at .96, or something less than one per Cent, upon Gold; at 1.48 or something less than one and a half per Cent; upon silver. The resolution of the 8th of August 1786 proceeds upon the idea of a deduction of half percent from Gold, and of 2 percent from silver as an indemnification for the expense of coining. This is inferred from a report of the late Board of Treasury upon which that resolution appears to have been founded.

Upon the supposition, that the expense of coinage ought to be defrayed out of the Metals, there are two ways in which it may be effected; one by a reduction of the quantity of fine Gold and silver in the Coins; the other by establishing a difference between the value of those Metals in the Coins and the Mint price of them in bullion.

The first method appears to the Secretary inadmissible. He is unable to distinguish an operation of this sort from that of raising the denomination of the Coin; a measure, which has been disapproved by the wisest men of the nations in which it has been practiced, and condemned by the rest of the world. To declare that a less weight of Gold or silver shall pass for the same sum which before represented a greater weight, or to ordain that the same weight shall pass for a greater sum are things substantially of one nature. The consequence of either of them, if the change can be realized, is to degrade the money unit; obliging creditors to receive less than their just dues—and depreciating property of every kind: For it is manifest, that everything would in this case be represented by a less quantity of Gold and silver, than before. . . .

It is, however, not improbable that the effect meditated would be defeated by a rise of prices, proportioned to the diminution of the intrinsic value of the coins. This might be looked for in every enlightened commercial Country; but perhaps in none with greater certainty than in this; because in none are men less liable to be the dupes of sounds—in none has authority so little resource for substituting names to things.

A general revolution in prices, though only nominally and in appearance, could not fail to distract the ideas of the community, and would be apt to breed discontents as well among all those who live on the income of their money, as among the poorer classes of the people to whom the necessaries of life would seem to have become dearer. In the confusion of such a state of things, ideas of value would not improbably adhere to the Old Coins, which from that circumstance, instead of feeling the effect of the loss of their privilege as money, would perhaps bear a price in the market relatively to the new ones in exact proportion to weight. The frequency of the demand for the metals to pay foreign balances would contribute to this effect.

Among the evils attendant on such an operation, are these— Creditors both of the Public and of individuals would lose a part of their property—Public and Private Credit would receive a wound—the effective revenues of the Government would be diminished. There is scarcely any point in the economy of national affairs of greater moment than the uniform preservation of the intrinsic value of the money unit. On this the security and steady value of property essentially depend.

The second method, therefore, of defraying the expense of the Coinage out of the Metals, is greatly to be preferred to the other. This is to let the same sum of money continue to represent in the new Coins exactly the same quantity of Gold and silver, as it does in those now current—to allow at the mint such a price only for those metals as will admit of profit just sufficient to satisfy the expense of coinage—to abolish the legal currency of the foreign coins, both in public and private payments—and of course to leave the superior utility of the national coins for domestic purposes to operate the difference of market value, which is necessary to induce the bringing of bullion to the Mint. In this case, all property and labor will still be represented by the same quantity of Gold and Silver as formerly; and the only change which will be wrought will consist in annexing the office of money exclusively to the national coins; consequently, withdrawing it from those of foreign countries and suffering them to become, as they ought to be, mere articles of Merchandize.

The arguments for a coinage entirely free are, that it preserves the intrinsic value of the Metals; that it makes the expense of fabrication a general instead of a partial tax; and that it tends to promote the abundance of gold, and silver, which it is alleged will flow to that place where they find the best price, and from that place where they are in any degree undervalued. . . .

In what sense a free coinage can be said to promote the abundance of gold and silver, may be inferred from the instances . . . of the tendency of a contrary system to promote their exportation. It is, however, not probable that a very small difference of value between coin and bullion can have any effect which ought to enter into calculation. There can be no inducement of positive profit to export the bullion, as long as the difference of price is exceeded by the expense of transportation. . . .

Under an impression that a *small* difference between the value of the coin and the Mint price of bullion is the least exceptionable expedient for restraining the melting down, or exportation of the former, and not perceiving that if it be a very moderate one, it can be hurtful in other respects—The Secretary is inclined to an experiment of ½ per Cent on each of the Metals. The fact which has been mentioned with regard to the price of Gold bullion in the English Market seems to demonstrate that such a difference may safely be made. In this case, there must be immediate payment for the Gold and Silver offered to the Mint. How far ½ per Cent will go towards defraying the expense of the coinage cannot be determined beforehand with accuracy. It is presumed that on an economical plan it will suffice in relation to Gold. But it is not expected that the same rate in silver will be sufficient to defray the expense attending that Metal. Some additional provision may therefore be found necessary if this limit be adopted.

It does not seem to be advisable to make any greater difference in regard to silver than to gold: Because it is desirable that the proportion between the two Metals, in the Market should correspond with that in the Coins, which would not be the case if the mint price of one was comparatively lower than that of the other; and because also silver being proposed to be rated in respect to Gold somewhat below its general commercial value, if there should be a disparity to its disadvantage in the Mint prices of the two Metals, it would obstruct too much the bringing of it to be coined, and would add an inducement to export it. . . .

It is sometimes mentioned as an expedient, which consistently with a free coinage, may serve to prevent the evils desired to be avoided, to incorporate in the coins a greater proportion of alloy than is usual, regulating their value nevertheless according to the quantity of pure metal they contain. This it is supposed, by adding to the difficulty or refining them, would cause bullion to be preferred both for manufacture and exportation.

But strong objections lie against this Scheme: An augmentation of expense; An actual depreciation of the Coin; A danger of still greater depreciation in the public opinion; the facilitating of Counterfeits: While it is questionable, whether it would have the effect expected from it.

Considering therefore, the uncertainty of the success of the expedient, and the inconveniencies, which seem incident to it, it would appear preferable to submit to those of a free coinage. It is observable that additional expense, which is one of the principal of these, is also applicable to the proposed remedy.

It is now proper to resume and finish the answer to the first question; in order to which the three succeeding ones have necessarily been anticipated. The conclusion to be drawn from the observations which have been made on the subject is this, that the unit in the coins of the United States ought to correspond with 24 Grains and ¾ of a Grain of a pure Gold and with 371 Grains and ¼ of a Grain of pure silver, each answering to a dollar in the money of account. The former is exactly agreeable to the present value of Gold, and the latter is within a small fraction of the mean of the two last emissions of dollars; the only ones which are now found in common circulation, and of which the newest is in the greatest abundance. The alloy in each case to be 1/12 of the total weight, which will make the unit 27 Grains of standard Gold and 405 Grains of standard silver.

Each of these it has been remarked will answer to a Dollar in the money of account. It is conceived that nothing better can be done in relation to this than to pursue the tract marked out by the resolution of the 8th of August 1786. This has been approved abroad, as well as at home, and it is certain that nothing can be more simple or convenient than the decimal subdivisions.

There is every reason to expect that the method will speedily grow into general use when it shall be seconded by corresponding Coins. On this plan, the unit in the Money of account will continue to be, as established by that resolution, a Dollar, and its multiples, dimes, cents, and milles, or tenths, hundredths, and thousandths.

With regard to the number of different pieces which shall compose the coins of the United States, two things are to be consulted—convenience of circulation and cheapness of the coinage. The first ought not to be sacrificed to the last; but as far as they can be reconciled to each other, it is desirable to do it. Numerous and small (if not too minute) subdivisions assist circulation; but the multiplication of the smaller kinds increases expense; the same process being necessary to a small as to a large piece.

As it is easy to add, it will be most advisable to begin with a small number, 'till experience shall decide whether any other kinds are necessary. The following, it is conceived, will be sufficient in the commencement.

1 Gold piece, equal in weight and value to ten Units or Dollars.

1 Gold piece, equal to a tenth part of the former, and which shall be a unit or Dollar.

1 Silver piece, which shall also be a unit or dollar.

1 Silver piece, which shall be in weight and value a tenth part of the silver unit or Dollar.

1 Copper piece, which shall be of the value of a hundredth part of a dollar.

1 other Copper piece, which shall be half the value of the former.

It is not proposed, that the lightest of the two Gold Coins, should be numerous; as in large payments, the larger the pieces, the shorter the process of counting, the less the risk of mistake, and consequently the greater the safety and the convenience; and in small payments it is not perceived that any inconvenience can accrue from an entire dependence on the Silver and Copper Coins. The chief inducement to the establishment of the small gold piece is to have a sensible object in that Metal as well as in silver to express the unit. Fifty thousand at a time in circulation may suffice for this purpose.

The tenth part of a dollar is but a small piece, and with the aid of the copper coins will probably suffice for all the more minute uses of circulation. It is less than the least of the silver Coins now in general currency in England.

The largest copper piece will nearly answer to the halfpenny sterling and the smallest of course to the farthing. Pieces of very small value are a great accommodation and the means of a beneficial economy to the Poor, by enabling them to purchase in small portions and at a more reasonable rate the necessaries of which they stand in need. If there are only Cents, the lowest price for any portion of a vendible commodity, however inconsiderable in quantity, will be a Cent; if there are half Cents, it will be a half Cent; and in a great number of cases exactly the same things will be sold for a half Cent which if there were none would cost a Cent. But a half Cent is low enough for the *minimum* of price. Excessive minuteness would defeat its object. To enable the poorer classes to procure necessaries cheap is to enable them with more comfort to themselves to labor for less; the advantages of which need no comment.

The denominations of the silver Coins contained in the Resolution of the 8th of August 1786 are conceived to be significant and proper. The dollar is recommended by its correspondence with the present coin of that name for which it is designed to be a substitute; which will facilitate its ready adoption as such in the minds of the Citizens. The disme or tenth, the Cent or Hundredth, the Mille, or thousandth are proper, because they express the proportions which they are intended to designate. It is only to be regretted that the meaning of these terms will not be familiar to those who are not acquainted with the language from which they are borrowed. It were to be wished that the length and in some degree the clumsiness of some of the corresponding terms in English did not discourage from preferring them. It is useful to have names which signify the things to which they belong; and, in respect to objects of general use, in a manner intelligible to all. Perhaps it might be an improvement to let the dollar have the appellation either of Dollar or Unit (which last will be the most significant) and to substitute "tenth" for disme. In time, the Unit may succeed to the Dollar. The word Cent being in use in various transactions and instruments will without much difficulty be understood as the hundredth, and the half Cent of course as the two hundredth part.

The Eagle is not a very expressive or apt appellation for the largest gold piece, but nothing better occurs. The smallest of the two Gold Coins may be called the Dollar or Unit, in common with the silver piece with which it coincides.

The volume or size of each piece is a matter of more consequence than its denomination. It is evident that the more superficies or surface, the more the piece will be liable to be injured by friction or in other words the faster it will wear. For this reason it is desirable to render the thickness in proportion to breadth as great as may consist with neatness and good appearance. . . .

As it is of consequence to fortify the idea of the identity of the dollar, it may be best to let the form and size of the new one, as far as the quantity of matter (the alloy being less) permits, agree with the form and size of the present. The diameter may be the same.

The tenths may be in a mean between the Spanish $\frac{1}{8}$ and $\frac{1}{16}$ of a dollar.

The Copper Coins may be formed merely with a view to good appearance, as any difference in the wearing that can result from difference of form can be of little consequence in reference to that metal.

It is conceived, that the weight of the Cent may be eleven pennyweight, which will about correspond with the value of the Copper and the expense of Coinage. This will be to conform to the rule of intrinsic value, as far as regard to the convenient size of the Coins will permit; and the deduction of the expense of Coinage in this case will be the more proper, as the copper coins which have been current hitherto have passed 'till lately for much more than their intrinsic value.

It may perhaps be thought expedient according to general practice to make the copper coinage an object of profit; but where this is done to any considerable extent, it is hardly possible to have effectual security against counterfeits. This consideration, concurring with the soundness of the principle of preserving the intrinsic value of the money of a Country, seems to outweigh the consideration of profit.

The foregoing suggestions respecting the sizes of the several coins are made on the supposition that the Legislature may think fit to regulate this matter: Perhaps, however, it may be judged not unadvisable to leave it to executive discretion. . . .

The devices of the Coins are far from being matters of indifference, as they may be made the vehicles of useful impressions. They ought therefore to be emblematical, but without losing sight of simplicity. The fewer sharp points and angles there are, the less will be the loss by wearing. The Secretary thinks it best on this head to confine himself to these concise and general remarks.

The last point to be discussed respects the Currency of foreign Coins.

The abolition of this, in proper season, is a necessary part of the system contemplated for the national coinage. But this it will be expedient to defer 'till some considerable progress has been made in preparing substitutes for them. A graduation may therefore be found most convenient.

The foreign coins may be suffered to circulate precisely upon their present footing for one year after the mint shall have commenced its operations. The privilege may then be continued for another year to the Gold Coins of Portugal, England, and France, and to the silver coins of Spain. And these may still be permitted to be current for one year more at the rates allowed to be given for them at the Mint; after the expiration of which the circulation of all foreign coins to cease.

The monies which will be paid into the Treasury during the first year, being recoined before they are issued anew, will afford a partial substitute before any interruption is given to the preexisting supplies of circulation. The revenues of the succeeding year, and the coins which will be brought to the Mint in consequence of the discontinuance of their currency, will materially extend the substitute in the course of that year, and its extension will be so far increased during the third year by the facility of procuring the remaining species to be recoined, which will arise from the diminution of their current values, as probably to enable the dispensing wholly with the circulation of the foreign Coins after that period. The progress which the Currency of Bank bills will be likely to have made during the same time will also afford a substitute of another kind.

This arrangement, besides avoiding a sudden stagnation of circulation, will cause a considerable proportion of whatever loss may be incident to the establishment in the first instance to fall as it ought to do upon the Government, and will probably tend to distribute the remainder of it more equally among the community.

It may nevertheless be advisable in addition to the precautions here suggested, to repose a discretionary authority in the President of the United States to continue the Currency of the Spanish dollar at a value corresponding with the quantity of fine silver contained in it beyond the period above mentioned for the cessation of the circulation of the foreign coins. It is possible than an exception in favor of this particular species of coin may be found expedient: And it may tend to obviate inconveniencies if there be a power to make the exception in a capacity to be exerted when the period shall arrive. . . .

The organization of the Mint yet remains to be considered.

This relates to the persons to be employed, and to the services which they are respectively to perform. It is conceived that there ought to be

A Director of the Mint, to have the general superintendence of the business.

An Assay Master, or Assayer, to receive the Metals brought to the Mint, ascertain their fineness and deliver them to be coined.

A Master Coiner, to conduct the making of the Coins.

A Cashier, to receive and pay them out.

An Auditor, to keep and adjust the Accounts of the Mint.

Clerks, as many as the Director of the Mint shall deem necessary, to assist the different Officers.

Workmen, as many as may be found requisite.

A Porter.

In several of the European Mints there are various other Officers, but the foregoing are those only who appear to be indispensable. Persons in the Capacity of Clerks will suffice instead of the others, with the advantage of greater Economy.

The number of Workmen is left indefinite because at certain times it is requisite to have more than at others. They will, however, never be numerous. The expense of the establishment in an ordinary year will probably be from fifteen to twenty thousand dollars.

The remedy for errors in the weight and alloy of the Coins must necessarily form a part in the system of a Mint, and the manner of applying it will require to be regulated. The following account is given of the practice in England in this particular.

A certain number of pieces are taken promiscuously out of every fifteen pounds of Gold coined at the Mint, which is deposited for safe keeping in a strong Box called the pix. This box from time to time is opened in the presence of the Lord Chancellor, the Officers of the Treasury and others; and portions are selected from the pieces of each coinage, which are melted together, and the mass assayed by a jury of the Company of Goldsmiths. If the imperfection and deficiency both in fineness and weight fall short of a sixth of a Carat or 40 Grains of pure Gold upon a pound of standard, the Master of the Mint is held excusable, because it is supposed that no workman can reasonably be answerable for greater exactness. The expediency of some similar regulation seems to be manifest.

All which is humbly submitted.

Alexander Hamilton
Secy of the Treasury

# CHAPTER TWELVE

# Opinion on the Constitutionality of an Act to Establish a National Bank (February 23, 1791)

*Every power vested in a Government is in its nature sovereign, and includes by force of the term, a right to employ all the means requisite, and fairly applicable to the attainment of the ends of such power; and which are not precluded by restrictions & exceptions specified in the constitution; or not immoral, or not contrary to the essential ends of political society.*

JUST AS HAMILTON introduced his Mint Report in late January 1791, his plan for a national (or central) bank encountered difficulties. Congress enacted Hamilton's bank plan, but its opponents claimed the bill was unconstitutional because the Constitution had not authorized such an institution or even used the word "bank." The opposition was led by three powerful Virginians in high offices: Secretary of State Thomas Jefferson, Representative James Madison, and Attorney General Edmund Randolph. This high-level break in the ranks of President Washington's top advisers became the catalyst for the formation of the Jeffersonian Democratic Republican party to oppose Hamilton and the Federalists.

The act establishing the Bank of the United States was sitting on the president's desk awaiting his signature. He demurred. Although the legislation had passed the Senate with ease, Madison tried to derail it in the House of Representatives. While Madison lost that round, he and his Southern allies had one more opportunity. They could convince fellow Virginian George Washington, the president, not to sign the bill into law, but instead to veto it.

The anti-Bank advocates fought the issue on several grounds. Some Americans objected to all banks, and the national bank, a gigantic corporation for its time, magnified their reservations. Banks were labeled as anti-agrarian on the premise that the farmers were at the mercy of city institutions. Also banks possessed note issuing authority, and the national bank's paper would circulate nationwide, causing some opponents to fear a return of the rampant inflation of the Revolutionary War era once Bank-issued currency appeared. The Bank merited specific antagonism because of its large size. Detractors believed the Bank was so colossal that it was capable of many evils, including masking a scheme for pumping up debt prices by helping to pay off the national debt. The Bank was labeled a monopolistic monster, which would not only be an instrument of support of the wealthy but also corrupt the entire society. The bank fight also brought to the surface an issue that had been around since the adoption of the Constitution. The clash of the prerogatives of the individual states and the federal government always lurked somewhere near the surface of politics, and in this case it was whether the state legislatures or Congress should issue bank charters.

But these objections were not enough to derail Hamilton's bank in the Congress. So the president asked Jefferson and Randolph to submit to him their opinions as to whether the bank legislation was constitutional. Both cabinet officers said no. Jefferson's brief argued that

> the foundation of the Constitution [was] laid on this ground that 'all powers not delegated to the U.S. by the Constitution, nor prohibited by it to the states, are reserved to the states or to the people' [Xth Amendnt.]. To take a single step beyond the boundaries thus specially drawn around the powers of Congress is to take possession of a boundless field of power, no longer susceptible of any definition. The incorporation of a bank, and other powers assumed by this bill have not, in my opinion, been delegated to the U.S. by the Constitution.[1]

Hamilton's entire financial vision hung in the balance. Quite simply, Madison, Jefferson, and the attorney general, Edmund Randolph, argued that the Constitution had not granted the government the power to incorporate a bank. Madison's objection was inconsistent with his earlier views. In *Federalist No. 44* he argued in favor of federal authority, concluding that "no axiom is more clearly established in law, or in reason that whenever the end is required, the means are authorized; wherever a general power to do a thing is given, every particular power for doing it is included." Madison now expressed a polar opposite opinion, labeling the Constitution a document that strictly limited federal powers.

The president sent the opinions of Jefferson and Randolph to Hamilton, requesting his opinion in support of the bank bill and reminding him that he, the president, by law had only a week to make his decision. The pressure was therefore on Hamilton to produce a convincing retort.

Hamilton's response to Washington's request is considered by many historians and legal scholars as the benchmark argument for a broad interpretation of the Constitution. The core of Hamilton's argument with respect to the issue of constitutionality was that

> this *general principle* is *inherent* in the *very definition of Government* and *essential* to every step of the progress to be made by that of the United States; namely—that every power vested in a Government is in its nature *sovereign*, and includes by *force of the term*, a right to employ all *means* requisite and fairly *applicable* to the attainment of the ends of such power; . . . The power which can create the *Supreme law* of the land, in any case, is doubtless sovereign *as to such case*. This general & indisputable question puts at once an end to the *abstract* question—Whether the United States have power to *erect a corporation*?[2]

Hamilton had turned the tables on his opposition. Whereas Jefferson, Madison, and Randolph argued that the power to incorporate a bank was not available unless it was explicitly authorized by the Constitution, Hamilton retorted that a power was available to serve legitimate ends of government unless it was explicitly forbidden by the Constitution.

Washington signed the bank bill into law. What had swayed the president? Perhaps he saw the irony in the positions of the opposition: both Madison and Jefferson had upheld the doctrine of implied powers advanced by Hamilton when it suited their purposes. More likely, Washington was simply convinced by Hamilton's arguments that the affairs of his administration and the country needed a national bank, and he came down in favor of a broader interpretation of governmental powers.

Most important, however, was not the political infighting, but rather that Hamilton's view holding that implied governmental powers were a viable part of the Constitution had carried the day. This view, first enunciated most clearly in Hamilton's defense of the bank, went on to become a principle of constitutional law everywhere.

Hamilton had accomplished his objective. Another key component of his economic and financial plan had been adopted. He would comment a year later: "A mighty stand was made on the affair of the Bank. There was much commitment in that case. I prevailed."[3]

His opponents were defeated, at least for the time being. But they were far from accepting defeat and moving on. Instead, they increased their efforts to oppose him and his policies.

This document contains a total of 13,072 words; we have abridged it to 4,258 words.

23 February 1791

The Secretary of the Treasury having perused with attention the papers containing the opinions of the Secretary of State and Attorney General concerning the constitutionality of the bill for establishing a National Bank, proceeds according to the order of the President to submit the reasons which have induced him to entertain a different opinion.

It will naturally have been anticipated that in performing this task he would feel uncommon solicitude. Personal considerations alone arising from the reflection that the measure originated with him would be sufficient to produce it: The sense which he has manifested of the great importance of such an institution to the successful administration of the department under his particular care; and an expectation of serious ill consequences to result from a failure of the measure, do not permit him to be without anxiety on public accounts. But the chief solicitude arises from a firm persuasion that principles of construction like those espoused by the Secretary of State and the Attorney General would be fatal to the just & indispensible authority of the United States.

In entering upon the argument it ought to be premised that the objections of the Secretary of State and Attorney General are founded on a general denial of the authority of the United States to erect corporations. The latter indeed expressly admits that if there be any thing in the bill which is not warranted by the constitution it is the clause of incorporation.

Now it appears to the Secretary of the Treasury that this *general principle* is *inherent* in the very *definition* of *Government* and *essential* to every step of the progress to be made by that of the United States; namely—that every power vested in a Government is in its nature sovereign, and includes by *force* of the *term*, a right to employ all the *means* requisite, and fairly *applicable* to the attainment of the *ends* of such power; and which are not precluded by restrictions & exceptions specified in the constitution; or not immoral, or not contrary to the essential ends of political society.

This principle in its application to Government in general would be admitted as an axiom. And it will be incumbent upon those who may incline to deny it, to *prove* a distinction; and to show that a rule which in the general system of things is essential to the preservation of the social order is inapplicable to the United States. . . .

This general & indisputable principle puts at once an end to the *abstract* question—Whether the United States have power to *erect a corporation?* that is to say, to give a *legal* or *artificial capacity* to one or more persons, distinct from the natural. For it is unquestionably incident to *sovereign power* to erect corporations, and consequently to *that* of the United States in *relation to the objects* entrusted to the management of the government. The difference is this—where the authority of the government is general, it can create corporations in *all cases;* where it is confined to certain branches of legislation, it can create corporations only in those cases.

Here then as far as concerns the reasons of the Secretary of State & the Attorney General, the affirmative of the constitutionality of the bill might be permitted to rest. It will occur to the President that the principle here advanced has been untouched by either of them.

For a more complete elucidation of the point nevertheless, the arguments which they have used against the power of the government to erect corporations, however foreign they are to the great & fundamental rule which has been stated, shall be particularly examined. And after showing that they do not tend to impair its force, it shall also be shown that the power of incorporation incident to the government in certain cases does fairly extend to the particular case which is the object of the bill.

The first of these arguments is that the foundation of the constitution is laid on this ground "that all powers not delegated to the United States by the Constitution nor prohibited to it by the States are reserved to the States or to the people", whence it is meant to be inferred that Congress can in no case exercise any power not included in those enumerated in the constitution. And it is affirmed that the power of erecting a corporation is not included in any of the enumerated powers.

The main proposition here laid down in its true signification is not to be questioned. It is nothing more than a consequence of this republican maxim, that all government is a delegation of power. But how much is delegated in each case is a question of fact to be made out by fair reasoning & construction upon the particular provisions of the constitution—taking as guides the general principles & general ends of government.

It is not denied, that there are *implied,* as well as *express* powers, and that the former are as effectually delegated as the latter. . . .

To return—It is conceded that implied powers are to be considered as delegated equally with express ones.

Then it follows that as a power of erecting a corporation may as well be *implied* as any other thing; it may as well be employed as an *instrument* or *mean* of carrying into execution any of the specified powers, as any other instrument or mean whatever. The only question must be, in this as in every other case, whether the mean to be employed, or in this instance the corporation to be erected, has a natural relation to any of the acknowledged objects or lawful ends of the government. Thus a corporation may not be erected by congress for superintending the police of the city of Philadelphia because they are not authorized to *regulate* the *police* of that city; but one may be erected in relation to the collection of the taxes, or to the trade with foreign countries, or to the trade between the States, or with the Indian Tribes because it is the province of the federal government to regulate those objects & because it is incident to a general *sovereign* or *legislative power* to *regulate* a thing, to employ all the means which relate to its regulation to the *best* & *greatest advantage.*

A strange fallacy seems to have crept into the manner of thinking & reasoning upon the subject. Imagination appears to have been unusually busy concerning it. An incorporation seems to have been regarded as some great, independent, substantive thing—as a political end of peculiar magnitude & moment; whereas it is truly to be considered as a *quality, capacity,* or *mean* to an *end.* Thus a mercantile company is formed with a certain capital for the purpose of carrying on a particular branch of business. Here the business to be prosecuted is the end; the association in order to form the requisite capital is the primary mean. Suppose that an incorporation were added to this; it would only be to add a new *quality* to that association; to give it an artificial capacity by which it would be enabled to prosecute the business with more safety & convenience.

And it is the true one in which it is to be understood as used in the constitution. The whole turn of the clause containing it indicates that it was the intent of the convention, by that clause, to give a liberal latitude to the exercise of the specified powers. The expressions have peculiar comprehensiveness. They are—"to make *all laws,* necessary & proper for *carrying into execution* the foregoing powers & all *other powers* vested by the constitution in the *government* of the United States, or in any *department* or *officer* thereof" . . ..

It may be truly said of every government, as well as of that of the United States, that it has only a right to pass such laws as are necessary & proper to accomplish the objects entrusted to it. For no government has a right to do *merely what it pleases.* Hence by a process of reasoning similar to that of the Secretary of State, it might be proved that neither of the State governments has a right to incorporate a bank. It might be shown that all the public business of the State could be performed without a bank, and inferring thence that it was unnecessary it might be argued that it could not be done because it is against the rule which has been just mentioned. A like mode of reasoning would prove that there was no power to incorporate the Inhabitants of a town with a view to a more perfect police: For it is certain that an incorporation may be dispensed with, though it is better to have one. It is to be remembered that there is no *express* power in any State constitution to erect corporations. . . .

But while, on the one hand, the construction of the Secretary of State is deemed inadmissible, it will not be contended on the other, that the clause in question gives any *new* or *independent* power. But it gives an explicit sanction to the doctrine of *implied* powers, and is equivalent to an admission of the proposition that the government, *as to its specified powers* and *objects*, has plenary & sovereign authority, in some cases paramount to that of the States, in others coordinate with it. For such is the plain import of the declaration, that it may pass *all laws* necessary & proper to carry into execution those powers. . . .

But the doctrine which is contended for is not chargeable with the consequence imputed to it. It does not affirm that the National government is sovereign in all respects, but that it is sovereign to a certain extent: that is, to the extent of the objects of its specified powers.

It leaves therefore a criterion of what is constitutional, and of what is not so. This criterion is the *end* to which the measure relates as a *mean*. If the end be clearly comprehended within any of the specified powers, & if the measure have an obvious relation to that end, and is not forbidden by any particular provision of the constitution—it may safely be deemed to come within the compass of the national authority. There is also this further criterion which may materially assist the decision. Does the proposed measure abridge a preexisting right of any State, or of any individual? If it does not, there is a strong presumption in favor of its constitutionality; & slighter relations to any declared object of the constitution may be permitted to turn the scale.

The general objections which are to be inferred from the reasons of the Secretary of State and of the Attorney General to the doctrine which has been advanced have been stated and it is hoped satisfactorily answered. Those of a more particular nature shall now be examined. . . .

To erect a corporation is to substitute a *legal* or *artificial* to a *natural* person, and where a number are concerned to give them *individuality*. To that legal or artificial person once created, the common law of every state of itself *annexes* all those incidents and attributes which are represented as a prostration of the main pillars of their jurisprudence. It is certainly not accurate to say that the erection of a corporation is *against* those different *heads* of the State laws; because it is rather to create a kind of person or entity, to which *they* are inapplicable, and to which the general rule of those laws assign a different regimen. . . .

There are two points in the suggestions of the Secretary of State which have been noted that are peculiarly incorrect. One is that the proposed incorporation is against the laws of monopoly, because it stipulates an exclusive right of banking under the national authority. The other that it gives power to the institution to make laws paramount to those of the states.

But with regard to the first point, the bill neither prohibits any State from erecting as many banks as they please, nor any number of Individuals from associating to carry on the business: & consequently is free from the charge of establishing a monopoly: for monopoly implies a *legal impediment* to the carrying on of the trade by others than those to whom it is granted.

And with regard to the second point, there is still less foundation. The by-laws of such an institution as a bank can operate only upon its own members; can only concern the disposition of its own property and must essentially resemble the rules of a private mercantile partnership. They are expressly not to be contrary to law; and law must here mean the law of a State as well as of the United States. There never can be a doubt that a law of the corporation, if contrary to a law of a state, must be overruled as void; unless the law of the State is contrary to that of the United States; and then the question will not be between the law of the State and that of the corporation, but between the law of the State and that of the United States.

Another argument made use of by the Secretary of State is the rejection of a proposition by the convention to empower Congress to make corporations, either generally, or for some special purpose.

What was the precise nature or extent of this proposition, or what the reasons for refusing it, is not ascertained by any authentic document or even by accurate recollection. As far as any such document exists, it specifies only canals. If this was the amount of it, it would at most only prove that it was thought inexpedient to give a power to incorporate for the purpose of opening canals, for which purpose a special power would have been necessary. . . . Some affirm that it was confined to the opening of canals and obstructions in rivers; others, that it embraced banks; and others, that it extended to the power of incorporating generally. Some again allege that it was disagreed to because it was thought improper to vest in Congress a power of erecting corporations—others, because it was thought unnecessary to *specify* the power, and inexpedient to furnish an additional topic of objection to the constitution. In this state of the matter, no inference whatever can be drawn from it.

But whatever may have been the nature of the proposition or the reasons for rejecting it concludes nothing in respect to the real merits of the question. The Secretary of State will not deny that whatever may have been the intention of the framers of a constitution, or of a law, that intention is to be sought for in the instrument itself, according to the usual & established rules of construction. Nothing is more common than for laws to *express* and *effect* more or less than was intended. If then a power to erect a corporation in any case be deducible by fair inference from the whole or any part of the numerous provisions of the constitution of the United States, arguments drawn from extrinsic circumstances regarding the intention of the convention must be rejected. . . .

It is presumed to have been satisfactorily shown in the course of the preceding observations

1. That the power of the government, *as to* the objects entrusted to its management, is in its nature sovereign.
2. That the right of erecting corporations is one inherent in & inseparable from the idea of sovereign power.
3. That the position that the government of the United States can exercise no power but such as is delegated to it by its constitution does not militate against this principle.
4. That the word *necessary* in the general clause can have no *restrictive* operation, derogating from the force of this principle; indeed,

that the degree in which a measure is or is not necessary cannot be a *test* of *constitutional* right, but of expediency only.

5. That the power to erect corporations is not to be considered as an *independent* & *substantive* power, but as an *incidental* & *auxiliary* one; and was therefore more properly left to implication than expressly granted.

6. that the principle in question does not extend the power of the government beyond the prescribed limits because it only affirms a power to *incorporate* for *purposes within the sphere of the specified powers.*

And lastly, that the right to exercise such a power in certain cases is unequivocally granted in the most *positive* & *comprehensive* terms.

To all which it only remains to be added that such a power has actually been exercised in two very eminent instances: namely in the erection of two governments, One, northwest of the river Ohio, and the other south west—*the last, independent of any antecedent compact.*

And there results a full & complete demonstration that the Secretary of State & Attorney General are mistaken when they deny generally the power of the National government to erect corporations.

It shall now be endeavored to be shown that there is a power to erect one of the kind proposed by the bill. This will be done by tracing a natural & obvious relation between the institution of a bank and the objects of several of the enumerated powers of the government; and by showing that, *politically* speaking, it is necessary to the effectual execution of one or more of those powers. In the course of this investigation, various instances will be stated by way of illustration of a right to erect corporations under those powers.

Some preliminary observations may be proper.

The proposed bank is to consist of an association of persons for the purpose of creating a joint capital to be employed, chiefly and essentially, in loans. So far the object is not only lawful, but it is the mere exercise of a right which the law allows to every individual. The bank of New York which is not incorporated is an example of such an association. The bill proposes in addition that the government shall become a joint proprietor in this undertaking, and that it shall permit the bills of the company payable on demand to be receivable in its revenues & stipulates that it shall not grant privileges similar to those which are to be allowed to this company to any others. All this is in controvertibly within the compass of the discretion of the government. The only question is, whether it has a right to incorporate this company in order to enable it the more effectually to accomplish *ends* which are in themselves lawful.

To establish such a right, it remains to show the relation of such an institution to one or more of the specified powers of the government.

Accordingly it is affirmed, that it has a relation more or less direct to the power of collecting taxes; to that of borrowing money; to that of regulating trade between the states; and to those of raising, supporting & maintaining fleets & armies. To the two former, the relation may be said to be *immediate.*

And, in the last place, it will be argued that it is *clearly* within the provision which authorizes the making of all *needful* rules & *regulations* concerning the *property* of the United States, as the same has been practiced upon by the Government.

A Bank relates to the collection of taxes in two ways; *indirectly*, by increasing the quantity of circulating medium & quickening circulation, which facilitates the means of paying—*directly*, by creating a *convenient species* of *medium* in which they are to be paid. . . .

A Bank has a direct relation to the power of borrowing money because it is an usual and in sudden emergencies an essential instrument in the obtaining of loans to Government.

A nation is threatened with a war. Large sums are wanted, on a sudden, to make the requisite preparations. Taxes are laid for the purpose, but it requires time to obtain the benefit of them. Anticipation is indispensible. If there be a bank, the supply can at once be had; if there be none loans from Individuals must be sought. The progress of these is often too slow for the exigency: in some situations they are not practicable at all. Frequently when they are, it is of great consequence to be able to anticipate the product of them by advances from a bank.

The essentiality of such an institution as an instrument of loans is exemplified at this very moment. An Indian expedition is to be prosecuted. The only fund out of which the money can arise consistently with the public engagements is a tax which will only begin to be collected in July next. The preparations, however, are instantly to be made. The money must therefore be borrowed. And of whom could it be borrowed; if there were no public banks?

It happens that there are institutions of this kind, but if there were none, it would be indispensible to create one. . . .

The institution of a bank has also a natural relation to the regulation of trade between the States: in so far as it is conducive to the creation of a convenient medium of *exchange* between them, and to the keeping up a full circulation by preventing the frequent displacement of the metals in reciprocal remittances. Money is the very hinge on which commerce turns. And this does not mean merely gold & silver; many other things have served the purpose with different degrees of utility. Paper has been extensively employed. . . .

The relation of a bank to the execution of the powers that concern the common defense has been anticipated. It has been noted that at this very moment the aid of such an institution is essential to the measures to be pursued for the protection of our frontier. . . .

A Bank then whose bills are to circulate in all the revenues of the country is *evidently* a general object, and for that very reason a constitutional one as far as regards the appropriation of money to it. Whether it will really be a beneficial one, or not, is worthy of careful examination, but is no more a constitutional point in the particular referred to than the question whether the western lands shall be sold for twenty or thirty cents per acre.

A hope is entertained that it has by this time been made to appear to the satisfaction of the President that a bank has a natural relation to the power of collecting taxes; to that of borrowing money; to that of regulating trade; to that of providing for the common defense: and that as the bill under consideration contemplates the government in the light of a joint proprietor of the stock of the bank, it brings the case within the provision of the clause of the constitution which immediately respects the property of the United States.

Under a conviction that such a relation subsists, the Secretary of the Treasury with all deference conceives that it will result

184 Opinion on the Constitutionality of an Act to Establish a National Bank

as a necessary consequence from the position, that all the specified powers of the government are sovereign as to the proper objects; that the incorporation of a bank is a constitutional measure, and that the objections taken to the bill in this respect are ill founded. . . .

In all questions of this nature the practice of mankind ought to have great weight against the theories of Individuals.

The fact, for instance, that all the principal commercial nations have made use of trading corporations or companies for the purposes of *external commerce*, is a satisfactory proof that the Establishment of them is an incident to the regulation of that commerce.

This other fact, that banks are an usual engine in the administration of national finances, & an ordinary & the most effectual instrument of loans & one which in this country has been found essential, pleads strongly against the supposition that a government clothed with most of the most important prerogatives of sovereignty in relation to the revenues, its debts, its credit, its defense, its trade, its intercourse with foreign nations—is forbidden to make use of that instrument as an appendage to its own authority.

It has been stated as an auxiliary test of constitutional authority, to try whether it abridges any preexisting right of any state or any Individual. The proposed incorporation will stand the most severe examination on this point. Each state may still erect as many banks as it pleases; every individual may still carry on the banking business to any extent he pleases.

One thing which has been omitted just occurs, although it is not very material to the main argument. The Secretary of State affirms that the bill only contemplates a re-payment, not a loan to the government. But here he is certainly mistaken. It is true, the government invests in the stock of the bank a sum equal to that which it receives on loan. But let it be remembered that it does not, therefore, cease to be a proprietor of the stock; which would be the case if the money received back were in the nature of a repayment. It remains a proprietor still, & will share in the profit, or loss, of the institution, according as the dividend is more or less than the interest it is to pay on the sum borrowed. Hence that sum is manifestly, and, in the strictest sense, a loan.

# CHAPTER THIRTEEN

# Prospectus of the Society for Establishing Useful Manufactures (August 1791)

*The establishment of Manufactures in the United States . . . [is] of the highest importance to [our] prosperity.*

AS HAMILTON APPROACHED the second anniversary of his appointment to head the Treasury Department, he witnessed the fruits of his funding program. Investors expanded their portfolios to include more than Treasury bonds. New private ventures and corporations sprouted in 1791, with large pools of capital created for banks in Baltimore and Providence, navigation for the Susquehanna and Schuylkill rivers in Pennsylvania, and a manufacturing company in Connecticut. The Bank of the United States had been approved and had its initial public offering in July when scripts, or rights to purchase full shares in the BUS stock, sold out in minutes and were oversubscribed. Hamilton's vision for finance-led economic growth was unfolding, and investors were captivated by all the new securities and financial technologies.

Finance, however, was only one aspect of the economy. Hamilton realized that to become a true power the United States needed to rely on a domestic manufacturing base, which he saw as "of the highest importance to [our] prosperity." Countries that could supply their own needs were "in a state of highest political perfection." The proposed

Society for Establishing Useful Manufactures (SEUM) would obviate the high cost of exporting raw goods that were turned into manufactured goods, only to be sold back to Americans at an elevated premium. Barriers to American manufacturing were a lack of skilled labor and a dearth of capital. The latter was already being addressed as investors pooled their financial resources to invest in Hamilton-inspired public securities as well as private banks and corporations. The former could be solved by finding immigrants with the requisite skills and adopting new technologies represented "by the late improvements in the construction and application of Machines."

Hamilton's immediate plan to achieve manufacturing independence was twofold. First, quickly incorporate a private company to create American manufactured goods, a sort of demonstration project, or what in modern terms might be called a business or manufacturing incubator. Second, submit to Congress a formal report, which that body had requested of him in 1790, on how to promote American manufacturing. The *Report on the Subject of Manufactures* would follow several months later (see chapter 14).

The proposed SEUM would sell 5,000 shares at $100 each for a capital of $500,000 (Article 1). As usual, the plan had interlocking benefits to other Hamiltonian projects. For example, to purchase shares in the proposed SEUM an investor could tender Treasury bonds as well as cash (Article 2). Hamilton had employed this same idea some months earlier by making new Treasury bonds tenderable for the purchase of shares in the Bank of the United States. Hamilton even suggested another way to bolster the BUS by suggesting that any excess funds in the SEUM could be invested in Bank stock (Article 14).

Hamilton intended the SEUM to remain under private control, which he ensured by allowing the states and national government to invest in the venture if they wished, but with a cap of 100 votes each, or 2 percent of the 5,000 potential votes (Article 4). Unlike the BUS and BoNY charters, the SEUM would have one vote per share (Article 4). The SEUM also differed from those banks in that there was no limited liability clause, although the absence of such a clause often implied that stockholders had limited liability. Hamilton ensured that the SEUM would have an edge by making "the Stock and other property of the Corporation . . . exempt from Taxes" (Article 19).

Hamilton suggested the SEUM could try to incorporate in either New York, New Jersey, or Pennsylvania, but indicated a preference for

New Jersey. The stated reason was that it is "thickly populated—provisions are there abundant and cheap." The unstated reason was the Great Falls of the Passaic River at Paterson, New Jersey, whose water could provide constant power to the envisioned machines. Hamilton's prospectus became the basis for a generous charter of incorporation, which he also wrote, from the state of New Jersey.

Although manufacturing was only a small part of the nascent economy of the early 1790s, Hamilton's SEUM encouraged entrepreneurs and showed them a path forward. Hamilton was shaping both the public and private sectors. The SEUM commenced operations in Paterson, but unfortunately it did not meet expectations. The problem was not the idea but rather its leadership: it was derailed by the spectacular failure the following year of its first president, William Duer. Duer's malfeasance in 1792 would not just disrupt the SEUM, but shake the entire country and Hamilton's financial plan to the core (see chapter 15).

The SEUM did not fail. But it did not become a demonstration plant to exploit new manufacturing technologies and encourage other American entrepreneurs to follow its lead. Instead, it became a supplier of power to other firms that in the nineteenth century would make Paterson a major center of American manufacturing. On that model, which is akin to the modern business incubator model, the SEUM lasted into the twentieth century.

This document is not abridged.

[Philadelphia, August 1791]

The establishment of Manufactures in the United States when maturely considered will be found to be of the highest importance to their prosperity. It is an almost self-evident proposition that that community which can most completely supply its own wants is in a state of the highest political perfection. And both theory and experience conspire to prove that a nation (unless from a very peculiar coincidence of circumstances) cannot possess much active wealth but as the result of extensive manufactures.

While also it is manifest that the interest of the community is deeply concerned in the progress of this species of Industry, there is as little room to doubt that the interest of individuals may equally be promoted by the pursuit of it. What is there to hinder the profitable prosecution of manufactures in this Country, when it is notorious, that, independent of impositions for the benefit of the revenue and for the encouragement of domestic enterprise—the natural commercial charges of the greater part of those which are brought from Europe amount to from fifteen to thirty per Cent—and when it is equally notorious that provisions and various kinds of raw materials are even cheaper here than in the Country from which our principal supplies come?

The dearness of labor and the want of Capital are the two great objections to the success of manufactures in the United States.

The first objection ceases to be formidable when it is recollected how prodigiously the proportion of manual labor in a variety of manufactures has been decreased by the late improvements in the construction and application of Machines—and when it is also considered to what an extent women and even children in the populous parts of the Country may be rendered auxiliary to undertakings of this nature. It is also to be taken into calculation that emigrants may be engaged on reasonable terms in countries where labor is cheap, and brought over to the United States.

The last objection disappears in the eye of those who are aware how much may be done by a proper application of the public Debt. Here is the resource which has been hitherto wanted. And while a direction of it to this object may be made a mean of public prosperity and an instrument of profit to adventurers in the enterprise, it, at the same time, affords a prospect of an enhancement of the value of the debt; by giving it a new and additional employment and utility.

It is evident that various fabrics, under every supposed disadvantage, are in a very promising train. And that the success has not been still more considerable may be traced to very obvious causes.

Scarcely any has been undertaken upon a scale sufficiently extensive or with a due degree of system. To insure success it is desirable to be able to enter into competition with foreign fabrics in three particulars—quality, price, term of credit. To the first, workmen of equal skill is an essential ingredient. The means employed have not generally been adequate to the purpose of procuring them from abroad and those who have been procurable at home have for the most part been of an inferior class.

To cheapness of price, a capital equal to the purpose of making all necessary advances, and procuring materials on the best terms is an indispensable requisite—and to the giving of ⟨Credit⟩ a Capital capable of affording a surplus beyond what is required for carrying on the business is not less indispensable. But most undertakings hitherto have been bottomed on very slender resources.

To remedy this defect an association of the Capitals of a number of Individuals is an obvious expedient—and the species of Capital which consists of the public Stock is susceptible of dispositions which will render it adequate to the end. There is good reason to expect that as far as shall be found necessary money on reasonable terms may be procured abroad upon an hypothecation of the Stock. It is presumable that public Banks would not refuse their aid in the same way to a solid institution of so great public utility. The pecuniary aid even of Government though not to be counted upon, ought not wholly to be despaired of. And when the Stock shall have attained its due value so that no loss will attend the sale all such aids may be dispensed with. The Stock may then be turned into specie without disadvantage whenever specie is called for.

But it is easy to see that upon a good Capital in Stock an effective Credit may be raised in various ways which will answer every purpose in specie, independent of the direct expedient of borrowing.

To effect the desired association an incorporation of the adventurers must be contemplated as a mean necessary to their security. This can doubtless be obtained. There is scarcely a state which could be insensible to the advantage of being the scene of such an undertaking. But there are reasons which strongly recommend the state of New Jersey for the purpose. It is thickly populated—provisions are there abundant and cheap. The state having scarcely any external commerce and no waste lands to be peopled can feel the impulse of no supposed interest hostile to the advancement of manufactures. Its situation seems to insure a constant friendly disposition.

The great and preliminary desideratum then is to form a sufficient capital. This it is conceived, ought not to be less than Five hundred thousand Dollars. Towards forming this capital subscriptions ought immediately to be set on foot; upon this condition that no subscriber shall be bound to pay until an Act of Incorporation shall have been obtained—for which application may be made as soon as the sums subscribed shall amount to One hundred thousand Dollars.

As soon as it is evident that a proper Capital can be formed means ought to be taken to procure from Europe skillful workmen and such machines and implements as cannot be had here in sufficient perfection. To this the existing crisis of the affairs of certain parts of Europe appears to be particularly favorable. It will not be necessary that all the requisite workmen should be brought from thence. One in the nature of a foreman for each branch may in some branches suffice. In others it may be requisite to go further and have one for each subdivision. But numbers of workmen of secondary merit may be found in the United States; and others may be quickly formed.

It is conceived that there would be a moral certainty of success in manufactories of the following articles—

1st Paper and Pasteboard
2nd Paper hangings
3rd Sail cloth and other coarse linen cloths, such as sheetings, shirtings, diaper, oznaburgs &ca.
4th The printing of Cottons and linens; and as incident to this but on a smaller scale the manufacturing of the article to be printed.
5th Womens shoes of all kinds.
6th Thread, Cotton and Worsted Stockings.
7th Pottery and Earthen Ware.
8th Chip Hats
9th Ribbands & Tapes
10th Carpets
11th Blankets
12th Brass and Iron wire
13th Thread and Fringes

It will be unnecessary to enter into the details of the execution further than to observe that the employment of the labor-saving mills and machines is particularly contemplated.

In addition to the foregoing a brewery for the supply of the manufacturers, as a primary object, may be thought of.

When application shall be made for an act of Incorporation it ought to include a request that provision may be made for incorporating the Inhabitants of the district within a certain defined limit which shall be chosen by the Company as the principal seat of their factories and a further request that the Company may have permission to institute a lottery or lotteries in each year for the term of five years for a sum or sums not exceeding in one year One hundred thousand dollars. The State of Jersey if duly sensible of its interest in the measure will not refuse encouragements of this nature.

An incorporation of this sort will be of great importance to the police of the establishment. It may also be found eligible to vest a part of the funds of the Company in the purchase of ground on which to erect necessary buildings &c. A part of this ground divided into town lots may be afterwards a source of profit to the Company.

The lottery will answer two purposes. It will give a temporary command of Money and the profit arising from it will go towards indemnifying for first unproductive efforts.

The following scheme for the organization of the Company will probably be an eligible one—

1. The Capital of the Company as before remarked to consist of Five hundred thousand dollars, to be divided into Five thousand Shares, each share being One hundred Dollars, [The Company nevertheless to be at liberty to extend their capital to one Million of Dollars.]

2. Any person Co-partnership or body politic may subscribe for as many shares as he she or they may think fit. The sums subscribed to be payable—One half in the funded six per Cent Stock, or in three per Cent Stock at two dollars for one, and the other half in deferred Stock. The payments to be in four equal parts. The first at the time of subscription, the second in six months after, the third in six months after the second, and the fourth in six months after the third. Those who prefer paying in Specie to be permitted to do so, computing the funded six per Centum at par, and the deferred according to its present value at the time of payment discounting the interest thereupon during the suspension of payment at the rate of Six per Centum per annum.

3rd. The affairs of the Company to be under the management of thirteen Directors to be chosen annually on the first Monday of October in each year by plurality of suffrages of the Stockholders. The Directors by plurality of voices to choose from among themselves a Governor and Deputy Governor.

4th. The number of votes to which each Stockholder shall be entitled, shall be in proportion to the number of shares he shall hold that is to say one vote for each share. But neither the United States nor any State which may become a Subscriber shall be entitled to more than One hundred votes. The United States or any State nevertheless, which may subscribe for not less than One hundred Shares may appoint a Commissioner who shall have a right at all times to inspect the proceedings of the Company and the state of its affairs but without any authority to control. Every Subscriber may vote by Attorney duly constituted.

5th. There shall be a stated meeting of the Directors on every first Monday of January, April, July and October at the place which is the principal seat of the Manufactory. But the Governor for the time being or any three Directors may by writing under his or their hands, directed to the other Directors and left at their respective places of abode at least fourteen days prior to the day for Meeting, or by advertisement in one public Gazette printed in the State where the Corporation shall be established and in another public Gazette printed in the City of Philadelphia, and in another public Gazette printed in the City of New York for the space of thirty days prior to the time of Meeting convene a special meeting of Directors, for the purpose of transacting business of the company.

6th No Director shall receive any emolument unless the same shall have been allowed by the Stockholders at a General meeting. But the Directors may appoint such Officers and with such compensations as they shall think fit.

7th Not less than seven Directors, if the Governor or Deputy Governor be not one shall constitute a Board for the transaction of business. But if the Governor or Deputy Governor be one four shall suffice. In case it should at any time happen that there are two separate meetings of five or more Directors each, but both less than a majority of the whole, one having the

Governor, and the other the Deputy Governor, that at which the Governor shall be present shall be the legal one.

8th. The Directors to have power to make all Bye-laws, rules and regulations requisite for conducting the affairs of the Company.

9th At every annual Meeting of the Stockholders for the purpose of choosing Directors the Directors shall lay before them a general state of the affairs of the Company exhibiting the amount of its Stock, Debts and Credits, the different kinds of Manufactures carried on, the number of persons employed in each and their respective compensations together with an account of profit and loss.

10th. [The persons not exceeding five in number who at any general meeting shall have next after the Directors chosen the highest number of votes for Directors shall by force thereof be a committee of Inspection and shall have a right of access to all the books of the Company and of examination into all its affairs, and shall at each succeeding meeting report all such authentic facts as shall come to their knowledge to the Stockholders for their information.] The Stockholders may also if they think fit at any general meeting appoint by plurality of suffrages any five of their number for the purpose of making such inquiries and investigations as they may think necessary.

11th. The Stockholders at a General meeting may annul or alter any of the Regulations established by the Directors and make such others as they may think necessary.

12th. Any Board of Directors or either of the Committees above-mentioned may at any time call a general meeting of Stockholders; giving thirty days previous notice thereof in three Gazettes, one published in the state in which the Factory shall be established another in the City of Philadelphia and another in the City of New York.

13th. Every Cashier or Treasurer of the Corporation shall before he enters upon the duties of his Office give Bond with one or more sureties to the satisfaction of the Directors for the faithful execution of his duty in a sum not less than Twenty thousand Dollars.

14th. So much of the Capital Stock of the Company as may consist of public Debts shall be placed on the Books of the Treasury of the United States in the name of the Corporation; and every

Stockholder shall be entitled to a license under the Seal of the Corporation to inspect the account of the said Stock at his pleasure as far as may comport with the rules of the Treasury. This however shall not prevent the investment of the said Debt in Stock of the Bank of the United States, reserving to each Stockholder the like right of Inspection in relation to the Stock of the Company so invested.

15th  There shall be a yearly dividend of so much of the profits of the Company as the Directors shall think proper for the first five years, and after that period a half yearly dividend.

16th  The Stock of the Corporation shall be assignable and transferable according to such rules as shall be instituted in that behalf by its laws & Ordinances.

17th.  The Corporation shall be at liberty to make and vend all such Articles as shall not be prohibited by law: Provided that it shall only trade in such articles as itself shall manufacture in whole or part or in such as shall be received in payment or exchange therefor. Provided nevertheless that this shall not prevent the investment of any sums paid in specie in Stock of the United States or in Bank Stock.

18.  It shall be understood that a Majority of the Stockholders may at any time dissolve the Corporation; but this shall only be done at a general meeting which shall have been specially summoned for the purpose with public notice of the intent. And upon such dissolution the Directors for the time being shall be ipso facto trustees for settling all the affairs of the Corporation disposing of its effects paying its debts and dividing the surplus among the Stockholders in proportion to their respective interests in the Stock; unless the Stockholders at a General Meeting previous to such dissolution shall have nominated other persons as trustees; in which case those persons shall be trustees for the purposes aforesaid.

19.  The Stock and other property of the Corporation to be exempt from Taxes.

The management of the Affairs of this Company will require that an Agent should be appointed to Superintend all the different works and the disposition of the Articles manufactured in conformity to the general regulations of the Directors.

This Agent ought to have such a compensation as will command the services of a man every way competent and trustworthy. Such a man may doubtless be found. It is not necessary that he should be a technical man in any of the branches of manufacture; but a man of information, thoroughly a man of business, of probity, and diligence and energy.

We the Subscribers for ourselves respectively and not one for the other and for our respective heirs, executors and administrators do severally covenant promise and agree to and with each other and with the heirs Executors and Administrators of each other that we will respectively contribute and pay in the manner and at the times specified in the plan hereunto annexed the respective sums against our respective names hereunder set for the purpose of establishing a company for carrying on the business of manufactures in one of the States of New York New Jersey and Pennsylvania (giving a preference to New Jersey if an incorporation can be obtained from the said State on advantageous terms) according to the general principles of the plan aforesaid, but subject to such alterations as shall be agreed upon at any time previous to the obtaining an Act of Incorporation either in the principles or details thereof by the major part of us whose names are hereunto subscribed, or in the details thereof only, as shall be thought fit by the major part of the persons hereinafter named. And we do hereby jointly and severally constitute and appoint one and each of our Attorney's who or the major part of them or the major part of the survivors of them are hereby empowered as soon as the sum of One hundred thousand Dollars shall be subscribed hereto to make application on our behalf to either of the States aforesaid (giving such preference as aforesaid to the State of New Jersey) for an Act or Acts of Incorporation according to the principles of the plan aforesaid with such alterations in the details thereof as shall appear to them eligible, or with such alterations whatsoever, as shall be previously agreed upon by us; And further to take such measures at our joint expense as shall appear to them necessary and proper for engaging workmen in the several branches of manufacture mentioned in the said plan.

In testimony whereof We have hereunto subscribed and set our hands and seals, the day of      in the year of our Lord One thousand seven hundred and ninety One.

# CHAPTER FOURTEEN

# Report on the Subject of Manufactures (December 5, 1791)

*The expediency of encouraging manufactures in the United States, which was not long since deemed very questionable, appears at this time to be pretty generally admitted.*

THIS IS THE most misunderstood of Hamilton's major policy papers because after Hamilton's death, protectionists—people seeking to spur domestic manufacturing by protecting it from foreign competition (hence the name)—used, or rather abused, the report to support the notion that Hamilton wanted to impose high tariffs on foreign manufactured goods. In fact, Hamilton implemented low tariffs designed to supply the national government with revenue needed to service its debts and make its current payments.[1]

All of Hamilton's major public reports contained didactic components because in order to induce legislators and their constituents to follow his proposals, he first had to ensure that they understood the economic principles (or theories) and the realities involved. The *Report on Manufactures* is the most didactic of Hamilton's policy papers, in part because common prejudices against manufacturing, and for farming, were even stronger than prejudices against, and misconceptions about, banks and corporations. Because of all the didactic content, what some readers considered Hamilton's policy proposals were, in fact, his explanations of the likely effects of such proposals. His actual proposals come only at the very end and are the epitome of cautious policymaking.

Stimulating manufacturing could only be effected after the establishment of public credit and a stable money supply. That had been accomplished by late 1791. In our condensation of this report, we focus on Hamilton's evaluation of how his financial reforms had prepared the ground for new efforts to stimulate American manufacturing.

The final version of the report submitted to Congress runs 110 printed pages in the definitive *Papers of Alexander Hamilton*. By the final version, "the expedience of encouraging manufacturers in the United States" was "pretty generally admitted" because of the "embarrassments" and "restrictive regulations" that conspired to "abridge the vent of the increasing surplus of our Agricultural product." In addition, "the complete success, which has rewarded manufacturing enterprise, in some valuable branches" had removed many doubts.

Nevertheless, Hamilton conceded that there were still "respectable patrons of opinions, unfriendly to the encouragement of manufactures." He stated their objections faithfully before demolishing them. After conceding the importance of agriculture, Hamilton immediately attacked the notion, set forth by the Physiocrat economists of eighteenth-century France, that agriculture was "more productive than every other branch of Industry." In this, he leaned heavily on Scottish economist Adam Smith's critique of Physiocratic doctrine in his seminal *Wealth of Nations* (1776), which basically noted that both farmers and manufacturers add value to raw materials while conceding that the former found considerable aid from nature (sunlight, rain). At the same time, Hamilton criticized Smith's *laissez-faire* doctrines and his view (expressed in Book II, Chapter 5 of Smith's *Wealth of Nations*) that American attempts to restrict imports of European manufactures and manufacture on their own would retard their country's growth.

Hamilton was careful to point out that he was not arguing that *"manufacturing industry is more productive than that of Agriculture,"* merely that "the reverse of this proposition is not ascertained," so U.S. public policies need not remain enslaved to the notion of "the superior productiveness of Tillage." An economy with both farmers and manufacturers, Hamilton explained, was better than an economy comprised of just one or the other because they each produce what they were best at producing and trade with each other.

An economy with a manufacturing sector, he further explained, would enjoy seven additional benefits:

1. *Extension of the division of labor.* Quite simply, as Adam Smith argued, "the separation of occupations causes each to be carried to a much greater perfection, than it could possible [*sic*] acquire, if they were blended."
2. *Extension of the use of machinery.* Breaking complex tasks down into simpler components, as required by the division of labor, made it easier to mechanize them. Machines, of course, could do more work than people could, and more cheaply, freeing up those people to engage in activities less susceptible to automation, as another Scottish economist, Sir James Steuart, had argued and the recent experience of the "Cotton Mill invented in England" showed.
3. *Inclusion of more people in the workforce.* Manufacturing activities afforded "occasional and extra employment to industrious individuals and families" who would otherwise spend their downtime in leisure. Similarly, factories employed people not physically or mentally cut out for "the toils of the Country," including women and children.
4. *Promotion of immigration.* Many men, Hamilton claimed, would rather change countries than occupations. Many could be induced to come to America for higher wages, higher net profits (due to lower taxes and less regulation), and/or "a perfect equality of religious privileges."
5. *Allowing people to find the right occupation for them.* This might seem trivial, but Hamilton was quick to point out that matching workers with the occupations for which they are most suited was a "powerful mean[s] of augmenting the fund of national Industry" because "each individual can find his proper element, and can call into activity the whole vigor of his nature."
6. *Increasing the field for enterprise.* "Every new scene," Hamilton argued, "which is opened to the busy nature of man to rouse and exert itself, is the addition of a new energy to the general stock of effort." In other words, manufacturing would help to stimulate not just invention but innovation, and create a "spirit of enterprise" capable of animating the wheels of commerce.
7. *Increasing demand for agricultural goods.* The final version of the report made clear that manufacturers would increase reliable,

domestic demand for food, fibers, stimulants, spices, and all the other products of farm labor. If American farmers rely on foreign markets, they will suffer during times of peace and bumper crops if they do not have manufacturing townspeople to sell to. Moreover, Hamilton noted, manufacturers will seek out new plants of use to them that farmers will find useful to add to their crop rotations.

Next, Hamilton demolished the free trade argument that the United States should exploit its natural advantage in agriculture by concentrating on farming and trading its surpluses for manufactured goods from nations like Britain with a natural advantage in manufacturing, employing what economists call a "second best world" argument. "If the system of perfect liberty to industry and commerce were the prevailing system of nations," Hamilton conceded, then the free trade argument would be correct and the country should focus on agriculture. But free trade did not characterize "the general policy of Nations." In fact, if anything, the "prevalent" system was one "regulated by an opposite spirit." In the real world, the United States found it difficult to sell its "principal staples" to several nations "with which we have the most extensive intercourse."

In such a second best world, free trade was not the best policy because the United States could not "exchange with Europe on equal terms." Hamilton made clear that he was not complaining, as it was up to other countries to determine their own trade policies. But given the fact that "Europe will not take from us the products of our soil, upon terms consistent with our interest," it was the U.S. government's responsibility to "contract as fast as possible our wants of her," which of course meant encouraging domestic manufacturing.

As for allowing manufacturers to flourish "without the aid of government" as soon as market conditions allow, Hamilton again pointed to the real (second best) world, in which nations gave "bounties premiums and other artificial encouragements" to their manufacturers, before returning to the notion that most people will change occupations only when pushed to do so by circumstances. For both reasons, the "incitement and patronage of government" was necessary "to produce the desirable changes, as early as may be expedient."

If nothing else, government encouragement of manufacturing would signal to the rich and ingenious that manufacturing was safe from policies that might hurt it. Such signaling was important for new, and hence marginal, endeavors, Hamilton argued. Parting with Smith, Hamilton next argued that new industries needed government's "extraordinary aid and protection" if they were to compete successfully with long-established foreign rivals. Note, though, that Hamilton did not call for interminable protective tariffs for infant industries, as critics later claimed. Rather, he dropped the discussion of infant industries to focus on his second best world argument, claiming that "the greatest obstacle of all to the successful prosecution of a new branch of industry . . . consists . . . in the bounties premiums and other aids which are granted . . . by the nations, in which the establishments to be imitated are previously introduced." The only way to compete was to fight fire with fire and match the aids provided by competing governments.

For example, Hamilton alluded to governments that subsidized predatory pricing counterattacks launched by established manufacturers against upstart ones in other countries. The government of the upstarts had to "fortify adventurers against the dread of such combinations, to defeat their effects" as surely as it had to defend its own geographical frontiers.

Hamilton then disposed of the "scarcity of hands—dearness of labor—want of capital" canards employed by opponents of domestic manufacturing. The first two Hamilton admitted were "real . . . obstacles to the success of manufacturing enterprise in the United States," but only "within due limits." Several "large districts" of the United States were "pretty fully peopled" despite the "continual drain" of people to the frontier. Those districts were also not very conducive to agriculture. He may have been referring to New England, which soon became a hotbed of American manufacturing.

Moreover, women and children could work in factories powered by water and steam, rendering the need for numerous hands less dire. And ingenious and valuable workmen were already migrating to the United States from Europe. More would come once the government signaled that America was as friendly to manufacturers as it was to trade and navigation, two sectors of the economy that flourished despite the alleged scarcity of labor.

As more laborers became available, Hamilton reminded readers, upward pressures on wages would decrease. Moreover, the cheap, ample sources of water power in the United States also meant that fewer laborers would be needed. Add to that the benefits of lower taxes, cheaper raw materials, and lower transportation costs and other costs of doing business, and manufacturing, despite the higher wage bill, would become at least as profitable in the United States as abroad.

That left only finance, specifically inadequate capital, in the list of objections to the encouragement of American manufactures. Finance was Hamilton's bailiwick. He began here by noting that measuring "the real extent of the monied capital of a Country" was "very difficult." On top of that, the sum total of capital was only one of two key variables, the other being the "*velocity*" at which capital was employed, by which Hamilton meant something closely akin to the velocity of money in modern monetary theories. Clearly, Hamilton conceded, the nation did not possess enough capital to put all of its "immense tracts of land" under cultivation at the present time. But to do so would not be efficient or profitable. The real question was whether sufficient capital was available to finance "the successful prosecution of any species of industry which is likely to prove truly beneficial."

Hamilton then showed that the nation did, in fact, have sufficient capital to fund profitable projects. The new banks that he had been instrumental in creating displayed "a powerful tendency to extend the active Capital" of the country. Thanks to the funding of the national debt, foreign capital was now also available, and not just to finance international trade as in the colonial period. In addition to buying U.S. government bonds, foreigners had already invested in American agriculture and "in a few instances" even manufactures. Foreign investors need to earn higher returns in the United States than at home, but not so much as they need to earn in less stable, less creditworthy countries.

Foreign investors will of course be entitled to some of the profits of our industry, Hamilton noted, but they need not be looked upon with a "jealous eye" because they are more helpers than rivals. Moreover, foreign capital is somewhat sticky because of the transaction costs of repatriating. So profits earned speculating on the stock market will often be reinvested in agriculture, trade, infrastructure, or manufacturing. And of course some funds will go, as they already have, directly into infrastructure projects and manufacturing.

Some foreign capitalists will find the United States so attractive that they will immigrate here along with their riches. Many already have since the continent's founding, so the domestic stock of capital is larger than many believe. Its most palpable form takes that of the funded debt, a form of wealth that can easily be liquidated (sold for cash) or borrowed against. U.S. government bonds, in other words, are paper gold because any owner of them "can embrace any scheme of business, which offers, with as much confidence as if he were possessed of an equal sum in Coin." Here Hamilton is touting the efficacy of his recent financial reforms.

Some, including Adam Smith, believed that government bonds did not create new net capital, Hamilton conceded, and they were in a strict accounting sense correct. But, the Treasury Secretary countered, the debt created "an artificial increase of Capital" that served "as an engine of business, or as an instrument of industry and Commerce." So long as the capital employed returned more than the interest and principal returned, debt created a net gain—i.e., added "to the active capital of the Country." Moreover, the moderate taxation needed to repay the bonds created "a Motive to greater exertion" and hence increased capital.

Great Britain's economy, Hamilton contended, ran off of its funded debt, not its supply of specie. "Among ourselves appearances thus far favor the same Conclusion. Industry in general seems to have been reanimated" and in "many parts of the Union a command capital, which till lately, since the revolution at least, was unknown." Hamilton conceded, however, that the economic revival had other causes as well, including bank and private credit, which also served as liquid forms of capital.

Others will not admit that any good can come of the debt because they overestimate the debt's costs and underestimate its benefits, a delicate equation that of course varies with the size of the debt. If the debt grows too large, "the greatest part of it may cease to be useful as a Capital, serving only to pamper the dissipation of idle and dissolute individuals" and the "Interest upon it may become oppressive." Where that "critical point," when the debt becomes more burden than blessing, lies "cannot be pronounced," so it is imperative that "in every government" there should be "a perpetual, anxious and unceasing effort to reduce" the debt "as fast as shall be practicable." But the debt as it stands is already an "extensive . . . resource" and "capital to the Citizens of the United States."

Truth be told, the United States was already undergoing a growth of manufacturing establishments "with a rapidity which surprises."[2] Included in Hamilton's list were manufactories that turned skins into footwear, gloves, "sadlery of all kinds," trunks, parchment, and glue; iron ore into bar and sheet iron and steel as well as finished iron goods like nails, stoves, pots, anchors, scales, and carriage frames; wood into ships, cabinets, machinery, and barrels; flax and hemp into cordage, sailcloth, and twine; clay into bricks, tiles, and "Potters Wares"; grains into "Ardent Spirits, and malt liquors"; wood into paper and paper hangings; fur and wool into hats, "Womens Stuff and Silk shoes"; raw sugar into refined sugar; animal and seed oils into soap and candles; copper and brass into utensils for distillers, brewers, and sugar refiners as well as "Articles for household Use"; tin for wares "of Ordinary use"; wood and iron for carriages "of all kinds"; tobacco for snuff, chewing tobacco, and smoking tobacco; various materials for starch and hair powder, painters' colors, and gunpowder.

Those, Hamilton made clear, were "carried on as regular Trades, and have attained a considerable degree of maturity." On top of all that, "a vast scene of household manufacturing" was also evident throughout the country, where people manufactured various types of coarse clothing and beddings from cotton, flax, and wool. Some families so excelled at household manufacturing that they produced not only for their own use but also for sale locally and even, Hamilton claimed, internationally.

Any nation that would be great, Hamilton continued, needs to be able to make its own food, clothing, housing, and military goods, lest it ever be unable to attain those necessities again, as at times during the Revolution, during some "future war." Building this self-sufficiency, Hamilton argued, " 'tis the next great work to be accomplished," and particularly important if the nation was not going to build and maintain naval forces sufficient "to protect our external commerce."

Hamilton argued that the time was ripe to encourage domestic manufacturing because of the influx of money caused by "foreign speculations in the funds—and by the disorders, which exist in different parts of Europe." Instead of using the money to "give a temporary spring to foreign commerce," it ought to go into domestic manufacturing. Instead of allowing the present spirit of "speculation and enterprise" to lead to "pernicious effects," the government should channel it into manufacturing. Because of "the disturbed state of Europe," it will be relatively easy to acquire "the requisite workmen" via immigration.

In the next section of the report, Hamilton reviews the ways in which the government might encourage domestic manufacturing.

This section is explicitly didactic, historical, and comparative, and merely "introductory to a Specification of the objects which in the present state of things appear the most fit to be encouraged." Our condensation essentially lists only the topics, ranging from protective tariffs to improved transportation facilities, which Hamilton discusses at greater length in the report. We also leave out his extensive discussions of American raw materials and industrial products. We do include his warning that unenlightened tax policies could discourage the development of manufactures and ought to be avoided.

Hamilton closes the report by noting that the United States in 1791 was not a nation possessing great private wealth and that government aid to manufacturing could substitute for deficiencies of private investment in launching U.S. industrialization.

Congress enacted Hamilton's tariff proposals the following year, but for reasons other than the ones given in the report. The government needed more revenue for military purposes after one of its forces had been routed by Native American tribes in the Midwest. Over the next decades, however, federal and state governments enacted more of Hamilton's policies to promote manufacturing, and within a century the United States would surpass all other countries in manufacturing output.

The entire *Report on Manufactures* contains 32,826 words; our abridgment, focused on parts of it related to finance, contains 7,044 words.

[Philadelphia, December 5, 1791
Communicated on December 5, 1791]

[To the Speaker of the House of Representatives]
The Secretary of the Treasury in obedience to the order of ye House of Representatives, of the 15th day of January 1790, has applied his attention at as early a period as his other duties would permit to the subject of Manufactures; and particularly to the means of promoting such as will tend to render the United States, independent on foreign nations for military and other essential supplies. And he thereupon respectfully submits the following Report.

The expediency of encouraging manufactures in the United States, which was not long since deemed very questionable, appears at this time to be pretty generally admitted. The embarrassments which have obstructed the progress of our external trade have led to serious reflections on the necessity of enlarging the sphere of our domestic commerce: the restrictive regulations, which in foreign markets abridge the vent of the increasing surplus of our Agricultural produce, serve to beget an earnest desire that a more extensive demand for that surplus may be created at home: And the complete success which has rewarded manufacturing enterprise in some valuable branches, conspiring with the promising symptoms which attend some less mature essays, in others justify a hope that the obstacles to the growth of this species of industry are less formidable than they were apprehended to be; and that it is not difficult to find in its further extension a full indemnification for any external disadvantages which are or may be experienced, as well as an accession of resources favorable to national independence and safety.

There still are, nevertheless, respectable patrons of opinions unfriendly to the encouragement of manufactures. The following are, substantially, the arguments by which these opinions are defended.

"In every country (say those who entertain them) Agriculture is the most beneficial and *productive* object of human industry. This position, generally if not universally true, applies with peculiar emphasis to the United States on account of their immense tracts of fertile territory, uninhabited and unimproved. Nothing can afford so advantageous an employment for capital and labor as the conversion of this extensive wilderness into cultivated farms. . . ."

"To endeavor by the extraordinary patronage of Government to accelerate the growth of manufactures is in fact to endeavor, by force and art, to transfer the natural current of industry from a more to a less beneficial channel. Whatever has such a tendency must necessarily be unwise. Indeed it can hardly ever be wise in a government to attempt to give a direction to the industry of its citizens. This under the quick-sighted guidance of private interest will, if left to itself, infallibly find its own way to the most profitable employment: and 'tis by such employment that the public prosperity will be most effectually promoted. To leave industry to itself, therefore, is in almost every case the soundest as well as the simplest policy."

"This policy is not only recommended to the United States by considerations which affect all nations, it is, in a manner, dictated to them by the imperious force of a very peculiar situation. The smallness of their population compared with their territory—the constant allurements to emigration from the settled to the unsettled parts of the country—the facility with which the less independent condition of an artisan can be exchanged for the more independent condition of a farmer, these and similar causes conspire to produce, and for a length of time must continue to occasion, a scarcity of hands for manufacturing occupation, and dearness of labor generally. To these disadvantages for the prosecution of manufactures, a deficiency of pecuniary capital being added, the prospect of a successful competition with the manufactures of Europe must be regarded as little less than desperate. . . ."

"If contrary to the natural course of things an unseasonable and premature spring can be given to certain fabrics, by heavy duties, prohibitions, bounties, or by other forced expedients, this will only be to sacrifice the interests of the community to those of particular classes. Besides the misdirection of labor, a virtual monopoly will be given to the persons employed on such fabrics; and an enhancement of price, the inevitable consequence of every monopoly, must be defrayed at the expense of the other parts of the society. It is far preferable that those persons should be engaged in the cultivation of the earth, and that we should procure, in exchange for its productions, the commodities with which foreigners are able to supply us in greater perfection, and upon better terms."

This mode of reasoning is founded upon facts and principles which have certainly respectable pretensions. If it had governed the conduct of nations more generally than it has done, there is room to suppose that it might have carried them faster to prosperity and greatness than they have attained by the pursuit of maxims too widely opposite. Most general theories, however, admit of numerous exceptions, and there are few if any of the political kind which do not blend a considerable portion of error with the truths they inculcate. . . .

It is now proper to proceed a step further, and to enumerate the principal circumstances from which it may be inferred—That manufacturing establishments not only occasion a positive augmentation of the Produce and Revenue of the Society, but that they contribute essentially to rendering them greater than they could possibly be without such establishments. These circumstances are—

1. The division of Labor.
2. An extension of the use of Machinery.
3. Additional employment to classes of the community not ordinarily engaged in the business.
4. The promoting of emigration from foreign Countries.
5. The furnishing greater scope for the diversity of talents and dispositions which discriminate men from each other.
6. The affording a more ample and various field for enterprise.
7. The creating in some instances a new, and securing in all, a more certain and steady demand for the surplus produce of the soil.

Each of these circumstances has a considerable influence upon the total mass of industrious effort in a community. Together, they add to it a degree of energy and effect which are not easily conceived. . . .

It is a primary object of the policy of nations to be able to supply themselves with subsistence from their own soils; and manufacturing nations, as far as circumstances permit, endeavor to procure from the same source the raw materials necessary for their own fabrics. This disposition, urged by the spirit of monopoly, is sometimes even carried to an injudicious extreme. It seems not always to be recollected that nations who have neither mines nor manufactures can only obtain the manufactured articles of which they stand in need by an exchange of the products of their soils; and that, if those who can best furnish them with such articles are unwilling to give a due course to this exchange, they must of necessity make every possible effort to manufacture for themselves, the effect of which is that the manufacturing nations abridge the natural advantages of their situation through an unwillingness to permit the Agricultural countries to enjoy the advantages of theirs, and sacrifice the interests of a mutually beneficial intercourse to the vain project of *selling everything* and *buying nothing*.

But it is also a consequence of the policy, which has been noted, that the foreign demand for the products of Agricultural Countries is in a great degree rather casual and occasional, than certain or constant. To what extent injurious interruptions of the demand for some of the staple commodities of the United States may have been experienced from that cause must be referred to the judgment of those who are engaged in carrying on the commerce of the country; but it may be safely assumed that such interruptions are at times very inconveniently felt, and that cases not infrequently occur, in which markets are so confined and restricted as to render the demand very unequal to the supply. . . .

The foregoing considerations seem sufficient to establish, as general propositions, That it is the interest of nations to diversify the industrious pursuits of the individuals who compose them— That the establishment of manufactures is calculated not only to increase the general stock of useful and productive labor, but even to improve the state of Agriculture in particular; certainly to advance the interests of those who are engaged in it. . . .

If the system of perfect liberty to industry and commerce were the prevailing system of nations—the arguments which dissuade a country in the predicament of the United States from the zealous pursuits of manufactures would doubtless have great force. It will not be affirmed that they might not be permitted, with few exceptions, to serve as a rule of national conduct. In such a state of things, each country would have the full benefit of its peculiar advantages to compensate for its deficiencies or disadvantages.

But the system which has been mentioned is far from characterizing the general policy of Nations. The prevalent one has been regulated by an opposite spirit.

The consequence of it is that the United States are to a certain extent in the situation of a country precluded from foreign Commerce. They can indeed without difficulty obtain from abroad the manufactured supplies of which they are in want; but they experience numerous and very injurious impediments to the emission and vent of their own commodities. Nor is this the case in reference to a single foreign nation only. The regulations of several countries with which we have the most extensive intercourse throw serious obstructions in the way of the principal staples of the United States.

In such a position of things, the United States cannot exchange with Europe on equal terms; and the want of reciprocity would render them the victim of a system which should induce them to confine their views to Agriculture and refrain from Manufactures. A constant and increasing necessity on their part for the commodities of Europe, and only a partial and occasional demand for their own in return, could not but expose them to a state of impoverishment compared with the opulence to which their political and natural advantages authorize them to aspire.

Remarks of this kind are not made in the spirit of complaint. 'Tis for the nations, whose regulations are alluded to to judge for themselves, whether by aiming at too much they do not lose more than they gain. 'Tis for the United States to consider by what means they can render themselves least dependent on the combinations right or wrong of foreign policy.

It is no small consolation that already the measures which have embarrassed our Trade have accelerated internal improvements, which upon the whole have bettered our affairs. To diversify and extend these improvements is the surest and safest method of indemnifying ourselves for any inconveniences which those or similar measures have a tendency to beget. If Europe will not take from us the products of our soil upon terms consistent with our interest, the natural remedy is to contract as fast as possible our wants of her. . . .

The remaining objections to a particular encouragement of manufactures in the United States now require to be examined.

One of these turns on the proposition that Industry, if left to itself, will naturally find its way to the most useful and profitable employment: whence it is inferred that manufactures without the aid of government will grow up as soon and as fast as the natural state of things and the interest of the community may require.

Against the solidity of this hypothesis, in the full latitude of the terms, very cogent reasons may be offered. These have relation to—the strong influence of habit and the spirit of imitation—the fear of want of success in untried enterprises—the intrinsic difficulties incident to first essays towards a competition with those who have previously attained to perfection in the business to be attempted—the bounties premiums and other artificial encouragements with which foreign nations second the exertions of their own Citizens in the branches in which they are to be rivalled. . . .

The superiority antecedently enjoyed by nations who have pre-occupied and perfected a branch of industry constitutes a more formidable obstacle . . . to the introduction of the same branch into a country in which it did not before exist. To maintain between the recent establishments of one country and the long matured establishments of another country a competition upon equal terms, both as to quality and price, is in most cases impracticable. The disparity in the one, or in the other, or in both, must necessarily be so considerable as to forbid a successful rivalry without the extraordinary aid and protection of government.

But the greatest obstacle of all to the successful prosecution of a new branch of industry in a country in which it was before unknown consists, as far as the instances apply, in the bounties premiums and other aids which are granted in a variety of cases by the nations in which the establishments to be imitated are previously introduced. It is well known . . . that certain nations grant bounties on the exportation of particular commodities to enable their own workmen to undersell and supplant all competitors in the countries to which those commodities are sent. Hence the undertakers of a new manufacture have to contend not only with the natural disadvantages of a new undertaking, but with the gratuities and remunerations which other governments bestow. To be enabled to contend with success, it is evident that the interference and aid of their own government are indispensable. . . .

The objections to the pursuit of manufactures in the United States which next present themselves to discussion represent an impracticability of success arising from three causes—scarcity of hands—dearness of labor—want of capital.

The two first circumstances are to a certain extent real, and, within due limits, ought to be admitted as obstacles to the success of manufacturing enterprise in the United States. But there are various considerations which lessen their force, and tend to afford an assurance that they are not sufficient to prevent the advantageous prosecution of many very useful and extensive manufactories. . . .

The supposed want of Capital for the prosecution of manufactures in the United States is the most indefinite of the objections which are usually opposed to it.

It is very difficult to pronounce anything precise concerning the real extent of the monied capital of a Country, and still more concerning the proportion which it bears to the objects that invite the employment of Capital. It is not less difficult to pronounce how far the *effect* of any given quantity of money, as capital, or in other words, as a medium for circulating the industry and property of a nation, may be increased by the very circumstance of the additional motion which is given to it by new objects of employment. . . .

It is not obvious why the same objection might not as well be made to external commerce as to manufactures; since it is manifest that our immense tracts of land occupied and unoccupied are capable of giving employment to more capital than is actually bestowed upon them. It is certain, that the United States offer a vast field for the advantageous employment of Capital; but it does not follow that there will not be found, in one way or another, a sufficient fund for the successful prosecution of any species of industry which is likely to prove truly beneficial.

The following considerations are of a nature to remove all inquietude on the score of want of Capital.

The introduction of Banks . . . has a powerful tendency to extend the active Capital of a Country. Experience of the Utility of these Institutions is multiplying them in the United States. It is probable that they will be established wherever they can exist with advantage; and wherever they can be supported, if administered with prudence, they will add new energies to all pecuniary operations.

The aid of foreign Capital may safely and with considerable latitude be taken into calculation. Its instrumentality has been long experienced in our external commerce; and it has begun to be felt in various other modes. Not only our funds, but our Agriculture and other internal improvements have been animated by it. It has already in a few instances extended even to our manufactures.

It is a well-known fact, that there are parts of Europe which have more Capital than profitable domestic objects of employment. Hence, among other proofs, the large loans continually furnished to foreign states. And it is equally certain that the capital of other parts may find more profitable employment in the United States than at home. And notwithstanding there are weighty inducements to prefer the employment of capital at home even at less profit to an investment of it abroad, though with greater gain, yet these inducements are overruled either by a deficiency of employment or by a very material difference in profit. Both these Causes operate to produce a transfer of foreign capital to the United States. 'Tis certain, that various objects in this country hold out advantages which are with difficulty to be equaled elsewhere; and under the increasingly favorable impressions which are entertained of our government, the attractions will become more and More strong. These impressions will prove a rich mine of prosperity to the Country if they are confirmed and strengthened by the progress of our affairs. And to secure this advantage, little more is now necessary than to foster industry and cultivate order and tranquility at home and abroad.

It is not impossible that there may be persons disposed to look with a jealous eye on the introduction of foreign Capital, as if it were an instrument to deprive our own citizens of the profits of our own industry: But perhaps there never could be a more unreasonable jealousy. Instead of being viewed as a rival, it ought to be Considered as a most valuable auxiliary conducing to put in Motion a greater Quantity of productive labor, and a greater portion of useful enterprise than could exist without it. It is at least evident that in a Country situated like the United States, with an infinite fund of resources yet to be unfolded, every farthing of foreign capital which is laid out in internal ameliorations and in industrious establishments of a permanent nature is a precious acquisition.

And whatever be the objects which originally attract foreign Capital, when once introduced it may be directed towards any purpose of beneficial exertion which is desired. And to detain it among us, there can be no expedient so effectual as to enlarge the sphere within which it may be usefully employed: Though induced merely with views to speculations in the funds, it may afterwards be rendered subservient to the Interests of Agriculture, Commerce & Manufactures.

But the attraction of foreign Capital for the direct purpose of Manufactures ought not to be deemed a chimerical expectation. There are already examples of it, as remarked in another place. And the examples, if the disposition be cultivated can hardly fail to multiply. There are also instances of another kind which serve to strengthen the expectation. Enterprises for improving the Public Communications, by cutting canals, opening the obstructions in Rivers and erecting bridges have received very material aid from the same source.

When the Manufacturing Capitalist of Europe shall advert to the many important advantages which have been intimated in the Course of this report, he cannot but perceive very powerful inducements to a transfer of himself and his Capital to the United States. Among the reflections, which a most interesting peculiarity of situation is calculated to suggest, it cannot escape his observation, as a circumstance of Moment in the calculation, that the progressive population and improvement of the United States insure a continually increasing domestic demand for the fabrics which he shall produce, not to be affected by any external casualties or vicissitudes.

But while there are Circumstances sufficiently strong to authorize a considerable degree of reliance on the aid of foreign Capital towards the attainment of the object in view, it is satisfactory to have good grounds of assurance that there are domestic resources of themselves adequate to it. It happens that there is a species of Capital actually existing within the United States which relieves from all inquietude on the score of want of Capital—This is the funded Debt.

The effect of a funded debt as a species of Capital, has been Noticed upon a former Occasion; but a more particular elucidation of the point seems to be required by the stress which is here laid upon it. This shall accordingly be attempted.

Public Funds answer the purpose of Capital from the estimation in which they are usually held by Monied men; and consequently from the Ease and dispatch with which they can be turned into money. This capacity of prompt convertibility into money causes a transfer of stock to be in a great number of Cases equivalent to a payment in coin. And where it does not happen to suit the party who is to receive to accept a transfer of Stock, the party who is to pay is never at a loss to find elsewhere a purchaser of his Stock, who will furnish him in lieu of it with the Coin of which he stands in need. Hence in a sound and settled state of the public funds, a man possessed of a sum in them can embrace any scheme of business which offers, with as much confidence as if he were possessed of an equal sum in Coin.

This operation of public funds as capital is too obvious to be denied; but it is objected to the Idea of their operating as an *augmentation* of the Capital of the community that they serve to occasion the *destruction* of some other capital to an equal amount.

The Capital which alone they can be supposed to destroy must consist of—The annual revenue which is applied to the payment of Interest on the debt, and to the gradual redemption of the principal—The amount of the Coin which is employed in circulating the funds or, in other words, in effecting the different alienations which they undergo.

But the following appears to be the true and accurate view of this matter.

1st. As to the point of the Annual Revenue requisite for Payment of interest and redemption of principal.

As a determinate proportion will tend to perspicuity in the reasoning, let it be supposed that the annual revenue to be applied, corresponding with the modification of the 6 per Cent stock of the United States, is in the ratio of eight upon the hundred, that is in the first instance six on Account of interest, and two on account of Principal.

Thus far it is evident that the Capital destroyed to the capital created would bear no greater proportion than 8 to 100. There would be withdrawn from the total mass of other capitals a sum of eight dollars to be paid to the public creditor; while he would be possessed of a sum of One Hundred dollars ready to be applied to any purpose, to be embarked in any enterprise which might appear to him eligible. Here then the *Augmentation* of Capital, or the excess of that which is produced beyond that which is destroyed is equal to Ninety two dollars. To this conclusion, it may be objected that the sum of Eight dollars is to be withdrawn annually until the whole hundred is extinguished, and it may be inferred that in process of time a capital will be destroyed equal to that which is at first created.

But it is nevertheless true, that during the whole of the interval between the creation of the Capital of 100 dollars and its reduction to a sum not greater than that of the annual revenue appropriated to its redemption—there will be a greater active capital in existence than if no debt had been Contracted. The sum drawn from other Capitals *in any one year* will not exceed eight dollars; but there will be *at every instant of time* during the whole period in question a sum corresponding *with so much of the principal* as remains *unredeemed*, in the hands of some person or other, employed or ready to be employed in some profitable undertaking. There will therefore constantly be more capital in capacity to be employed than capital taken from employment. The excess for the first year has been stated to be Ninety two dollars; it will diminish yearly, but there always will be an excess until the principal of the debt is brought to a level with the *redeeming annuity*, that is, in the case which has been assumed by way of example, to *eight dollars*. The reality of this excess becomes palpable if it be supposed, as often happens, that the citizen of a foreign Country imports into the United States 100 dollars for the purchase of an equal sum of public debt. Here is an absolute augmentation of the mass of Circulating Coin to the extent of 100 dollars. At the end of a year the foreigner is presumed to draw back eight dollars on account of his Principal and Interest, but he still leaves Ninety two of his original Deposit in circulation, as he in like manner leaves Eighty four at the end of the second year, drawing back then also the annuity of Eight Dollars: And thus the Matter proceeds; The capital left in circulation diminishing each year and coming nearer to the level of the annuity drawn back. There are, however, some differences in the ultimate operation of the part of the debt which is purchased by foreigners and that which remains in the hands of citizens. But the general effect in each case, though in different degrees, is to add to the active capital of the Country.

Hitherto the reasoning has proceeded on a concession of the position that there is a destruction of some other capital to the extent of the annuity appropriated to the payment of the Interest and the redemption of the principal of the debt, but in this too much has been conceded. There is at most a temporary transfer of some other capital to the amount of the Annuity from those who pay to the Creditor who receives; which he again restores to the circulation to resume the offices of a capital. This he does either immediately by employing the money in some branch of

Industry, or immediately by lending it to some other person who does so employ it or by spending it on his own maintenance. In either supposition there is no destruction of capital, there is nothing more than a suspension of its motion for a time; that is, while it is passing from the hands of those who pay into the Public coffers, & thence through the public Creditor into some other Channel of circulation. When the payments of interest are periodical and quick and made by instrumentality of Banks, the diversion or suspension of capital may almost be denominated momentary. Hence the deduction on this Account is far less than it at first sight appears to be.

There is evidently as far as regards the annuity no destruction nor transfer of any other Capital than that portion of the income of each individual which goes to make up the Annuity. The land which furnishes the Farmer with the sum which he is to contribute remains the same; and the like may be observed of other Capitals. Indeed as far as the Tax which is the object of contribution (as frequently happens, when it does not oppress by its weight) may have been a Motive to *greater exertion* in any occupation; it may even serve to increase the contributory Capital: This idea is not without importance in the general view of the subject.

It remains to see, what further deduction ought to be made from the capital which is created by the existence of the Debt, on account of the coin which is employed in its circulation. This is susceptible of much less precise calculation than the Article which has been just discussed. It is impossible to say what proportion of coin is necessary to carry on the alienations which any species of property usually undergoes. The quantity indeed varies according to circumstances. But it may still without hesitation be pronounced from the quickness of the rotation, or rather of the transitions, that the *medium* of circulation always bears but a small proportion to the amount of the *property* circulated. And it is thence satisfactorily deducible that the coin employed in the Negotiations of the funds and which serves to give them activity as capital is incomparably less than the sum of the debt negotiated for the purposes of business.

It ought not, however, to be omitted that the negotiation of the funds becomes itself a distinct business which employs, and by employing diverts a portion of the circulating coin from other pursuits. But making due allowance for this circumstance, there is no reason to conclude that the effect of the diversion of coin in the whole operation bears any considerable proportion to the amount of the Capital to which it gives activity. The sum of the debt in circulation is continually at the Command of any useful enterprise—the coin itself which circulates it is never more than momentarily suspended from its ordinary functions. It experiences an incessant and rapid flux and reflux to and from the Channels of industry to those of speculations in the funds.

There are strong circumstances in confirmation of this Theory. The force of Monied Capital which has been displayed in Great Britain, and the height to which every species of industry has grown up under it, defy a solution from the quantity of coin which that kingdom has ever possessed. Accordingly it has been Coeval with its funding system, the prevailing opinion of the men of business and of the generality of the most sagacious theorists of that country that the operation of the public funds as capital has contributed to the effect in question. Among ourselves appearances thus far favor the same Conclusion. Industry in general seems to have been reanimated. There are symptoms indicating an extension of our Commerce. Our navigation has certainly of late had a Considerable spring, and there appears to be in many parts of the Union a command of capital which till lately, since the revolution at least, was unknown. But it is at the same time to be acknowledged that other circumstances have concurred, (and in a great degree) in producing the present state of things, and that the appearances are not yet sufficiently decisive to be entirely relied upon.

In the question under discussion, it is important to distinguish between an *absolute increase of Capital or an accession of real wealth*, and *an artificial increase of Capital* as an engine of business, or as an instrument of industry and Commerce. In the first sense, a funded debt has no pretensions to being deemed an increase of Capital; in the last, it has pretensions which are not easy to be controverted. Of a similar nature is bank credit and in an inferior degree every species of private credit.

But though a funded debt is not in the first instance an absolute increase of Capital or an augmentation of real wealth;

yet by serving as a New power in the operation of industry it has within certain bounds a tendency to increase the real wealth of a Community, in like manner as money borrowed by a thrifty farmer to be laid out in the improvement of his farm may in the end add to his Stock of real riches.

There are respectable individuals who from a just aversion to an accumulation of Public debt are unwilling to concede to it any kind of utility, who can discern no good to alleviate the ill with which they suppose it pregnant; who cannot be persuaded that it ought in any sense to be viewed as an increase of capital lest it should be inferred that the more debt the more capital, the greater the burthens the greater the blessings of the community.

But it interests the public Councils to estimate every object as it truly is; to appreciate how far the good in any measure is compensated by the ill; or the ill by the good. Either of them is seldom unmixed.

Neither will it follow that an accumulation of debt is desirable because a certain degree of it operates as capital. There may be a plethora in the political as in the Natural body; There may be a state of things in which any such artificial capital is unnecessary. The debt too may be swelled to such a size as that the greatest part of it may cease to be useful as a Capital, serving only to pamper the dissipation of idle and dissolute individuals: as that the sums required to pay the Interest upon it may become oppressive, and beyond the means which a government can employ consistently with its tranquility to raise them; as that the resources of taxation to face the debt may have been strained too far to admit of extensions adequate to exigencies which regard the public safety.

Where this critical point is cannot be pronounced, but it is impossible to believe that there is not such a point.

And as the vicissitudes of Nations beget a perpetual tendency to the accumulation of debt, there ought to be in every government a perpetual, anxious and unceasing effort to reduce that which at any time exists as fast as shall be practicable consistently with integrity and good faith.

Reasoning on a subject comprehending ideas so abstract and complex, so little reducible to precise calculation as those which enter into the question just discussed, are always attended with a danger of running into fallacies. Due allowance ought therefore to be made for this possibility. But as far as the Nature of the subject admits of it, there appears to be satisfactory ground for a belief that the public funds operate as a resource of capital to the Citizens of the United States, and, if they are a resource at all, it is an extensive one. . . .

If then it satisfactorily appears that it is the Interest of the United states generally, to encourage manufactures, it merits particular attention that there are circumstances, which Render the present a critical moment for entering with Zeal upon the important business. The effort cannot fail to be materially seconded by a considerable and increasing influx of money in consequence of foreign speculations in the funds—and by the disorders, which exist in different parts of Europe.

The first circumstance not only facilitates the execution of manufacturing enterprises, but it indicates them as a necessary mean to turn the thing itself to advantage, and to prevent its being eventually an evil. If useful employment be not found for the Money of foreigners brought to the country to be invested in purchases of the public debt, it will quickly be re-exported to defray the expense of an extraordinary consumption of foreign luxuries; and distressing drains of our specie may hereafter be experienced to pay the interest and redeem the principal of the purchased debt.

This useful employment too ought to be of a Nature to produce solid and permanent improvements. If the money merely serves to give a temporary spring to foreign commerce, as it cannot procure new and lasting outlets for the products of the Country, there will be no real or durable advantage gained. As far as it shall find its way in Agricultural ameliorations, in opening canals, and in similar improvements it will be productive of substantial utility. But there is reason to doubt whether in such channels it is likely to find sufficient employment, and still more whether many of those who possess it would be as readily attracted to objects of this nature as to manufacturing pursuits, which bear greater analogy to those to which they are accustomed, and to the spirit generated by them.

To open the one field as well as the other will at least secure a better prospect of useful employment for whatever accession of money there has been or may be.

There is at the present juncture a certain fermentation of mind, a certain activity of speculation and enterprise which if properly directed may be made subservient to useful purposes; but which if left entirely to itself, may be attended with pernicious effects.

The disturbed state of Europe inclining its citizens to emigration, the requisite workmen will be more easily acquired than at another time; and the effect of multiplying the opportunities of employment to those who emigrate may be an increase of the number and extent of valuable acquisitions to the population arts and industry of the Country. To find pleasure in the calamities of other nations would be criminal; but to benefit ourselves by opening an asylum to those who suffer in consequence of them is as justifiable as it is politic.

A full view having now been taken of the inducements to the promotion of Manufactures in the United States accompanied with an examination of the principal objections which are commonly urged *in opposition*, it is proper in the next place to consider the means by which it may be effected. . . .

In order to a better judgment of the Means proper to be resorted to by the United states, it will be of use to Advert to those which have been employed with success in other Countries. The principal of these are.

I   Protecting duties—or duties on those foreign articles which are the rivals of the domestic ones, intended to be encouraged. . . .

II   Prohibitions of rival articles or duties equivalent to prohibitions. . . .

III   Prohibitions of the exportation of the materials of manufactures. . . .

IV   Pecuniary bounties. . . .

V   Premiums. . . .

VI   The Exemption of the Materials of manufactures from duty. . . .

VII   Drawbacks of the duties which are imposed on the Materials of Manufactures. . . .

VIII   The encouragement of new inventions and discoveries at home, and of the introduction into the United States of such as may have been made in other countries, particularly those which relate to machinery. . . .

IX  Judicious regulations for the inspection of manufactured commodities. . . .

X  The facilitating of pecuniary remittances from place to place is a point of considerable moment to trade in general, and to manufactures in particular, by rendering more easily the purchase of raw materials and provisions and the payment for manufactured supplies. A general circulation of Bank paper, which is to be expected from the institution lately established, will be a most valuable mean to this end. But much good would also accrue from some additional provisions respecting inland bills of exchange. If those drawn in one state payable in another were made negotiable everywhere, and interest and damages allowed in case of protest, it would greatly promote negotiations between the Citizens of different states by rendering them more secure; and with it the convenience and advantage of the Merchants and manufacturers of each.

XI  The facilitating of the transportation of commodities.

Improvements favoring this object intimately concern all the domestic interests of a community; but they may without impropriety be mentioned as having an important relation to manufactures. There is perhaps scarcely anything which has been better calculated to assist the manufactures of Great Britain than the ameliorations of the public roads of that Kingdom, and the great progress which has been of late made in opening canals. Of the former, the United States stand much in need; and for the latter they present uncommon facilities. . . .

The foregoing are the principal of the means by which the growth of manufactures is ordinarily promoted. It is, however, not merely necessary that the measures of government, which have a direct view to manufactures should be calculated to assist and protect them, but that those which only collaterally affect them in the general course of the administration should be guarded from any peculiar tendency to injure them.

There are certain species of taxes which are apt to be oppressive to different parts of the community, and among other ill effects have a very unfriendly aspect towards manufactures. All Poll or Capitation taxes are of this nature. They either proceed according to a fixed rate which operates unequally and injuriously to the industrious poor; or they vest a discretion in certain officers to make estimates and assessments which are necessarily vague, conjectural and liable to abuse. They ought therefore to be abstained from in all but cases of distressing emergency.

All such taxes (including all taxes on occupations) which proceed according to the amount of capital *supposed* to be employed in a business, or of profits *supposed* to be made in it are unavoidably hurtful to industry. It is in vain that the evil may be endeavored to be mitigated by leaving it, in the first instance, in the option of the party to be taxed to declare the amount of his capital or profits. . . .

Arbitrary taxes, under which denomination are comprised all those that leave the *quantum* of the tax to be raised on each person to the *discretion* of certain officers are as contrary to the genius of liberty as to the maxims of industry. In this light, they have been viewed by the most judicious observers on government who have bestowed upon them the severest epithets of reprobation as constituting one of the worst features usually to be met with in the practice of despotic governments. . . .

In countries where there is great private wealth much may be effected by the voluntary contributions of patriotic individuals, but in a community situated like that of the United States, the public purse must supply the deficiency of private resource. In what can it be so useful as in prompting and improving the efforts of industry?

All which is humbly submitted
Alexander Hamilton
Secy of the Treasury

# CHAPTER FIFTEEN

# To William Seton (February 10 and March 22, 1792)

*Every existing bank ought within prudent limits to abridge its operations. The superstructure of Credit is now too vast for the foundation. It must be gradually brought within more reasonable dimensions or it will tumble.*

BY JANUARY 1792 Hamilton's financial revolution was riding high: domestic and foreign debt healthy, the national bank commencing operations the previous month, the U.S. dollar set as the account of value (if not quite yet the medium of exchange), the Society for the Establishment of Useful Manufactures open for business, and the delivery to Congress of his *Report on the Subject of Manufactures*.

Then came a setback. By March the major cities of Philadelphia, New York, and Boston were in turmoil because U.S. securities markets had their first crash. Government debt securities, for example, lost nearly a quarter of their value in two weeks. It would be the first of many Wall Street crashes in our nation's history.

The crisis, which came when the modern U.S. markets were less than two years old, is off the screens of most scholars, including financial historians. In part that is because Treasury Secretary Hamilton managed the crisis incredibly well. Hence there was almost no economic fallout for the economy. Hamilton stemmed the panic, and the financial system quickly recovered.[1] But the political fallout was vicious. Thomas Jefferson, James Madison, and their allies were appalled at the chaos and bankruptcies brought on by speculation in Hamilton's newly created Treasury bonds as well as the stocks of the Bank of New York and Bank of the United States.

In our first letter to William Seton, who was cashier of the Bank of New York and Hamilton's eyes and ears in that city, dated February 10, Hamilton saw trouble brewing from speculative trading and wild plans to launch new banks to fuel the speculation. He suggested a gradual reduction in credit to reduce the speculation. Our second letter displays that when the crisis hit, Hamilton exhibited a financial creativity of an uncommonly high order as well as an instinct for what needed to be done to resolve a financial panic.

Speculative machinations resulted in wild trading in securities markets, first in the summer of 1791 and again in the early months of 1792. Speculators—none more prominent than his own former employee and number two man at the Treasury Department, William Duer—tried to control, even corner, the markets for government bonds and bank stocks by borrowing large sums from whoever would lend, rich and poor alike. When he became short of funds, Duer stole from the newly created Society for Establishing Useful Manufactures (see chapter 13), of which he was the president.

Although Hamilton's letter was to Seton at the Bank of New York, one can reasonably assume that he would also have mentioned his concerns to the recently created Bank of the United States in Philadelphia, located near the Treasury Department in what was then the nation's capital, particularly as he mentioned "every existing bank." Evidence also exists that several of the other banks were curtailing credit in the first days of the panic. Philadelphia securities broker Clement Biddle claimed that "all the Banks on the Continent" were involved in the restrictive process.[2] Hamilton is the only one who could have coordinated the restriction of credit. His words sound like those of a modern central bank head, bringing to mind, for example, Federal Reserve chairman Alan Greenspan's December 1996 comments about "irrational exuberance" in U.S. securities markets.

Hamilton's prescription was not followed, as the "superstructure of credit" was not "gradually" brought to "more reasonable dimensions." Instead, the Bank of the United States, which Hamilton hinted to Seton was experiencing difficulties, rapidly reduced its credit creation, which shortly caused the bubble to burst. Duer and other speculators were unable to repay their loans, and their defaults triggered panic as everyone who could began to hoard cash. Markets went into free fall, and paralysis gripped finance in New York, Philadelphia, and Boston. A confederate of Duer lamented from jail that one "can scarcely imagine the present distress in the town, + all confidence lost, no credit, failures every day . . . at present every countenance is gloomy, all confidence between individuals is lost, credit at a stand, and distress and general bankruptcy to be daily expected—for everyone gambled more or less on these cursed speculations."[3]

In the second letter, dated March 22, we find two of Hamilton's innovative solutions to allay the crisis. Hamilton first acknowledges the panic and suggests he is open to transferring funds to the Bank of New York to pay the upcoming quarterly interest on U.S. debt. He next refers to the "Sinking Fund." This August 1790 creation, outlined toward the end of Hamilton's January 1790 public credit report (see chapter 13), was a pool of funds to be raised to assist in paying down the national debt over time. Hamilton had established the sinking fund as part of his plan to restore public credit; he also could use it in emergencies such as the March, 1792, crash to purchase U.S. debt securities to inject liquidity into panicked markets through what today would be termed central bank open market operations. Hamilton, however, had only one of the five votes of the sinking fund commissioners, and he needed two more votes to use the money. The other voters were Vice-President John Adams, Secretary of State Thomas Jefferson, Attorney General Edmund Randolph, and Chief Justice of the Supreme Court John Jay. Jay was not in Philadelphia, and therefore Hamilton sent for him. Four days later, with Jay still absent and Thomas Jefferson dissenting, Hamilton received the votes of Adams and Randolph to utilize some of the sinking fund money. Hamilton refers in this paragraph to being "in the market," which is a reference to his attempts to buy government bonds to support the market.

Given that money from the sinking fund was unavailable at the time of this letter and might not be enough alone to stem the crisis, Hamilton needed another plan, and herein lies the genius of this letter. Hamilton developed a strategy to stop troubles in the financial system from spilling over into the "real" or nonfinancial part of the economy without subsidizing those who caused the panic in the first place.

Central banking theorists have long called this strategy Bagehot's rules because they believed that it was first articulated by Walter Bagehot, founding editor of *The Economist* (the same weekly newsmagazine that bears that name today), in his 1873 book, *Lombard Street*. Bagehot believed that the Bank of England, the British central bank, needed to follow his rules, which simply stated that during times of widespread financial distress, the lender of last resort (the central bank) should lend freely, but at a high rate of interest (sometimes called a penalty rate), to all borrowers who could post good collateral for such loans. This letter demonstrates that Hamilton had developed the same idea, which solves the so-called moral hazard problem of a central bank in supporting financial markets, eight decades before Bagehot's famous articulation.

Bagehot's two rules are in the letter—namely, to lend on what in normal times is considered good security (U.S. government bonds), but at a penalty rate of 7 percent (the New York usury ceiling) when the normal rate banks charged was 6 percent. It is true that Hamilton places a limit of $1 million on these credits. But $1 million was quite a large sum in 1792, and even the Bank of England in Bagehot's day, as well as before and after, did not have the capability of unlimited lending.

Hamilton understood that Seton and the Bank of New York would be reluctant to lend in the panic for fear of incurring losses if the collateral they accepted for loans continued to decline in value. So, after naming the values at which the various Treasury bonds were to be accepted as collateral for the bank's loans, Hamilton combined his Bagehot-like plan with a repurchase (repo) feature. Should the Bank of New York for whatever reason get stuck with the collateral, the Secretary of the Treasury would take at least half of it off the bank's hands at the prices he had named. But Hamilton thought that eventuality "not supposable," or in other words, highly unlikely. Hamilton asked the bank to act as the lender of last resort in New York, the epicenter of the crisis, because it was then the only bank in New York. The Bank of the United States would open its New York branch the following month, and that, too, may have alleviated the crisis.

Lenders of last resort recently have strayed from the strict use of Hamilton's rule. In 2008, in response to the financial panic, central banks used all means necessary—lowering interest rates to zero, lending on almost any collateral, and using billions of taxpayer dollars to prop up banks and other institutions. The concern is always the message that sends: if central banks always aid those in financial distress, it essentially tells the largest market participants to take big risks and reap the big rewards that go with them. That is "moral hazard."

Although bailing out failing companies in the way just described is politically controversial, central bankers during and after the crisis of 2007–2009 justified their actions by arguing that everyone is better off if the contagion of financial panic and failure is stopped before it causes a large decline in overall economic activity, or possibly another Great Depression. While the argument is plausible, Hamilton's rule, strictly applied, provides an alternative strategy that may stop panic without encouraging excessive risk-taking. First, central banks that follow Hamilton's rule lend only at a penalty rate—i.e., at a rate higher than the one prevailing before the panic—so emergency borrowers are not subsidized. Second, the rule carefully differentiates companies that are bankrupt (liabilities greater than assets) from those merely suffering from a temporary lack of liquidity (insufficient cash to keep up current payments) by insisting on sufficient strong collateral backing for all emergency loans. Application of the rule stops the spread of panic by reassuring all prudently managed companies that they will be able to acquire sufficient cash to continue operations, while simultaneously forcing bankrupt companies to cease operations.

Hamilton alleviated the crisis of 1792 with a variety of measures. Employing the sinking fund, he bought securities in the open market in Philadelphia and through the Bank of New York in New York. He instructed banks not to raid each other's specie reserves, as they were tempted to do in a panic; in panics, financial institutions that normally compete need to cooperate with one another. He released information that the U.S. government had a received a new loan from the Dutch on favorable terms, news that had a calming effect. Lastly, as we have seen, he suggested to the Bank of New York (and presumably the other banks) that they extend their loans if it could be done with government bonds as collateral. With these steps, the panic of 1792, Wall Street's first crash, was short-lived. Normal trading soon resumed, and prices recovered.

Hamilton's financial genius surfaces in these letters. First, he was prescient in see the bubble forming, and second, when it burst, he created a plan involving a series of measures that stemmed the panic and saved the financial system. While the overall long-term trend in U.S. economic history has been one of strong growth, it has all too often been punctuated by vicious downturns and depressions caused by financial speculation. Central bankers could learn from this case study, in which Hamilton prevented catastrophe by bold, creative, and novel steps.

The two letters here are not abridged.

Philadelphia
Feby. 10. 179[2]

My Dear Sir
I have received your letter of the 6th instant. The full and confidential communication you make is equally acceptable and necessary.

I sincerely hope the Petitioners for a New Bank may be frustrated; but I fear more than I hope. General Schuyler will do everything in his power against them. Every day unfolds the mischievous tendency of this mad scheme. The enemies to Banks & Credit are in a fair way of having their utmost malignity gratified.

It is certainly necessary, that if an independent branch of the Bank of the U States be carried into effect in your City, there should be a good understanding between the two institutions. But I tell you in the *strictest confidence* that there are circumstances which must of necessity postpone this operation, and which are opening the eyes of certain folks to the expediency of a coalition.

I am under a necessity of authorizing the Treasurer to draw upon you for One hundred thousand Dollars. It is a necessary aid to the Bank of the U States which feels more than you do the effects of certain machinations. *This* for your *own breast* exclusively. I advance it upon terms which will insure its restoration to you *in specie*, if a branch is established; so that it will not eventually affect your safety. I may be compelled to go further; but it will be on the same conditions.

You will understand that all the money which you may receive for bills or otherwise, on account of the U States, subsequent to the 31st of January last shall be received from you in bills of the Bank of the United States. And that no order shall issue to derange this engagement.

You appear to me to mistake a point, which is, that in the case of an establishment of a branch, you will have to pay the Bank of the U States the amount of their deposit in specie. They certainly cannot make a difficulty about receiving their own Notes. This idea I think you may safely proceed upon. At all events no distress will be permitted to arise to you on this account.

The state of things however requires unusual circumspection. Every existing bank ought within prudent limits to abridge its operations. The superstructure of Credit is now too vast for the foundation. It must be gradually brought within more reasonable dimensions or it will tumble. Adieu My Dear Sir

Most sincerely    Yrs

A Hamilton


Philadelphia, March 22, 1792

My Dear Sir

In the present state of things it would be *satisfactory* to me and I think would ensure accommodation to the Bank, if you would undertake to pay the Quarter's Interest at the Bank. In this case I would direct the Commissioner of Loans to deposit the Dividend book with you for the purpose. As the time is almost arrived an immediate answer is necessary.

I need not tell you how much I have participated in the distress of your City—how much I have felt for our unfortunate friend Duer—I should have come to your aid on the spot but for a difference of Opinion among the Trustees of the Sinking Fund. I am now in the market—and hope if necessary to be enabled to come into it with more power—Mr. Jay has been sent for—This rather in confidence or only for discreet communication.

If your distress continues would not the following plan be advisable for your institution?

Let deposits of stock [US government bonds] be received to an amount not exceeding a million—Six per Cents at *par* three per Cents at 10 shillings on the pound and deferred at 12 shillings— Let credits be passed on your books in favor of the Depositors for the amounts, according to those values, transferable at the Bank as in the case of deposits in the Bank of Amsterdam—and if required receipts may be given to the parties. Let the terms of the deposit be that the Depositors may withdraw their Stock at any time paying in specie the sums credited whenever the Credits have been transferred—with a right to the Bank after six months to sell the Stock and pay them the overplus. Let the Bank engage at the end of six months to pay the amount of these Credits in Gold or Silver; for the undertaking which let them receive a compensation in Interest at the rate of 7 per Centum per annum.

I take it for granted in the prevailing disposition of your City, transfers of these Credits under the promise of the Bank to pay in Specie at the end of six months would operate as Cash in mutual payments between Individuals—while the Bank would be safe from the danger of a run & undoubtedly safe eventually.

To render the operation more perfectly safe to the Bank, I will engage at the expiration of six months to take off your hands at the rate specified to the amount of 500,000 Dollars—in case the parties should not redeem & there should be no adequate demand. Which, however, is not supposable.

I have thought a good deal of this plan & I really believe it is a good one & will tend to obviate the necessity of ruinous sacrifice of the Public Stock by parties indebted—Such as it is however I give it to you. Perhaps a change in your affairs may render it unnecessary.

Yours with great regard
A Hamilton

# CHAPTER SIXTEEN

# Report on a Plan for the Further Support of Public Credit (January 16, 1795)

*Credit, public and private, is of the greatest consequence to every Country. Of this, it might be emphatically called the invigorating principle.*

THIS IS ONE of the more neglected of Hamilton's state papers, but also among the most significant because it was both a history of Hamilton's tenure as Treasury Secretary and a guide to future policy. James Madison, in a letter to Thomas Jefferson dated February 15, 1795, derided it as an "arrogant valedictory Report." Some academic and other opponents of Hamilton have ignored it ever since, because it tended to destroy misconceptions about Hamilton's policies common among his detractors, especially those who erroneously claimed that Hamilton wanted to keep the United States perpetually indebted for large sums.

In fact, the report laid out a "*definitive plan* for the *Redemption* of the public debt," so "that credit as far as may be practicable" would be placed "*on grounds which cannot be disturbed*," and for the prevention of "*that progressive accumulation of Debt which must ultimately endanger* all Government." Later passages of the report contain a paean to the role of credit, both public and private, in strengthening a government and making an economy grow. To Hamilton, credit was a new power in the world, essential to economic and political modernization.

As usual, Hamilton provided ample context for his policy proposals. In this case, he provided a fiscal history of the new nation in three parts, the first covering "the revenues which have been established," the second the provisions for funding the debt, and the third "provisions for reimbursing and extinguishing the Debt."

The first part contains descriptions of fifteen different revenue acts, many of which Hamilton had drafted for Congress, plus reference to the unreliability of the sale of western lands at twenty cents an acre because of uncertainties about the quality of the land and "the boundary line between the United States & the Indians." These descriptions are not included in our condensation of the report.

The second describes ten laws related to the funding and repayment of the national debt, also left out of our condensation.

Hamilton summarized the revenue and debt acts into thirteen "leading features" of "the fiscal system of the United States":

1. Federal revenues came entirely from tariffs on imports, tonnage of ships, excises on domestically distilled spirits and a tax on stills, postage, fees on patents, Bank of the United States stock dividends, sales at auction, licenses to retail wines and spirits, taxes on domestically manufactured snuff and sugar, and a carriage tax.

2. Most of the tariffs, tonnage duties, liquor excises and still taxes, postage, patent fees, and bank stock were permanent, but the others were limited to the end of the next session of Congress two years after passage.

3. The tariffs, tonnage duties, and domestic distilling taxes were "subject to . . . permanent dispositions," including $0.6 million for operation of the federal government, interest on foreign loans, interest on the original debt of the United States, interest on assumed debt, and interest on balances due to creditor states, in that order.

4. Any surplus in the liquor distillation duties was to be applied to the reduction of the public debt, but the others were not subject to "*such ultimate appropriation.*"

5. Postage and bank stock dividends had no permanent appropriation.

6. Temporary duties were charged with $1.3 million plus interest on $1 million authorized to be borrowed "*for the expenses of foreign intercourse.*"

7. The entire foreign debt and most of the domestic debt were "bottomed on certain specified revenues pledged or hypothecated for the payment of the Interest upon them and thus constitute the FUNDED DEBT of the United States."

8. The funded domestic debt consisted of three types of bonds ("Stock"), one now bearing 6 percent interest (Sixes), another bearing 6 percent interest after 1800 (Deferred), and a third bearing 3 percent interest (Threes), all payable quarterly.

9. Sixes and Deferreds could be redeemed no faster than 8 percent per year "on Account both of principal & interest," but Threes were "redeemable at pleasure."

10. The deadline for subscribing to the domestic debt passed on 31 December 1794, and "no further provision has been made for the unsubscribed residue."

11. The funding act expressly confirmed the rights of creditors who chose not to subscribe to the new loan (Sixes, Deferreds, Threes) and gave "an *expectation* to them of *further* and *other* arrangements."

12. Western land sales were earmarked for redemption of the public debt.

13. In addition, a sinking fund run by five principal officers of the United States was instituted, funded by any surplus of tariffs and tonnage duties, $2 million of authorized borrowings, and the interest on the public debt purchased or otherwise paid into the Treasury.

The national debt represented by securities (Sixes, Deferreds, Threes, and various old loans not subscribed to the new ones) amounted to $76.01 million. In addition, the federal government in 1795 owed $1.4 million to the Bank of the United States for its stock and various "loans which are temporary anticipations of the Revenue." The total current revenue of the federal government Hamilton calculated at $6.55 million, and its expenditures, computing Army and Navy spending based on Indian and Algerine (Algerian) wars, amounted to $5.68 million.

In the next few years, the government would have to start paying interest on the Deferreds, but that might be offset by the operations of the sinking fund and the "sales of Western Lands." If $3 million could be raised from those lands, and certain other assumptions came to pass,

Hamilton calculated that the United States could pay off the entire national debt in thirty years, give or take, adding, "Some Auxiliary provisions which will be proposed may greatly accelerate that result."

That led Hamilton to make ten suggested policy changes in the form of "Propositions," followed by explanations of each. In summary terms, the propositions and explanations were:

1. Government creditors should be allowed until the end of 1795 to subscribe to the new loan under somewhat improved terms.
2. New emission bills of credit—i.e., those emitted by resolution of Congress on 18 March 1780—should be funded at 5 percent for thirty years because they read, in part: "The United States *insure* the *payment* of the within Bill and will draw Bills of exchange for the interest annually if demanded." They were initially sold at less than their par or face value, though, indicating that buyers did not expect contract fulfillment, so "a compromise" seemed in order to Hamilton. The sum was only $95,574.
3. The foreign debt should be repaid by a new domestic loan because "the payment of Interest and installments of principal of our foreign debt in the Countries where it was contracted is found by experience to be attended with difficulty, embarrassment, some loss, and a degree of casualty which occasionally puts in jeopardy the National Credit,"
4. Temporary duties should be made permanent and appropriated in like manner. The $0.6 million for the government's general expenses should be postponed until after the payment of interest on the debt. The object was to "give moral certainty to the adequateness of the fund for paying the interest upon the Debt and for its ultimate Redemption."
5. Ten very technical changes in debt funding were all geared toward appropriating surplus revenues to repayment of the national debt via the sinking fund, with an exception for years of "war with any foreign European power." Washington was right in his annual message on the state of the union about "the danger to every Government from the progressive accumulation of Debt." Excessive debt, Hamilton stated, is "the NATURAL DISEASE of all Governments" because they are wont to compete with other governments and because of a desire, "founded in the Constitution of man, to shift off the burden from the

present to a future day; a propensity which may be expected to be strong in proportion as the form of the State is popular." People always want to pay off the debt until the taxman cometh. Often men will call for debt reduction as "an *abstract thesis*" but oppose the taxes necessary to "discharge old debts." "These contradictions are in human nature," Hamilton assured his readers. The proposed changes would make it more difficult for our nature to get the better of us, enabling us to pay off the national debt "with reasonable celerity" and "give IMMORTALITY TO PUBLIC CREDIT." Hamilton reiterated his belief, stated in his January 1790 Report on Public Credit, that new debts should always be matched by a means for extinguishing them. Britain had adopted a similar rule within the last few years, but the United States was much better situated to do likewise if it acted soon. The goal of the fifth proposition was to pay off the national debt in thirty years, give the commissioners of the sinking fund the goal of doing so, and make fulfillment of the promise "*a part of the contract with the Creditors*" even in the case of war, given that some trade "through Neutral powers" would always be possible. What Hamilton wanted was "the inviolable application of an adequate sinking fund" because that was "the only practicable security against an excessive accumulation of debt," as shown by the experience of some countries that "diverted" money from their sinking funds "when immediate exigencies press." Hamilton thought his suggestions would render it better for the government to tax and then borrow during an emergency rather than to "Plunder" the sinking fund. "There is no cause to hesitate about the inviolable appropriation of funds to the extinction of an existing debt within no less term than 30 Years," especially in a young, growing nation like the United States. Such strong credit would be cheap even during the largest war that we can imagine. So Congress should adopt the principle that "with the creation of debt should be incorporated the means of extinguishment," including "reimbursement of the PRINCIPAL."

6. The sinking fund commissioners, with the President's approbation, should be authorized to borrow up to $1 million per year, the interest "to be defrayed out of the permanent Revenues." This is because "the receipts" from taxes "come too slowly into the Treasury" to meet payments punctually.

7. Internal revenues from snuff, refined sugars, auction sales, retail distilled spirits licenses, and the carriage tax should be continued until January 1800, and thence until the end of the next session of Congress. This is because public revenues should "be commensurate in duration with the object which they are to accomplish and no more."

8. Funds unexpended for more than two years after the end of the calendar year in which they were appropriated shall be carried to the surplus fund account. This, Hamilton explained, was designed to "terminate an embarrassment," the tying up of public funds for long periods. If further appropriations past the deadline are needed, new estimates and appropriations can always be made.

9. Except for creditors who dissented, all priorities established in the revenue acts funding the national debt would cease at the end of 1796. Thereafter, "appropriations shall constitute a common or consolidated Fund chargeable indiscriminately and without priority." The proposition was to make public accounting simpler, more accurate, and more rapidly available. The rights of creditors would not really be affected by this change, so it was "presumed that" none would "dissent."

10. Provision should be made for calling in all the old debt certificates for new ones "of equivalent tenor." All certificates not presented within two years would be barred from receiving interest. This was to ascertain precisely the amount of the unfunded debt and to weed out "forgeries and counterfeits."

Hamilton saved for the end of the report a final proposition that he believed was "of great importance to the Public Credit." As usual, he offered "some preliminary observations" so that lawmakers would fully grasp the rationale for the proposal, which related "to the right of taxing the public funds" and to "sequestering them in time of war." Hamilton averred that he had assumed it "an Axiom" that the government had no right to do either, but two resolutions asserting such rights that passed in the House in 1794 had challenged that assumption.

The government may be supposed to have the right to tax any or all species of property, Hamilton said, but the debt of the government imposing the tax "must form an exception," or it would be possible for the government de facto to reduce some or all of its obligations. The government had never explicitly promised not to tax its own bonds, but it did do so "in substance" by explicitly promising a certain interest payment. "To Tax the funds is manifestly either to *take* or to *keep back* a portion of the principal or interest *stipulated to be paid*," Hamilton argued, hence an *ex post facto* tax would constitute a breach of contract. In short, it was "against the rules both of Law & reason to admit by *implication*; in the construction of a contract, a principle which goes in destruction of it."

A tax on all money balances would be acceptable, Hamilton admitted, but the government would have to tax everyone the same, not just public creditors, and it could not deduct the tax from the interest payment. But a tax on transactions, when bondholders sell to other investors, is not acceptable because "stock in its *creation* is *made transferrable*." The right to sell the obligation to a new owner is a major part of the contract, and of the value of the bond. To tax transfers, therefore, is to tax the bond itself and is no less objectionable than withholding interest payments as just discussed.

Government creditors are not tax exempt. They can be, and are, taxed just as other citizens are.

Admitting a right of the government to tax its funds "would cost much more than it was worth" because the government would find it very costly to sell its bonds or otherwise borrow in the future as "the money lender would exact exorbitant premiums" in expectation of such a tax. More likely, "there would be no borrowing at all upon such terms," so the government would have to expressly renounce its right to tax "in every future loan."

The right of a Government to sequester or confiscate property in its funds in time of war," Hamilton continued, "involves considerations analogous to these which regard the right of taxing them." Confiscation, after all, is just a 100 percent tax. Foreign holders of a U.S. government bond "stand upon equal ground with the Citizen" and have an equal claim upon the faith of the Government.

To own property, people must "be protected & secured in the enjoyment" of it by national governments. Once a foreigner is allowed to purchase property in a nation, that nation's government promises to protect it, which is "an engagement which no state of things between the two nations can justly or reasonably affect."

"No well informed man," Hamilton reminded readers, "can cast a retrospective eye over the progress of the United States, from their infancy to the present period, without being convinced that they owe in a great degree, to the fostering influence of Credit their present mature growth."

Mercantile credit and bills of credit spurred growth in the colonial period; credit helped to win the Revolution; credit also may "claim a principal agency in that increase of national and individual welfare, since the establishment of the present Government." Moreover, credit is essential to the nation's future well-being because it is a "young Country with moderate pecuniary Capital and not a very various industry," and hence it could be overwhelmed by a country "more advanced in both" unless it was able to "borrow at pleasure considerable sums on moderate terms." To Hamilton, "War without Credit would be more than a great calamity, it would be ruin."

In addition to being "one of the main pillars of the public safety," credit was "among the principal engines of useful enterprise and internal improvement," and "little less useful than Gold or silver, in Agriculture, in Commerce, in the Manufacturing and mechanic arts." Hamilton then supplied quotidian, though fictional, examples: a man purchases land on credit, "another sets up in trade," while a third "commences business as a manufacturer or Mechanic, with skill, . . . without Money" but with credit enough "to procure the tools, the materials and even the subsistence of which he stands in need, 'till his industry has supplied him with Capital." And, of course, "public and private Credit are closely allied, if not inseparable," so "a shock to public Credit would . . . diminish the antecedent resources of private Credit."

After all, "Credit is an *entire thing*. Every part of it has the nicest sympathy with every other part. Wound one limb, and the whole Tree shrinks and decays." Therefore, measures that hurt public credit, even if just foreign bondholders, hurt everyone. "Hence the Government, by sequestering the property of foreign Citizens in the public funds at the commencement of a war, would impair at least if not destroy that Credit, which is the best resource in war."

Yes, credit can be abused, but so can everything, including the precious metals, agriculture, trade, and manufacturing, and "even Liberty itself" can degenerate "into licentiousness." But Hamilton warned against throwing out the baby with the bathwater: " 'Tis Wisdom in every case, to cherish what is useful and guard against its abuse."

In the case of the public debt, that means following Hamilton's suggestions and avoiding "every temptation to run in debt founded on the hope of evading the Just claims of Creditors." Hence, there should "be an express renunciation by Law of all pretension of right, to tax the public funds, or to sequester at any time, or on any pretext, the property which foreign Citizens may hold therein."

Hamilton's strictures on public credit in this report are well worth revisiting today. The national debt of the United States doubled in the decade after 2007, and it rose twenty-fold after 1980. As he said, "credit can be abused," and he cautions us against such abuse.

This document has been abridged from 25,675 words to 12,772 words.

### Report on a Plan for the Further Support of Public Credit
[Philadelphia, January 16, 1795
Communicated to the House on January 19, 1795
Communicated to the Senate on January 21, 1795]

[To the Speaker of the House of Representatives and the President of the Senate]
The Secretary of the Treasury respectfully makes the following report to the House of Representatives

The President of the United States, with that provident concern for the public welfare which characterizes all his conduct, was pleased in his speech to the two Houses of Congress at the opening of the present session to invite their attention to the adoption of a *definitive plan* for the *Redemption* of the public debt, and to the Consummation of *whatsoever may remain unfinished of our System of Public Credit* in order to place that credit as far as may be practicable *on grounds which cannot be disturbed*, and to prevent *that progressive accumulation of Debt which must ultimately endanger* all Government.

It was at the same time very justly intimated that the period which has elapsed since the commencement of our Fiscal Measures (now more than four years) has so far developed our resources as to open the way to the important work: And it is matter of solid Consolation that the result, presenting a State of our finances prosperous beyond expectation, solicits the public councils to enter with zeal and decision upon measures commensurate with the greatness of the Interests to be promoted.

Under the influence of this conviction, in conformity with the suggestions of the President, and pursuant to the duty which the

Constitution of the Department, as by Law established, enjoins upon the Secretary of the Treasury; He has employed himself in digesting and preparing the materials of a Plan for the attainment of the invaluable ends which are recommended; And he now respectfully submits them to the consideration of Congress.

Towards a clear and distinct conception of the means necessary to the accomplishment of those ends, it will be useful in the first place to review what has been heretofore done.

This will be presented under three heads—

1st. The revenues which have been established:
2ndly The Provisions for funding the Debt and for the payment of interest upon it:
3rdly The provisions for reimbursing and extinguishing the Debt. . . .

The foregoing review of the Laws, which constitute the fiscal system of the United States, displays these prominent points as the leading features of that system.

1 That all the current revenues of the United States are derived from these sources (Vizt.) IMPORTED ARTICLES, The TONNAGE of SHIPS and VESSELS, SPIRITS distilled within the United States & STILLS, The POSTAGE of LETTERS, FEES on PATENTS, DIVIDENDS of Bank Stock, SNUFF manufactured within the United States, SUGAR refined within the United States, SALES AT AUCTION, LICENSES to retail Wines & distilled Spirits, CARRIAGES for the CONVEYANCE OF PERSONS.

2nd That of these Revenues, the principal part of the duties on imported Articles, those on the Tonnage of Ships or Vessels, those on distilled Spirits & Stills, those on the postage of Letters, Patent fees, the dividends of Bank Stock, are permanent (the three first being commensurate with the existence of the Debt, for the payment of the Interest of which they are pledged, the 4th. and 5th. having no limit assigned in the laws, and the last being commensurate with the duration of the property in the Stock)—all the others temporary, being limited to continue no longer than 'till the end of the session of *Congress next* after the *expiration* of two years from the respective times of passing the laws which establish them.

3rd That the permanent duties on imported articles, the Tonnage duties, the duties on Spirits distilled within the United States and on Stills, are subject to these permanent dispositions.

1rst To an Annual reservation of 600,000 Dollars for the support of the Government of the United States and their common defense.

2nd To an appropriation of so much as may be necessary to pay the Interest on the foreign loans provided for by the funding Act.

3rd To an appropriation of so much as may be necessary to pay the interest on the Stock created by the Loan in domestic debt, or more properly in the *original* debt of the United States.

4th To an appropriation of so much as may be necessary to discharge the interest on the Stock created by the loan in the Debts of the respective States.

5. To an appropriation of so much as may be necessary to pay the interest on the Balances due to creditor States.

which dispositions establish PRIORITIES according to the order in which they are here enumerated.

4th That the surplus if any of the duties on Spirits distilled within the United States and on Stills has an ultimate appropriation, that is, to the reduction of the public Debt; *but that the surpluses of the other duties have no such ultimate appropriation.*

5th That the duties on the postage of Letters and the net dividends on Bank Stock have *no permanent or particular appropriation.*

6th That the temporary duties *are charged* with a specific Sum of 1,292,137 Dollars & 38 Cents and with the payment of *Interest on a sum of 1,000,000 of dollars authorized to be borrowed for the expenses of foreign intercourse.*

7th That the whole of the Foreign debt, and all that part of the Domestic debt being now nearly the whole, which consists of the Stock created by Loans in the original debt of the United States and in the particular debts of the Several States and by the balances due to Creditor States, are *bottomed on certain specified revenues pledged* or *hypothecated* for the payment of the *Interest* upon them and *thus* constitute the FUNDED DEBT of the United States.

8th That the funded DOMESTIC Debt of the United States consists of three species of Stock, one bearing a present interest of 6 per Cent per annum, another bearing an equal interest after the year 1800, a third bearing a present Interest of three per centum per Annum; the interest in each case payable *quarter Yearly.*

9th That the six per Cent Stock present and deferred can be redeemed in no greater proportion than at the rate of 8 per Centum per annum of the *original* sum on Account both of principal & interest; but the three per cent Stock is redeemable at pleasure.

10th That the provision for subscribing to the Loan in Domestic Debt expired on the last of December 1794, & that *no further provision* has been made for the unsubscribed residue.

11th That the FUNDING ACT *expressly confirms the contracts and rights* of the Creditors of the United States who shall not *think fit to subscribe to the loan*, and gives an *expectation* to them of *further* and *other* arrangements upon the event of the propositions made to them.

12th That the proceeds of all the Lands of the United States in the western Territory are appropriated to the redemption of all that part of the public debt, for which *prior to the funding* Act, or *by virtue thereof,* the United States were or are liable.

13th That, in addition to this, a regular SINKING FUND has been successively constituted, to be applied under the direction of five principal Officers of the United States with the approbation of the president, hitherto composed of three parts 1st the Surplus of the duties on imports & Tonnage to the end of 1790; 2ndly. the proceeds of loans not exceeding 2.000.000 of Dollars authorized to be borrowed for the purpose (these two funds to be invested in purchases) and 3rdly (in which the two former resolve themselves) the Interest on the public debt *purchased redeemed* or paid into the Treasury, together with the surpluses, if any, of monies appropriated for Interest; to be applied 1st to *purchases* of the debt *till* the fund is equal to two per centum of the *outstanding Stock* bearing a present interest of 6 per Cent, 2nd to the *redemption* of that Stock, & lastly to purchases of any *unredeemed* residue of the public debt. But there is *reserved out of this fund a sum not exceeding* 8 per Centum per annum, towards the payment of Interest & reimbursing of principal of the loans made for purchases of the Debt.

To this recapitulation of the leading features of our fiscal system, it may be useful to add a summary exhibition of certain results, which appear more in detail or are deducible from the Tables or Statements annexed to this Report.

The particulars and amount of the debt of the United States are as follow

| | | | |
|---|---|---|---|
| Foreign Debt as per Statements B & C | | 14 599 129.35 | |
| | deduct installments of foreign Debt in the Year 1795 to be paid out of proceeds of foreign loans | <u>853.750.</u> | 13,745 379.35 |
| Funded Domestic Debt (Vizt) | | | |
| 1. | Arising from original domestic Debt subscribed to loan proposed by Funding Act | | |
| | Stock bearing a present interest of 6 per Ct. | 17,912,138.01. | |
| | Stock bearing a future interest of ditto | 8,538,228.97. | |
| | Stock bearing an Interest of 3 per Ct. | 12.275.347.55. | |
| 2 | Arising from State Debts assumed | | |
| | Stock bearing a present interest of 6 per Ct. | 7,908,374.19. | |
| | Stock bearing a future interest of ditto | 3,940,608.96. | |
| | Stock bearing an Interest of 3 per Ct. | 5,994,115.70. | |
| 3. | Arising from Balances to Creditor States | | |
| | Stock bearing a present Interest of 6 per Ct. | 2,345,056. | |
| | Stock bearing a future Interest of do: | 1,172,528. | |
| | Stock bearing an Interest of 3 per Ct. | <u>703,516.80</u> | 60,789,914.18 |
| Unsubscribed Debt (Viz) | | | |
| Principal exclusive of loan office Certificates bearing interest on nominal Value | | 1.072.583.40 | |
| Interest thereupon including Indents | | 452,826.74 | |

(*continued*)

(*Continued*)

| | |
|---|---|
| Principal of Loan Office Certificates bearing interest on Nominal Sum | 27,935. |
| Interest thereupon | 7,830. |
| | 1.561.175.14 |
| Total *Unredeemed* Debt Dollars | 76.096.468.67 |

This is exclusive of a sum of 1.400,000 Dollars due to the Bank of the United States, on Account of the loan of 2.000,000 had of that institution pursuant to the 11 Section of the Act by which it is incorporated and which is not included in the mass of the debt because it is more than counterbalanced by a greater value in Stock. It is also exclusive of those loans which are temporary anticipations of the Revenue.

The particulars & Amount of the annual current revenues of the United States are as follow.

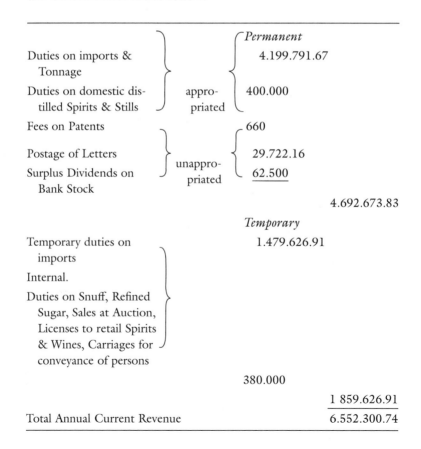

| | | | |
|---|---|---|---|
| | | *Permanent* | |
| Duties on imports & Tonnage | appro- priated | 4.199.791.67 | |
| Duties on domestic dis- tilled Spirits & Stills | | 400.000 | |
| Fees on Patents | unappro- priated | 660 | |
| Postage of Letters | | 29.722.16 | |
| Surplus Dividends on Bank Stock | | 62.500 | |
| | | | 4.692.673.83 |
| | | *Temporary* | |
| Temporary duties on imports | | 1.479.626.91 | |
| Internal. | | | |
| Duties on Snuff, Refined Sugar, Sales at Auction, Licenses to retail Spirits & Wines, Carriages for conveyance of persons | | | |
| | | 380.000 | |
| | | | 1 859.626.91 |
| Total Annual Current Revenue | | | 6.552.300.74 |

The particulars and amount of the annual Stated Expenditure of the United States, computing the Army and Navy establishments on the Scale of an Indian and Algerine War are as follow

| | |
|---|---|
| Interest on the foreign Debt | 638.480.58 |
| Interest on Domestic funded Debt | 2,339.241.50 |
| Interest on unfunded Debt | 66,031.10 |
| Interest on Temporary loans | 100.000. |
| Expenses of the Civil Government including foreign intercourse | 475.249.53 |
| Expenses of Military Land Service | 1.311.975.29 |
| Expenses of Military Naval Service | 441.508.80 |
| Miscellany | 109.357.04 |
| Total Annual Expenditure Dolls. | 5,681.843.84 |

This sum is liable to be increased by the interest which will begin to accrue on the deferred Stock the first of January 1801, being on the present amount of that Stock 871,401 Dollars & 92 Cents.

The Annual force of the sinking fund as depending on ascertained funds may be stated as follows.

| | |
|---|---|
| Interest for a Year on sums already carried to its Credit | 68.225.55 |
| Interest for a year on debt [to] foreign Officers in a course of payment including arrears of Interest to be carried to the credit of this fund | 13 439.49 |
| Interest for a year on the unexpended Surplus of the Revenues at the end of the year 1790 being 411,659 dollars 49 Cents, supposing this to be invested by purchase in an equal sum of present 6 per Cent Stock. | 24.699.56 |
| Dollars | 106.364.60 |

It is further liable to be increased by an investment in purchases of 865.098 Dolls and 11 Cents, which together with the sums from that source already invested in purchases and payments will amount to 2.000.000 of Dollars, the sum authorized to be borrowed by purchases of the Debt.

But as this auxiliary depends on an operation not only future but in some degree casual, it cannot be taken into an estimate of the actual strength of the fund.

The proceeds of the sales of Western Lands must also be considered as an eventual resource.

There are other contingent sources of augmentation not computed, because they are contingent: But on the other hand the fund is liable to be reduced by a sum reserved out of it for the payment of principal and interest of the two Millions authorized to be borrowed for purchases not exceeding 8 per Centum per annum.

The Sum applicable in the first instance to the redemption of that portion of the funded Debt which bears a present interest of 6 per Centum, excluding that standing to the Credit of the Commissioners of the Sinking fund, is as follows

| | |
|---|---|
| of Transferrable Stock | 516.410.24 |
| of Untransferrable Stock arising from Balances to Creditor States | 46.901.12 |
| Dollars | 563.311.36 |

The Sum applicable in the first instance, that is on the 1st day of January 1802, to the redemption of that portion of the funded debt now called deferred Stock; excluding that Standing to the Credit of the Commissioners of the Sinking fund, will be as follows

| | |
|---|---|
| Of transferrable Stock | 249.576.75 |
| Of Untransferrable Stock arising from Balances to Creditor States | 23.450.56 |
| Dolls | 273.027.31 |

These sums would complete the redemption of the whole amount of the Stock to which they are applicable within Twenty three Years after the redemption in each case was begun; within which terms, they would discharge the whole of the public Debt except the foreign debt, the unsubscribed Debt, and the three per Cent Stock.

If the redemption of the present 6 per Cent Stock, commence the first of January 1796 and the redeeming fund be commensurate with the whole of the unredeemed Stock bearing a present Interest of six per Cent and transferrable, the Revenue set free in the Year 1818, for operations upon the residue of the Debt will be 2039394 Dolls. & 36 Cents.

If the Redemption of the deferred debt commence the first of January 1802, when it may rightfully commence, and the redeeming fund be commensurate with the whole of that Stock, unredeemed and transferrable, the Revenue set free in the year 1824 for operations upon the residue of the Public Debt, if any remain, will be 998307 Dols & 02 Cents.

The Revenue set free by these successive redemptions, would be sufficient to redeem the whole of the present foreign Debt in six years, that is within a term of 28 Years from the proposed time; for commencing the Redemption, or the 1st of January 1796, and after extinguishing the foreign debt would more than discharge the whole of the balances to Creditor States and the whole of the unfunded Debt in two years more.

If the proceeds of the Lands in the Western Territory should be equal to three Millions of Dollars, and the three per Cent Stock can be purchased at an average of twelve shillings in the pound, that fund would suffice to pay off the principal of the three per Cent Stock in something more than twenty five years.

It follows that if the force of the sinking fund be rendered equal, exclusive of the proceeds of the Sales of Western Lands, to the Redemption of the present unredeemed Transferrable Stock, commencing the first of January 1796, as to that bearing a present Interest of 6 per Centum, and the first of January 1802, as to that bearing a future Interest of 6 per Centum, and if the proceeds of the Sales of Western Lands, should prove equal to 3,000,000 of dollars, and can be brought into action for purchases of the 3 per Ct. Stock at the rate abovementioned at any time before the year 1801, the whole of the present Debt of the United States foreign and Domestic (the funds appropriated being during the whole period adequate in productiveness and inviolably applied) would be extinguished in 30 Years. And there would then revert to the United States an Annual income of 4435320 Dollars & 89 Cents.

Some Auxiliary provisions which will be proposed may greatly accelerate that result.

On the basis of the foregoing data, the Secretary of the Treasury proceeds to submit to the consideration of Congress certain propositions which appear to him necessary to be adopted to complete our system of Public Credit. These will be followed by some explanatory remarks.

### Ist. Proposition

That further provision be made with regard to the yet unsubscribed debt of the United States. . . .

### II Proposition

That provision be made for taking upon loan to the United States, by subscription at the Treasury, the outstanding and unbarred new emission Bills of Credit. . . .

### III Proposition

That provision be made for converting by a new Loan the whole of our present *foreign* into *Domestic* Debt. . . .

And lastly, that the commissioners of the sinking fund be empowered with the approbation of the President to provide by new loans for the reimbursement of any installment or part of Principal of the present foreign debt. . . .

### IV. Proposition

That the temporary duties on Imports be made coextensive in duration with those now permanent & be appropriated in like manner; and that the reservation of 600000 Dollars annually out of the duties on imports & Tonnage for the support of the Government of the United States and their common defense be postponed till after the appropriations for the interest of the funded Debt foreign and domestic, [including the new Loans to be made thereupon,] & for the SINKING FUND.

### V. Proposition

That the following provisions be added to those heretofore made for reimbursing & redeeming the debt of the United States. . . .

## VI. Proposition

That Power be given to the Commissioners of the sinking fund, with the approbation of the President, to borrow from time to time such sums as may be necessary in anticipation of the Revenues appropriated for the purpose, not exceeding in one year one Million of dollars, to be reimbursed within a year from the time of each Loan; for the payment of the interest which shall annually accrue on the Public Debt.

The Interest upon each loan to be defrayed out of the permanent Revenues.

## VII. Proposition

That the internal revenues from snuff, and refined sugar, Sales at Auction, Licenses to sell by retail foreign Distilled Spirits and Wines, and from Carriages for the conveyance of Persons, be continued to the first day of January 1800; [and thence until the end of the session of Congress next thereafter;] and that the reimbursement of the principal of the Loan of 1,000,000 of Dollars authorized to be borrowed for defraying the expenses of foreign intercourse be charged upon this fund.

## VIII Proposition

That in regard to any Sum which shall have remained *unexpended* upon any appropriations, other than for the payment of the interest of the funded Debt and for the purposes of the Sinking fund, for more than two years after the end of the Calendar year in which the act of appropriation shall have been passed, such appropriation shall be deemed to cease and determine, and the sum unexpended upon it shall be carried to an account to be denominated "THE SURPLUS FUND"; But no appropriation shall be so deemed to have ceased or determined till after the year 1795, unless it shall appear to the Secretary of the Treasury that the object of such appropriation has been fully satisfied, in which case it shall be Lawful for him to cause to be carried the unexpended residue thereof, to the Account aforesaid.

## IX Proposition

That Provision be made that all PRIORITIES heretofore established in the appropriations for the funded debt as between the different parts of the said debt shall after the year 1796 cease, with respect to all Creditors of the United States, who do not before the expiration of the said period signify their dissent therefrom; and that thenceforth with the exception only of the debts of those Creditors who shall so signify their dissent, the revenues charged with these appropriations shall constitute a common or consolidated Fund chargeable indiscriminately and without priority.

### X. Proposition
That Provision be made for calling in all outstanding Loan office Certificates, Certificates called final Settlements, and Indents of Interest, and for issuing in Lieu of them other Certificates of equivalent tenor; establishing that all which shall not be presented for exchange within the term of two years shall be barred.

### Remarks upon the First proposition
The experiment has now been fully tried, and with nearly complete success, of the disposition of the Public Creditors to accept the terms offered by the funding Act. Those who still decline have probably made a final election to abide by their original Contracts.

It remains to fulfill them as to the future. This the Moral obligation of the Contracts, the new and peremptory sanction given to them by the present Government, and the essential maxims of Public Credit unite to demand: and while these cogent motives affecting intimately the permanent Character and general interest of the United States recommend the measure, there is now no longer any inducement from situation to procrastinate.

The present advanced State of the National finances, and the inconsiderable Magnitude of the still unsubscribed debt, render it of little if of any consequence to obtain upon it the temporary accommodation of deferring the payment of a part of the interest *accruing* according to Contract. . . .

### Remarks on the II. Proposition
The Certificates or bills of Credit called New emission Money were emitted pursuant to a resolution of Congress of the 18th.

March 1780, which directs them to be emitted upon the funds of individual States, to bear an interest of five per Centum per annum payable in Specie at the Redemption of the Bills, or at the election of the Holder, *annually at the continental Loan Offices, in Sterling bills drawn by the United States upon their Commissioners in Europe*, and pledges the faith of the United States for the payment of the said Bills, *in case any State on whose funds they should be emitted should by the events of War be rendered incapable to redeem them;* directing also an endorsement to be made on *each bill* in these words "The United States *insure* the *payment* of the within Bill and will draw Bills of exchange for the interest annually if demanded, according to a resolution of Congress of the 18th. of March 1780."

These resolutions and the endorsement upon the Bills engage the absolute promise of the United States for the payment of the interest indefinitely, and their eventual guarantee of the principal, in case any State on whose funds the Bills should be emitted should by the events of War be rendered incapable to redeem them; which is in effect, though not in form, an absolute guarantee of the principal; for the United States are bound to pay the interest *perpetually* 'till that is discharged.

Good faith demands that the United States should supply the omissions of the States which issued the Bills, by providing themselves at least for the interest upon them. . . .

**Remarks on the IIIrd. Proposition**

The payment of Interest and installments of principal of our foreign debt in the Countries where it was contracted is found by experience to be attended with difficulty, embarrassment, some loss, and a degree of casualty which occasionally puts in jeopardy the National Credit. Loans for reimbursement of principal must be made beforehand as the market suits and necessarily involve double interest for a greater or less time.

The procuring of Bills to be remitted for payment of Interest cannot be depended upon in coincidence with the periods of payment, which co-operating with distance renders inconvenient anticipations necessary.

The remitting in commodities would be liable to other casualties and to some peculiar objections; and whatever mode be adopted, it may be frequently not practicable to deposit in season the necessary funds on the spot without great sacrifices.

If therefore the place of these payments could with consent of the Creditors, upon an equitable indemnification to them for the transfer, be changed to the United States, the operation would be in various lights beneficial. It has occurred that the present posture of the affairs of Europe might favor a plan of this kind and perhaps produce some collateral advantages. . . .

### Remark on the IVth. Proposition

The object of this proposition is to give moral certainty to the adequateness of the fund for paying the interest upon the Debt and for its ultimate Redemption—making a reasonable allowance for the casualties to which it is exposed.

### Remarks on the Vth. proposition

There is no sentiment which can better deserve the serious attention of the Legislators of a Country than the one expressed in the Speech of the President, which indicates the danger to every Government from the progressive accumulation of Debt.

A tendency to it is perhaps the NATURAL DISEASE of all Governments; and it is not easy to conceive anything more likely than this to lead to great & convulsive revolutions of Empire.

On the one hand, the exigencies of a Nation creating new causes of expenditure, as well from its own as from the ambition, rapacity, injustice, intemperance and folly of other Nations, proceed in unceasing and rapid Succession. On the other, there is a general propensity in those who administer the affairs of a government, founded in the Constitution of man, to shift off the burden from the present to a future day, a propensity which may be expected to be strong in proportion as the form of the State is popular.

To extinguish a Debt which exists and to avoid contracting more are ideas almost always favored by public feeling and opinion; but to pay Taxes for the one or the other purpose, which are the only means of avoiding the evil, is always more or less unpopular. These contradictions are in human nature. And the lot of a Country would be enviable indeed in which there were not always men ready to turn them to the account of their own popularity or to some other sinister account.

Hence it is no uncommon spectacle to see the same men Clamoring for Occasions of expense, when they happen to be in unison with the present humor of the community, whether well or ill directed, declaiming against a Public Debt, and for the reduction of it as an *abstract thesis*, yet vehement against every plan of taxation which is proposed to discharge old debts or to avoid new by defraying the expenses of exigencies as they emerge.

These unhandsome arts throw artificial embarrassment in the way of the administrators of Government; and Co-operating with the desire which they themselves are too apt to feel to conciliate public favor by declining to lay even necessary burthens, or with the fear of losing it by imposing them with firmness serve to promote the accumulation of debt by leaving that which at any time exists without adequate provision for its reimbursement, and by preventing the laying with energy new Taxes when new Occasions of expense Occur. The consequence is that the public Debt swells 'till its magnitude becomes enormous, and the Burthens of the people gradually increase 'till their weight becomes intolerable. Of such a state of things great disorders in the whole political economy, convulsions & revolutions of Government are a Natural offspring.

There can be no more sacred obligation, then, on the public Agents of a Nation than to guard with a provident foresight and inflexible perseverance against so mischievous a result. True patriotism and genuine policy cannot, it is respectfully observed, be better demonstrated by those of the United States at the present juncture than by improving efficaciously the very favorable situation in which they stand for extinguishing with reasonable celerity the actual debt of the Country, and for laying the foundations of a system which may shield posterity from the consequences of the usual improvidence and selfishness of its ancestors: And which if possible may give IMMORTALITY to PUBLIC CREDIT.

Fortunately for the first object, the circumstances in our foreign affairs, which during the last session impelled to an extension of the national revenues, have left little more to do than to apply the existing means with decision and efficacy.

The second object will depend on the establishment of wise principles in that application; fitted to become a permanent precedent in the fiscal system of the Country.

The first report of the Secretary on the subject of the Public Debt, of the 9th. of January 1790, suggests the Idea of "*incorporating* as a *fundamental maxim* in the SYSTEM of PUBLIC CREDIT of the United States, *that the creation of Debt should always be accompanied with the means of extinguishment*—that this is the true secret for rendering public credit immortal, and that it is difficult to conceive a situation in which there may not be an adherence to the Maxim" and it expresses an unfeigned solicitude that this may be attempted by the United States and that they may commence their measures for the establishment of credit with the observance of it.

No opportunity has been lost by the secretary, as far as he could contribute to the event, to reduce this principle to practice; and important steps towards it have been from time to time taken by the legislature.

But much remains to be done to give it full effect. The present state of things encourages and invites to the consummation of the plan. And the Secretary about to leave the office he holds feels it a peculiar duty to make a final effort to promote that invaluable end.

This is the object of the 5th. Proposition aided by the preliminary provisions of the 4th. This proposition aims at two principal points—

1 To constitute a fund sufficient in every supposable event for extinguishing the whole of the present debt of the United States foreign and domestic in a period not exceeding thirty years.
2 To fix its destination unchangeably by not only appropriating it permanently under the direction of Commissioners and vesting it in them as property in trust, but by making its faithful application, *a part of the contract with the Creditors.* . . .

Its necessity rests upon these cogent reasons.

The inviolable application of an adequate sinking fund is the only practicable security against an excessive accumulation of debt, and the essential Basis of a permanent national Credit.

Experience has shown in Countries the most attentive to the principles of Credit that a simple appropriation of the sinking fund is not a complete barrier against its being diverted when immediate exigencies press. The causes which have been stated with another view tempt the administrators of Government to lay hold of this resource rather than resort to new taxes.

This indicates the utility of endeavoring to give by additional sanctions inviolability to the fund.

But will those proposed answer the end? They are the most efficacious that can be imagined, and they are likely to be entirely efficacious.

They cannot be disregarded without, by breach of faith and contract, destroying Credit, and that at a juncture when it is most indispensable. The Emergences which induce a diversion of the fund are those in which loans, and consequently Credit, are most needed.

But will it be safe to put the fund so entirely out of the command of the Government? May there not be situations in which the command of it may be requisite to the safety of the state?

This is not conceivable. The Amount of the sinking fund will in the situations which create extraordinary demands for Money be always inconsiderable compared even with a single years expenditure. The current revenues of a nation do not in such cases suffice.

Plunder or Credit must supply the deficiency. The first presupposes a subversion of all social order. The second will find its best support and greatest efficacy in adhering steadily to the principles of such a Fund. An Annuity of 7 Dollars will pay the Interest upon and discharge a Capital of 100 Dollars bearing 6 per Ct Interest in 33⅓ years nearly. The situation of a Country must be not a little exhausted if it cannot create yearly by new Revenues during the continuance of a Foreign War an annuity on the above scale sufficient to fund the Loans of which it may stand in need. Ten Millions of Dollars will with order and economy maintain in this Country an Army of 50.000 Men for a year. Viewing our geographical position, is there a prospect of any war expensive beyond this ratio? If not, an annuity of 700.000 Dollars created each year of the War would suffice. But it would be wise in such an event to carry Taxation *in the first instance* to the full extent of the ability of the State, which would proportionally contract the necessity for borrowing and consequently the extent of the annuities necessary for loans.

If a nation can find embarrassment in creating the revenues requisite on this scale, it must arise from her having reached a stage when from the neglect of the principle now inculcated, the mass of her Debt has become so enormous as to strain her faculties in order to a provision for it.

The United States are in a Situation altogether different. An inspection of the list of their Revenues discovers that they have a large field of resource unexplored. Their Youth, and large tracts of unsettled Land & land in the infancy of improvement assure them a great and rapid increase of means. Even their actual revenues without additions must with the progress of the country considerably increase. And though war may interrupt—the temporary interruption being removed by the restoration of peace, their increasing productiveness suspended for a time must resume its vigor and growth. In a given number of years a considerable augmentation is certain.

The Government of this Country may therefore adopt, fearless of future embarrassment, a principle which being adopted will ultimately furnish resources for future exigencies, without an increase of burthen to the Community.

To explain this last idea—It will readily be perceived that the funds pledged for paying the Interest and Sinking the principal of a portion of the Debt existing or Created at a particular time will within a certain period extinguish that portion of Debt.

They will then be liberated and will be ready for any future use, either to defray current expenditures or be the Basis of new Loans, as circumstances may dictate. And after a course of time it is a reasonable presumption that the fund so successively liberated will be adequate to new exigencies as they occur.

Moreover, the last clause of the proposition authorizes the deriving aid from the sinking fund for new Loans whenever the state of the fund admits of it consistently with the accomplishment of the purposes; that is, when it is sufficient 1st. to make good the stipulated payments on account of the principal of the Debt as they accrue. 2nd to purchase in the market all that part of the Public Debt of which there is no stipulation of payment by installment (as the three per Cent Stock) within a period of 30 Years.

This, while it secures the extinction of the existing debt within a reasonable term, by preventing too great a proportion of the public revenue from being tied up by the sinking fund gives due weight to the consideration of providing for future emergencies. . . .

Every system of Public Credit must assume it as a fundamental principle that the resources of the Country are equal to its probable exigencies, and that it will possess ability to pay the debts which it contracts.

If this be so, there is no cause to hesitate about the inviolable appropriation of funds to the extinction of an existing debt within no less term than 30 Years.

Indeed, as before intimated, it cannot be doubted that the resources of a credit built upon a foundation so solid as that which is recommended will more than replace even in the earliest stages of our affairs the use of the additional funds withdrawn from the Command of the Government to effect it, and in the eventual operation will give a more abundant command of funds than it can otherwise have. The successive liberation of the revenues successively pledged, after accomplishing their object, will afford resources that may almost be said to be inexhaustible.

It should be recollected too, that the public arrangements may, under a great pressure, anticipate the approaching period of such a liberation by intermediate temporary Loans, to be replaced by those funds when they are free.

This proposition exemplifies, as to the past, the nature of the maxim which has been supposed capable of giving immortality to credit, namely, that with the *creation* of debt should be incorporated the *means* of extinguishment; which means are two-fold, the establishing *at the time of contracting a* debt funds for the *reimbursement* of the PRINCIPAL, as well as for the *payment* of INTEREST within a DETERMINATE PERIOD—The making it a PART OF THE CONTRACT that the FUNDS SO ESTABLISHED shall be INVIOLABLY applied to the object.

It is believed that it would be happy for the United States if Congress would adopt this principle as a rule in all future Loans, never to be departed from: And a good evidence of this determination will be to apply it [as far as may be] to the past.

This would be at the same time an antidote against what may be pronounced the most plausible objections to the system of *funding* public Debts; which are, that by facilitating the means of supporting expense, they encourage to enterprises which produce it, and by furnishing in credit a substitute for revenue, likely to be too freely used to avoid the odium of laying new Taxes, they occasion a tendency to run in debt.

Though these objections to funding Systems, which giving the greatest possible energy to public Credit, are a great source of National strength security and prosperity, are very similar to those which speculative men urge against national and individual opulence, drawn from its abuses, and though perhaps upon a careful analysis of facts they would be found to have much less support in them than is imagined, inasmuch as they attribute to those systems effects which are to be ascribed more truly to the passions of men and perhaps to the genius of particular governments; yet as they are not wholly unfounded it is desirable to guard as far as possible against the dangers which they suppose without renouncing the advantages which those systems undoubtedly afford.

It will readily be seen that the maxim for making concurrent provision for the principal as well as interest in the act of contracting debt, if by *precedent and habit* it can be rendered a RULE OF ADMINISTRATION, by implicating a greater portion of the revenue in every such operation than would be requisite for a mere provision for interest, will control proportionally the disposition to defer the burthen to futurity and create a greater necessity for circumspection in incurring expense.

This is probably the true expedient for uniting a due regard to the present accommodation of the community with a due care not to overburden posterity—the full energy of public Credit with a salutary restraint upon the abuses of it. . . .

### Remarks on the VI. Proposition

This will be a useful and important provision. It has reference to a circumstance repeatedly adverted to, the long credits given upon the principal branches of Revenue; from which it happens that though the *fund itself* or the *product* of the revenue is more than adequate to an appropriation, yet the receipts upon it come too slowly into the Treasury to answer the end without anticipation by temporary Loans. Its propriety depends on the principle suggested under the last head of having all the means of complete execution organized in the system of Public Credit.

### Remarks on the VIIth. Proposition

It is a good rule of caution that no more of the public revenues should be rendered permanent than is necessary to give moral certainty to the provisions which may be regarded as the pillars of public Credit.

This idea will, it is believed, be satisfied by giving permanency to the now temporary duties on Imports. . . .

### Remarks on the VIIIth. Proposition

This is to terminate an embarrassment which has been experienced. Appropriations are frequently made for objects the extent of which is not precisely known or in a degree casual. To leave them indefinite as to time is sometimes to tie up unnecessarily a portion of the public funds which may ultimately not be wanted at all for the purpose of the original appropriation.

It will do away this inconvenience and promote perspicuity in the Treasury Accounts of appropriations if an ultimate period is fixed when each appropriation shall be deemed to have ceased. Should further appropriations appear necessary for the same objects, new estimates can be presented and new appropriations made. . . .

### Remarks on the IXth Proposition

This proposition is calculated to give simplicity to the public Accounts of Stock and Revenue which will be conducive to correctness dispatch and economy. . . .

### Remarks on the Xth Proposition

It is important to the fiscal calculations to ascertain positively the extent of every portion of the public debt. At present the amount of *these* several items of it is deduced from accounts of the late war of various Officers & Offices—in some instances conducted with little order. There is not therefore sufficient certainty. Indeed it is probable from the length of time which has elapsed without their appearing that the computed amount exceeds the real.

Besides, they are from their nature subject to forgeries and counterfeits, which implies a danger of loss to the public 'till their circulation is finally terminated. The proposition accordingly, besides the obtaining of better information, aims at obviating this danger.

Allowing sufficient time for bringing them in to be exchanged for Certificates of equivalent tenor, while it is a measure tending to Public information and security, it can be liable to no reasonable objection on the part of the Creditors.

The Secretary of the Treasury has reserved for the conclusion of this Report a proposition which appears to him of great importance to the Public Credit and which after some preliminary observations will be offered to consideration.

It relates to the right of taxing the public funds and to that of sequestering them in time of war.

A proposition on either of these points would have been deemed superfluous had there never been discussions asserting a right to do the one and the other, and even the expediency of exercising that right. The *negative* of both the pretensions, from the habit of regarding *it* as incapable of being disputed, had acquired in the mind of the Secretary so much the force of an Axiom as to have precluded even the mention of the subject in the plan which he originally submitted for funding the public Debt. He should otherwise have thought it an indispensable duty to suggest as a matter of primary consequence to the System of Credit contemplated in the plan, the express renunciation of those pretensions: For they are (as he believes) not only unwarranted by principle or usage, but entirely subversive of the sound maxims of public Credit.

A persuasion that this would always be a *truth granted* in the councils of the United States is his apology for the omission.

Even now he should think it useless to depart from his silence on the point had not the discussions alluded to create some alarm in places where all the circumstances are not well understood, which it is the interest of the Country to dispel.

The confidence justly to be reposed in the collective wisdom of this government forbids the supposition by one acquainted with its constitution that the security of the Creditor can need in this particular a further sanction. It is presumed to be impossible that any *final* act can ever give so deep a wound to the national interest and character as to derogate from a principle which may be placed among the most sacred in the administration of a Government.

Is there a right in the Government to tax its own funds?

The pretense of this right is deduced from the general right of the legislative power *to make all the property of the State contributory to its exigencies.*

But this right is obviously liable to be restricted by the *engagements* of the *Government*; it cannot be justly exercised in contravention of them. They must form an exception.

It will not be denied that the general right in question could and would be abridged by an express promise not to tax the funds. This promise indeed has not been given in terms.

But it has been given in substance. When an individual lends money to the state—the State stipulates to repay him the principal lent with a certain interest, or to pay a certain Interest indefinitely till the principal is reimbursed, or it stipulates something equivalent in another form. In our case, the Stipulation is in the second form.

To Tax the funds is manifestly either to *take* or to *keep back* a portion of the principal or interest *stipulated to be paid.* To do this on whatever pretext is *not to do what is expressly promised*; It is not to pay that precise principal or that precise Interest which has been engaged to be paid.

It is therefore to violate the promise given to the lender.

But is not the stipulation to the lender with a tacit reservation of the general right of the Legislature to raise contributions on the property of the State?

This cannot be supposed because it involves two contradictory things; an *obligation to do* and a *right not to do*; an obligation to *pay a certain sum* and a *right* to *retain it in the shape of a Tax.* It is against the rules both of Law & reason to admit by *implication* in the construction of a contract a principle which goes in destruction of it.

The Government by such a construction would be made to say to the lender "I want a sum of money for a national purpose, which all the citizens ought to contribute proportionally, but it will be more convenient to them and to me to borrow the money of you. If you will lend it, I promise you faithfully to allow you a *certain rate* of interest while I keep the money, and to *reimburse the principal* within a determinate period, *except so much of the one and the other as I may think fit to withhold in the shape of a tax.*"

Is such a construction either natural or rational? does it not in fact nullify the promise, by the reservation of a right not to perform it?

Is it to be presumed without being expressed that such can be the understanding of a lender when he parts with his Money to a Government?

The contrary is so much the more presumable, that nothing short of an express reservation can support the pretention to tax the fund.

It may be replied that the Creditor might be willing to rely upon the equity of Government not to abuse its right by exacting from him excessive contributions.

This, if true, does not obviate the difficulty of supposing the coexistence of an *obligation* and a *right* destructive the one of the other in interpreting the sense of a Contract when nothing of the Kind is said.

It is *possible* that a creditor might be willing so to contract; yet it is still necessary in order to determine that he has done it to find some provisions or expressions in the Contract indicating the intention; to render what is stipulated Compatible with what is reserved.

But it is not probable that an individual would be willing to lend upon such terms. He would justly apprehend that in great emergencies a *right* having no *limit* but the *opinion* of the party possessed of the *power* would be abused, and that the convenience of laying hold of a fund already prepared and at hand supported by a claim of right would be a temptation to abuse not easy to be resisted. However well-disposed to contribute in common with his fellow Citizens on all the ordinary objects of property or income, he would be unwilling to subject himself to a special burthen in the peculiar character of creditor of the State. He would prefer to employ his Money in other ways; even to lend it to private persons, where it might be more likely to escape the hand of the Fiscal Power.

Let the question be tried by another analysis.

*Public Debt* can scarcely in legal phrase be defined either *property in possession* or in *action*. It is evidently not the first till it is reduced to possession by payment. To be the second would suppose a *legal power* to *compel* payment by *suit*—does such a power exist? The true definition of public debt is *a property subsisting in the faith of the Government*. Its essence is promise. Its definite value depends upon the reliance that the promise will be definitely fulfilled. Can the Government rightfully tax its promises? Can it put its own faith under contribution? where or *what* is the value of the debt if such a right exist?

Suppose the Government to contract with an individual to convey to him a hundred acres of Land upon the condition of paying a hundred Dollars. When he came to pay the 100 Dollars & demand his title, could the Government require of him to pay fifty more as a Tax upon the land before it would consent to give him the Title? Who would not pronounce this to be a breach of contract, a fraud, which nothing could disguise?

This case is parallel with that under examination, with circumstances that fortify the right of the lending Creditors. The Government agrees with him that for 100 Dollars which he delivers to the Government, it will deliver to him at the end of each year six Dollars.

Here the six dollars *to be delivered* answer to the land *to be conveyed*, with this stronger ground of right that the consideration for them has actually been given and received. Yet when the Creditor comes to demand his Six dollars, he is told that he cannot have them except with the reservation of one dollar, as a tax upon the six, or that he cannot have them except upon the condition of returning one dollar as that tax? What is this but to say that his Title to the money in this case, as to the land in the other, must depend upon his paying or allowing a *further* consideration for it not contemplated in the contract? Can there be a doubt that this also would be a breach of Contract—a fraud?

The true rule of every case of property founded on contract with the Government is this—

It must first be reduced into possession, and then it will become subject in common with other similar property to the right of the Government to raise contributions upon it. It may be said that the Government may fulfil this principle by paying the interest with one hand, and taking back the amount of the tax with the other.

But to this the answer is, that to comply truly with the rule the tax must be upon all the money of the community, not upon the particular portion of it which is paid to the public Creditors, and it ought besides to be so regulated as not to include a *lien* of the tax upon the fund. The creditor should be no otherwise acted upon than as every other possessor of *money*, and consequently the money he receives from the public can then only be a fit subject of taxation, when it is entirely separated and thrown undistinguished into the common mass. A different practice would amount to an evasion of the principle contended for and to oppression. A Rent or Annuity liable before it passes, or in the act of passing, or at the moment of passing from one proprietor to another, to a deduction or drawback at the pleasure of the party from whom it is to pass is an imaginary thing, destitute both of shape and substance.

When a Government enters into contract with an individual, it deposes as to the matter of the contract its constitutional authority, and exchanges the Character of Legislator for that of a moral Agent, with the same rights and obligations as an individual. Its promises may be Justly considered as excepted out of its *power to legislate*, unless in aid of them. It is in Theory impossible to reconcile the two ideas of a *promise which obliges* with a *power to make a Law which can vary the effect of it*. This is the great principle that governs the question, and abridges the general right of the Government to lay taxes by excepting out of it a species of property which subsists only in its promise.

There are persons who admitting the general rule conceive a distinction to exist between a tax upon the funds, which must be paid at all events, and a tax upon alienations of them, which will only be to be paid when they are transferred from one to another. The latter they think justifiable because it is in the option of the Creditor to avoid the Tax by avoiding the alienation. But the difference between the two cases is only a difference in the degree of violation.

The Stock in its *creation* is *made transferrable*. This quality constitutes a material part of its value, and the existence of it is a part of the contract with the Government which has undertaken itself to conduct the operation of transferring by its own officers and consequently at its own expense. It is as completely a breach of contract to derogate from this quality in diminution of the value of Stock by encumbering the transfer with a charge or tax, as it is to take back in the same shape a portion of the principal or interest. It is obvious too that this may be carried so far as essentially to destroy the transferrable capacity. But what is a tax upon transfers other than the faculty of taking away from the actual proprietor of Stock a portion of his principal, whenever his interests or his necessities demand a transfer in derogation from the full enjoyment of the right to transfer and from the express promise of the Government to pay him or his alienee? For it is upon the seller, not upon the buyer, that such a tax will fall. And where is the substantial difference on the ground of contract between this and a direct tax upon the fund itself. The value of it is as certainly impaired by the one as by the other.

But shall the proprietor of money in the funds then be exempt from his proportion of the burthens which other Citizens bear?

This will not be the consequence of the principle. As a consumer of which his income is the instrument, he will pay his proportion of the Taxes on consumption. As a holder of any other species of property procured by that income or otherwise which is liable to a tax, he must also contribute his proportion.

But without undue refinement, the lender of money to the Public may be affirmed to have paid his tax when he lends his money. Relying upon the engagement of the government express or implied that he will receive what is promised him without defalcation, he is content with a less interest than he would take if subject to any such defalcation, and especially if it was to be arbitrary as to its extent. In this lower rate of Interest he may be truly said to pay his Tax or to purchase an exemption from it. Here also we find what is decisive on the point of expediency.

If the Government had a right to tax its funds, the exercise of that right would cost much more than it was worth. The money lender would exact exorbitant premiums, not only as an indemnification for the use which the Government might probably make of its right, and which in practice would be likely to be qualified by some regard to equality of contribution, but as an equivalent for insurance against the risk or possibility of a more extensive use.

Hence the Government would be likely to pay much more in premiums upon its loans than it would draw back in Taxes, and the former being supposed but equal to the latter, there would be no advantage in exercising the right.

But it will be perhaps more safe to affirm that there would be no borrowing at all upon such terms. The first precedent of a tax upon the funds might be expected to compel the Government to an express renunciation of the right in every future loan. Solid capitalists would not be much inclined to adventure their money upon so precarious a footing as is implied in a power of taxing their credits.

These reflections lead readily to an estimate of the impressions which would be produced by the example of an imposition on the funds. Regarded either as a positive breach of contract, or as a deviation from the maxims of credit, the effect upon it would be nearly equally fatal. Whatever might be excused to a time of revolution, to a defect of means, or to some extraordinary peculiarity of situation—no excuse would be admitted for a *deliberate* departure from principles at a time too of National prosperity, in a flourishing State of our finances, after the foundations of a regular system had been laid. The departure would argue an incorrectness, an instability, or a depravity of Views calculated to give a lasting shock to Credit. The United States must henceforth tread with the most cautious Step.

A renunciation of the right in future might not speedily heal the wound which an example of its exercise had given. Durable suspicions might fasten on the Wisdom or the integrity of the Government; which might occasion to it no inconsiderable loss and embarrassment before a course of contrary experience could obliterate them.

The right of a Government to sequester or confiscate property in its funds in time of war involves considerations analogous to these which regard the right of taxing them.

Whether the foreigner be himself the original lender or the proprietor of Stock in its constitution *transferrable without discrimination*, he stands upon equal ground with the Citizen. He has equal claim upon the faith of the Government. In the second case—As the Substitute of the original lender, the promise made attaches immediately upon him. Indeed the certificates which issue upon every transfer, and which may be called the public Bonds, designate him as the Creditor and expressly invest him with the correspondent rights.

To sequester or confiscate the Stock is as effectually a breach of the contract to pay as to absorb it by a Tax. It is to annihilate the promise under the sanction of which the foreigner became a proprietor.

But does not the general right of War to seize & confiscate enemy-property extend the property of the Citizens of one nation in the funds of another; the two Nations being at war with each other?

Resorting to principle as the guide, This question may on solid grounds be answered in the negative.

The right to seize & confiscate individual property in National Wars excludes all those cases where the individual derives his title from the enemy sovereign or nation: For the right to property always implies the right to be protected & secured in the enjoyment of that property. And a nation by the very act of permitting the Citizen of a foreign country to acquire property within its territory, whether to Lands, funds or to any other thing, tacitly engages to give protection and security to that property and to allow him as full enjoyment of it as any other proprietor; an engagement which no state of things between the two nations can justly or reasonably affect.

Though politically right that in wars between nations, the property of private persons which depend on *Laws of their own Country*, or on *circumstances foreign to the Nation with which their own is at war*, should be subject to seizure & confiscation by the enemy Nation: Yet it is both politically and morally wrong that this should extend to property acquired *under the faith of the Government and the Laws of that enemy Nation.*

When the Government enters into a contract with the Citizen of a foreign country it considers him *as an individual in a state of Nature, and Contracts with him as such.* It does not contract with him as *the member of another society.*

The contracts therefore with him cannot be affected by his political relations to that society. War, whatever right it may give over his other property, can give none over that which he derives from those contracts. The character, in which they are made with him, the faith pledged to him personally, virtually exempt it.

This principle which seems critically correct would exempt as well the INCOME as the CAPITAL of the property. It protects the use as effectually as the thing. What in fact is property but a fiction without the beneficial use of it? In many cases indeed the income or annuity is the property itself: And though general usage may control the principle, it can only be as far as the usage clearly goes. It must not be extended by analogy.

Some of the most approved Publicists, admitting the principle, qualify it with regard to the income of Lands, which they say may be sequestered "to hinder the remittance of it to the Enemy's country."

But the same authority affirms that a State at War "does not *so much as touch* the sums which it owes to the Enemy. *Everywhere* in case of a war funds credited to the Public are *exempt* from confiscation and SEIZURE" These expressions clearly exclude sequestration as well as confiscation.

The former no less than the latter would be inconsistent with the declaration that a State at war does not *so much as touch* the sums which it owes to the enemy, and that funds Credited to the Public are exempt from SEIZURE. And on full enquiry it is believed that the suggestion, thus understood, is founded in fact.

Usage then, however it may deviate in other particulars, in respect to Public funds concurs with principle in pronouncing, that they cannot rightfully be sequestered in time of War.

The usages of war still savor too much of the ferocious maxims of the times when war was the chief occupation of man. Enlightened reason would never have pronounced that the persons or property of foreigners found in a Country, at the breaking out of a war between that Country and his own, were liable to any of the rigors which a State of war authorizes against the persons and goods of an enemy. It would have decreed to them an inviolable sanctuary in the faith of those permissions and those Laws by which themselves & their property had come under the jurisdiction where they were found. It would have rejected the Treachery of converting the indulgencies and even rights of a previous state of amity into snares for innocent individuals.

Happily, however, the practice of latter times has left several of those maxims little more than points of obsolete doctrine. They still retain their rank in Theory; but usage has introduced so many qualifications as nearly to destroy their operation.

This appears from the acknowledgements of writers, from the barrenness of modern history in examples of the application of those doctrines—from the opinions known to be generally current in Europe—and from a variety of articles which are constant formulas in the Treaties of the present Century.

The United States are every way interested in the mitigation of the rigor of the ancient maxims of war. They cannot better demonstrate their wisdom than by their moderation in this respect. Particularly interested in maintaining in their greatest purity & energy the principles of Credit, they cannot too strictly adhere to all the relaxations of those maxims which favor the rights of Creditors.

No temporary advantage can compensate for the evils of a different course of Conduct.

Credit, public and private, is of the greatest consequence to every Country. Of this, it might be emphatically called the invigorating principle. No well-informed man can cast a retrospective eye over the progress of the United States from their infancy to the present period without being convinced that they owe in a great degree to the fostering influence of Credit their present mature growth.

This Credit has been of a mixed nature, Mercantile and public, foreign and Domestic. Credit abroad was the trunk of our Mercantile credit, from which issued ramifications that nourished all the parts of Domestic Labor and industry. The bills of Credit emitted from time to time by the different local Governments which passed current as money co-operated with that resource. Their united force quickening the energies and bringing into action the capacities for improvement of a new Country was highly instrumental in accelerating its growth.

Credit, too, animated and supported by the general zeal, had a great share in accomplishing, without such violent expedients as generating universal distress would have endangered the issue, that Revolution of which we are so justly proud, and to which we are so greatly indebted.

Credit, likewise, may no doubt claim a principal agency in that increase of national and individual welfare since the establishment of the present Government, which is so generally felt and acknowledged, though the causes of it are not as generally understood.

It is the constant auxiliary of almost every public operation—has been an indispensable one in those measures by which our frontiers have been defended; and it would not be difficult to demonstrate that in a recent and delicate instance it has materially contributed to the safety of the State.

There can be no time, no state of things, in which Credit is not essential to a Nation, especially as long as nations in general continue to use it as a resource in war. It is impossible for a Country to contend on equal terms, or to be secure against the enterprises of other nations without being able equally with them to avail itself of this important resource. And to a young Country with moderate pecuniary Capital and not a very various industry, it is still more necessary than to Countries more advanced in both; a truth not the less weighty for being obvious and frequently noticed.

Public Credit has been well defined to be, "a faculty to borrow at pleasure considerable sums on moderate terms, the art of distributing over a succession of years the extraordinary efforts found indispensable in one, a mean of accelerating the prompt employment of all the abilities of a nation and even of disposing of a part of the overplus of others."

This just and ingenious definition condenses to a point the principal arguments in favor of public Credit, and displays its immense importance.

Let any man consult the actual course of our pecuniary operations, and let him then say whether Credit be not eminently useful. Let him imagine the expense of a single campaign in a war with a great European power, and let him then pronounce whether Credit would not be indispensable. Let him decide whether it would be practicable at all to raise the necessary sum by taxes within the year, and let him Judge what would be the degree of distress and oppression which the attempt would occasion to the community. He cannot but conclude that war without Credit would be more than a great calamity—would be ruin.

But Credit is not only one of the main pillars of the public safety—it is among the principal engines of useful enterprise and internal improvement. As a substitute for Capital it is little less useful than Gold or silver, in Agriculture, in Commerce, in the Manufacturing and mechanic arts.

The proof of this needs no labored deduction. It is matter of daily experience in the most familiar pursuits. One man wishes to take up and Cultivate a piece of land—he purchases upon *Credit*, and in time pays the purchase money out of the produce of the soil improved by his labor. Another sets up in trade; in the *Credit* founded upon a fair character he seeks and often finds the means of becoming at length a wealthy Merchant. A third commences business as a manufacturer or Mechanic with skill, but without Money. Tis by *Credit* that he is enabled to procure the tools, the materials and even the subsistence of which he stands in need, 'till his industry has supplied him with Capital; and even then he derives from an established and increased credit the means of extending his undertakings.

Among the Circumstances which recommend Credit, and indicate its importance in the whole System of internal exertion and amelioration, it is impossible to pass unnoticed its unquestionable tendency to moderate the rate of interest—a Circumstance of infinite value in all the operations of labor and Industry.

If the individual Capital of this Country has become more adequate to its exigencies than formerly, 'tis because individuals have found new resources in the public *Credit*, in the funds to which *that* has given value and activity. Let Public Credit be prostrated, and the deficiency will be greater than before. Public and private Credit are closely allied, if not inseparable. There is perhaps no example of the one being in a flourishing, where the other was in a bad state. A shock to public Credit would therefore not only take away the additional means which it has furnished, but by the derangements, disorders, distrusts, and false principles which it would engender and disseminate, would diminish the antecedent resources of private Credit.

The United States possess an immense mass of *improvable matter*. The developments of it continually going on may be said to enlarge the field of Improvement as it progresses: And though the active Capital of the Country has no doubt considerably increased, it is probable that it does not bear at present a *much* greater proportion to the objects of employment than it has done at any former period. Credit, upon this hypothesis, of every kind is nearly as necessary to us now as it ever was. But at least it may be affirmed with absolute certainty that to a Country so situated, Credit is peculiarly useful and important.

If the United States observe with delicate caution the maxims of Credit, as well towards foreigners as their own Citizens, in connection with the general principles of an upright, Stable, and Systematic administration, the strong attractions which they present to foreign Capital will be likely to ensure them the command of as much as they may want in addition to their own for every species of internal amelioration. Can it be doubted that they would derive from this, in a course of time, advantages incomparably greater than any, however tempting, that could partially result from a disregard of those maxims, or from the exercise of a questionable right, which should even appear to derogate from them?

Credit is an *entire thing*. Every part of it has the nicest sympathy with every other part. Wound one limb, and the whole Tree shrinks and decays. The security of each Creditor is inseparable from the security of all Creditors. The boundary between foreigner and Citizen would not be deemed a sufficient barrier against extending the precedent of an invasion of the rights of the former to the latter. The most judicious and cautious would be most apt to reason thus, and would only look for stronger shades of apparent necessity or expediency to govern the extension. And in affairs of Credit, the opinion of the Judicious and cautious may be expected to prevail. Hence the Government, by sequestering the property of foreign Citizens in the public funds at the commencement of a war, would impair at least if not destroy that Credit which is the best resource in war.

'Tis in vain to attempt to disparage Credit by objecting to it its abuses. What is there not liable to abuse or misuse?

The precious metals, those great springs of labor and industry, are also the ministers of extravagance, luxury and corruption. Commerce, the nurse of Agriculture and manufactures, if over-driven leads to bankruptcy and distress. A fertile soil, the principal source of human comfort, not unfrequently begets indolence and effeminacy. Even Liberty itself degenerating into licentiousness, produces a frightful complication of ills, and works its own destruction.

'Tis Wisdom in every case to cherish what is useful and guard against its abuse. 'Twill be the truest policy in the United States to give all possible energy to Public Credit by a firm adherence to its strictest maxims, and yet to avoid the ills of an excessive employment of it by true economy and system in the public expenditures, by steadily cultivating peace, and by using sincere, efficient and persevering endeavors to diminish present debts, prevent the accumulation of new, and secure the discharge within a reasonable period of such as it may be matter of necessity to contract. 'Twill be wise to cultivate and foster private Credit by an exemplary observance of the principles of public Credit, and to guard against the misuse of the former by a speedy and vigorous administration of Justice, and by taking away every temptation to run in debt founded on the hope of evading the Just claims of Creditors.

As an honorable evidence of this disposition, and with a view to quiet the alarms which have been excited, and to silence for ever a question which can never be agitated without serious inconvenience—

The Secretary of the Treasury in the last place respectfully submits—

That there be an express renunciation by Law of all pretension of right to tax the public funds, or to sequester at any time, or on any pretext, the property which foreign Citizens may hold therein. This renunciation is the more essential with regard to the object of the third proposition, as the Amsterdam and Antwerp loans already include an equivalent stipulation which they would be unwilling to relinquish without a similar stipulation in the New Loan.

In the commencement of this Report it was the intention to submit some propositions for the improvement of the several branches of the public Revenue, but it is deemed advisable to reserve this part of the subject, for a future communication.

All which is respectfully submitted.

Treasury Department
January 16. 1795
Alexander Hamilton
Scy of the Treasury

# CHAPTER SEVENTEEN

# The Defense of the Funding System (July 1795)

*Credit may be called a new power in the mechanism of national affairs. It is a great and a very useful one, but the art of regulating it properly, as is the case with every new and great contrivance, has been till lately imperfectly understood.*

HAMILTON'S RESIGNATION FROM the office of Secretary of the Treasury became effective on the first day of February, 1795. He left Philadelphia, the capital, to resume his private law practice in New York. Freed from the time-consuming duties of a federal cabinet officer, he turned to drafting this document to explain and justify in considerable detail the policies he had formulated and implemented to restore public credit during his first year in office, 1789–1790. The document is a first draft that was never completed. There are blanks and gaps in it that he hoped to fill in later, and it tails off at the end virtually in the middle of a thought. The incomplete manuscript would not be published for another century.

Perhaps for that reason, scholars and biographers have not given the document the attention it deserves. Despite being an incomplete first draft, it is one of the most insightful of any of Hamilton's writings. It gives snapshots of the dire economic and financial situation of the country in 1789, and also in 1795 when the situation had much improved. It shows how his mind worked in formulating the problems he faced and his solutions to those problems. It is a response, sometimes caustic, to his critics, who were legion in the charged political atmosphere of the time. At the same time, it is philosophical in stating his realistic view of human nature and the implications of that nature for a "true politician," that is, a statesman, seeking to improve the condition of his country and the happiness of its people. And it is rich in its discussion of moral obligation and the sanctity of contracts.

In essence, Hamilton defends two key aspects of his debt restructuring program. First, he defends the new federal government's immediate assumption of debts of the states into the national debt. Second, he defends the "funding" of the entire national debt, meaning the pledging of specified government revenues to the payment of interest on the debt and toward its eventual redemption.

In his defense of immediate assumption, Hamilton notes that the Constitution created dual sovereignties of the federal government and the states, implying that that each had powers of taxation. If instead the Constitution had subordinated state power of taxation to that of the federal government, Hamilton says, it "would probably have been an insuperable obstacle to the adoption of the constitution." But concurrent, overlapping taxing powers of the federal and state governments "involved inherent and great difficulties . . . the Gordian Knot of our political situation." Hamilton foresaw that a competition between federal and state governments for tax revenues could well lead to animosities and dissolution of the union just as it was forming.

"To me," Hamilton says, "there appeared but one way of untying or severing [the Gordian Knot], which was in practice to leave the states under as little necessity as possible of exercising the power of taxation." Assumption of state debts into the national debt did exactly that, and it helped avoid "the weakness and embarrassment incident to fifteen or perhaps to 50 different systems of taxation." Moreover, since federal revenues derived mostly from customs and tonnage duties would make payments due on the national debt, tax burdens at the state level would be lightened, there would be an equalization of the tax burdens of all citizens, and the most indebted states, which were Massachusetts and South Carolina, would get immediate relief.

Despite these advantages, assumption was still controversial when Hamilton wrote in 1795. "It is a curious fact which has not made its due impression," he says, "that in every state the people have found relief from assumption while an incomparably better provision than before existed has been made for the state debts."

More caustically, Hamilton describes the vociferous opposition to assumption emanating from the state of Virginia: "The effect of energy and system is to vulgar and feeble minds a kind of magic which they do not comprehend. . . . The people of several parts of the state, relieved and happy by the effects of the assumption, execrate the measure with its authors to which they owe a blessing."

Hamilton then turns to defending the funding of the national debt, which he says was "the theme of much declamation and invective." Some alleged that funding and assumption had created the large national debt. Hamilton deemed that a ridiculous charge. Assumption had merely shifted debts from the states to the nation without increasing the total amount of debt. And funding strengthened the nation's credit, which resulted in lower interest costs. According to Hamilton's critics, however, having better credit was a negative because "by facilitating Credit they [funding systems] encourage enterprises which produce expense by furnishing in credit a substitute for revenue; they . . . avoid the unpopularity of laying new taxes and . . . occasion a tendency to run in debt; consequently a progressive accumulation of debt and its perpetuation; at least till it is crushed beneath the load of its own enormous weight." Hamilton's answer was that it was good, not bad, to have a good credit rating, but there could be "abuses of a thing intrinsically good."

The attack on the funding system, Hamilton argues, was really an attack on credit itself. But to Hamilton, "credit may be called a new power in the mechanism of international affairs." Abuses could be avoided by "regulating it properly." That could be done by coupling borrowing with levying taxes to pay the interest on new debt plus a little more to redeem the principal: "The rule of making cotemporary provision for the extinguishment of principal as well as for the payment of interest in the art of contracting new debt is the desideratum—the true panacea." Here Hamilton reiterates the notion he first mentioned in *The Continentalist* fifteen years earlier and then fleshed out in his January 1790 and January 1795 Public Credit Reports (see chapters 4, 9, and 16). It was his plan for making public credit "immortal."

Even if his critics were right that credit could be abused, Hamilton says, "it will not follow that it can be renounced by any one nation while nations in general continue to use it. It is so immense a power in the affairs of war that a nation without credit would be in great danger of falling a victim in the first war with a power possessing a vigorous and flourishing credit."

But good credit did not just make a government strong by giving it the ability to fight wars successfully. It also could energize an economy and make it grow. Toward the end of The Defense, Hamilton observed that credit was doing exactly that at the time of his writing in mid-1795: "Whoever will impartially look around will see that the great body of the new Capital created by the Stock [public debt] has been employed in extending commerce, agriculture, manufactures, and other improvements. Our own *real* navigation has been much increased. Our external commerce is carried on much more upon our own capitals than it was—our marine insurances in a much greater proportion are made by ourselves. Our manufactures are increased in number and carried on upon a larger scale. Settlements of our waste land are progressing with more vigor than at any former period. Our Cities and Towns are increasing rapidly by the addition of new and better houses. Canals are opening, bridges are building with more spirit & effect than was ever known at a former period. The value of lands has risen everywhere."

Energized by public and private credit, the U.S. economy was off and running in 1795, and the run would continue for more than two centuries. It was finance-led growth, which was, despite the criticisms and venom Hamilton encountered, rather pleasing to the principal architect of U.S. financial modernization.

The never completed Defense of the Funding System contained 24,616 words; our abridgment runs to 11,198 words.

**The Defense of the Funding System**
[New York, July 1795]

In speaking of the public debt hereafter, to avoid circumlocution I shall denominate the original debt of the U States the general Debt & the separate debts of the respective States the particular Debts. As often as these terms occur they are to be understood in this sense.

The operation of these circumstances generated a variety of different sects holding different opinions. The parties in and out of Congress on the subject of a provision for the public debt may be thrown into five classes: I Those who were for providing for the general debt exclusively of the particular debts on the basis of the subsisting contracts. II Those who were for providing separately for the general debt on the principle of a discrimination between original holders and alienees. III Those who were for providing separately for the general debt without that discrimination at arbitrary rates of interest inferior to the stipulated rules. IV Those who were for providing for the general debt on the basis of the subsisting contracts and for assuming the particular debts upon an equal provision. V Those who were for providing for the general debt at arbitrary rates of interest inferior to the stipulated rates and for assuming the state debts upon an equal provision. . . .

It is easy to perceive that such a heterogeneous mass of opinions not merely speculative but actuated by different interests and passions could not fail to produce much embarrassment to the person who was to devise the plan of a provision for the public debt—if he had been provident enough to sound the ground and probe the state of opinions.

It was proper for him to endeavor to unite two ingredients in his plan, intrinsic goodness and a reasonable probability of success.

It may be thought that the first was his only concern—that he ought to have devised such a plan as appeared to him absolutely the best, leaving its adoption or rejection to the chance of events and to the responsibility of those whose province it was to decide.

But would not this have been to refine too much? If a plan had been offered too remote from the prevailing opinions—incapable of conciliating a sufficient number to constitute a majority—what would have been the consequences? The Minister would have been defeated in his first experiment. Before he had established any reputation for a knowledge of the business of his department, he might be sure that the blame of his ill-success would have fallen on his want of skill, not upon the ignorance or perverseness of those who had rejected his plan. Placed in a back ground he would have lost confidence and influence. A retreat or the disgrace of remaining in office without weight or credit or an adequate prospect of being useful would have been his alternative. The public interest might have been still more injured. The public deliberations left without any rallying point would been the more apt to be distracted between jarring, incoherent, and indigested projects, and either to conclude nothing or to conclude on something manifestly contrary to the public interests. That this is a natural inference is proved by the diversity and still more by the crudity of the opinions which have been enumerated, and by the zeal with which considerable men afterwards and since have maintained opinions which would disgrace pupils not yet out of the alphabet of political science.

Had a single session passed after the subject had been once seriously entered upon without some adequate provision for the debt, the most injurious consequences were to have been expected.

With but a slight dawning of previous confidence, such a delay arising from the conflict of opinions after a public display of the very unsound and heretical notions which were entertained by too many would have excited something very like despair in the Creditors and would have thrown complete discredit on the debt. The value in the market would have sunk to almost nothing, to the great prejudice of those who had lately through confidence in the new Government purchased at high prices. . . . No mortal could foresee the result. A total failure to provide for the debt was possible. A provision for it on terms destructive of principle & replete with injustice to the creditors was the least ill result to have been anticipated.

Those who from a horrible sentiment of injustice or the manias of false opinions regard the public debt with detestation as a nuisance and a curse and every creditor as a criminal, those who would have delighted in the disgrace of a government they had resisted and vilified, might have looked forward with malignant pleasure to this wreck of the public Debt. But every virtuous enlightened man would have foreseen in it the complicated mischief of ruined Credit—the prostration abroad and at home of the Character of the new Government—its possible subversion and with it that of the Union—and let it be added a severe blow to the general security of property.

In hinting at the possible subversion of the Government, it may be proper to explain the foundation of this idea. The public Creditors, who consisted of various descriptions of men, a large proportion of them very meritorious and very influential, had had a considerable agency in promoting the adoption of the new Constitution for this peculiar reason among the many weighty reasons which were common to them as citizens and proprietors, that it exhibited the prospect of a Government able to do justice to their claims. Their disappointment and disgust quickened by the sensibility of private interest could but have been extreme. There was another class of men and a very weighty one who had had great share in the establishment of the constitution, who though not personally interested in the debt, considered the maxims of public credit as of the essence of good government, as intimately connected, by the analogy and sympathy of principles, with the security of property in general, and as forming an insepa-rable portion of the great system of political order. These men from sentiment would have regarded their labors in supporting the constitution as in a great measure lost—they would have seen the disappointment of their hopes in the unwillingness of the government to do what they esteemed justice and to pursue what they called an honorable policy, and they would have regarded this failure as an augury of the continuance of the fatal system which had for some time prostrated the national honor interest and happiness. The disaffection of a part of these classes of men might have carried a considerable reinforcement to the enemies of the government. The lukewarmness of the residue would have left them a clearer stage to direct their assaults against it. . . .

In pursuing too far the idea of absolute perfection in the plan to be proposed unaccommodated to circumstances, the chance of an absolutely bad issue was infinitely enhanced, and of the evils connected with it. . . .

I grant that the idea of accommodation was not to be carried so far as to sacrifice to it any essential principle. This is never jus-tifiable. But with the restriction of not sacrificing principle, was it not right and advisable so to shape the course as to secure the best prospect of effecting the greatest possible good?

To me this appeared the path of policy and duty, and I acted under the influence of that impression.

Thus guided, I resolved to give the following features to my plan.

First To embrace in the provision, upon equal terms, the particular debts of the individual States as well as the general debt of the U States.

2dly To *fund* the whole by *pledging* for the payment of interest certain specified revenues adequate to the object, to continue pledged until the redemption or reimbursement of the principal of the Debt.

3d To provide in the first instance for the foreign part of the general debt in exact conformity with the contracts concerning it. To endeavor to effect a new, more manageable, and more convenient modification of the domestic part of the general debt with consent of the Creditors upon the ground of certain equivalents to be offered to them.

Fourthly To take as the basis of the provision for the domestic part of the general debt the contracts with the Creditors as they stood at the time of the adoption of the new Constitution . . .; bottoming the provision on this principle, that those contracts were to be fulfilled as far and as fast as was practicable & were not to be departed from without the free consent of the Creditors.

5thly To provide for the arrears of interest which had accumulated upon the same terms with the principal, constituting them a new Capital.

Sixthly To endeavor to carry these ideas into effect by opening two loans on the terms proposed, one for the domestic part of the general debt, the sums subscribed thereto to be paid in the principal and arrears of interest of the old debt, another for the particular debts of the respective States, the sums subscribed thereto to be paid in the principal and arrears of interest of those debts.

Seventhly. To endeavor to establish it as a rule of administration that the creation of debt should always be accompanied with a provision for its extinguishment; and to apply the rule as far as it could be applicable to a new *provision* for an *old* debt by incorporating with it a fund for sinking the debt.

Eighthly. As an incident to the whole, to provide for the final settlement of Accounts between the United & Individual States, charging the latter with the sums assumed for them by the subscriptions in state-debt which should be made to the proposed loan. . . .

Let us now review under each head the reasons which led to this plan, and the means and modes of execution.

I. As to the uniting in the provision upon equal terms the particular debts of the several States with the general debt of the U States.

It appeared to me that this measure would be conducive to the greatest degree of justice and was essential to policy.

I use a qualified and comparative mode of expression in the first case because from the past course and then existing state of things, perfect justice was unattainable. The object consequently was to pursue such a plan as would procure the greatest practicable quantum of Justice.

The true rule for conducting the expenses of the Revolution which established independence seems to have been this. That as the benefits to be derived from it would be individually equal to the citizens of every state, so the burthens ought also to be individually equal among the citizens of all the states according to individual property and ability. That for this purpose all the expenses of the war ought to have been defrayed out of a common Treasury supplied by contributions of all the individuals of the U States, levied under the common authority according to equal rules, by loans either direct by borrowing or indirect and implied by emissions of paper money, operated upon the *joint credit* of the Union & by bringing into common stock all auxiliary or adventitious resources as waste lands, confiscated property &c.

This was the true justice of the case and the true national ground—a ground which perhaps might well have been taken by those first assemblies of the Union convened by the direct commission of the people with plenary power to take care of the Nation, but which was never but partially taken & was successively abandoned in compliance with the un-national demands of state claims—the aristocracy of state pretensions.

But instead of this course, that which was pursued was a compound of incoherent principles. A part of the general expenditure was defrayed on the general credit of the U States immediately by the emissions of bills of credit and by loans of individuals mediated by the contracts of various officers and Agents who obtained services & supplies on the credit of the Union and gave certain paper evidences of them. Another part was defrayed in consequence of requisitions upon the states of men, money, provisions, and other articles of supply according to certain estimated or conjectural quotas to be raised & furnished by the states separately. A third part was defrayed by the spontaneous exertions of the states themselves for local defense, for enterprises independently undertaken to annoy the common enemy, divest him of acquisitions, or make acquisitions upon him. Each State enjoyed the exclusive benefit of its extra resources, waste lands & confiscated property. Geographical lines thus made a substantial difference in the condition of the citizens of one common country, engaged in a common cause.

It was impossible that such a state of things should not have led to very disproportionate exertions and contributions—should not have produced and left very unequal burthens on the citizens of different states. . . .

Very different also was the care and accuracy of the different states in recording and preserving the evidences of their contributions. Some states kept an account of everything, others only of those things which they had furnished upon regular authorization of the Union. Others kept very loose & imperfect accounts of anything—and others lost by accidents of the war the records and vouchers which they had taken.

Add to all this the circumstances of the valuable aids which some states were able to derive more than others from auxiliary resources, particularly of waste land & confiscated property—two obvious consequences will result.

First that it was impossible that in the course of the War there could have been any proportional equality between the exertions, contributions, and burthens of the citizens of the different States.

Secondly that it was impossible by any after adjustment to restore the equilibrium & produce retrospective equality.

All then that could be rationally aimed at was to pursue such a course as promised *most certainly* the *greatest degree* of Justice.

The option lay between three modes of proceeding.

One—To refer the obtaining of ultimate justice to a final settlement of Accounts between the United and Individual States upon the best and most equitable principles which were practicable, and to provide for the balances which would be established in favor of certain states by that settlement.

A second: to exonerate all the states from Debt by the assumption of the still existing debts, and to abandon a settlement as impracticable on certain and equitable principles.

Another: To exonerate the states from debt by the assumption of their still existing debts; to charge each with the sums assumed upon its account—and to attempt an ultimate equalization by the settlement of Accounts.

The first & second plans were those contrasted by official propositions & deliberations, & will be considered together by way of comparison with each other: first with regard to Justice & secondly with regard to policy.

The first plan, which was that vehemently insisted upon by those who opposed the assumption of the State Debts, appeared to me liable to some conclusive objections on the score of justice.

I It would have left certain states greatly indebted, deprived of the most easy & productive sources of revenue by the occupation of them in a provision for the general debt, to struggle for an indefinite and uncertain period with a heavier load of debt than they were able to bear, depending for relief on the precarious issue of a final settlement of Accounts and a provision for the balances.

II It was uncertain in the nature of the thing and so considered by all parties not only when a settlement could be effected, but whether any settlement would ever be practicable. The peace took place in 1783. In 1790 very little more than the formal measures of settlement had been devised, and scarcely any impression made on the business.

III It was altogether a chapter of accidents whether a settlement would bring the expected and the just relief. From the circumstances which have been mentioned, a settlement must have been of necessity an artificial and arbitrary thing. It was impossible for any to be made on truly equitable or satisfactory principles. The greatest portion of human intellect & justice was unequal to it because Adequate data were wanting. . . .

In such a posture of things, consequently it might well have happened that an indebted state well entitled to relief by a balance in its favor might have been disappointed by the issue of the settlement.

Not to assume the State Debts, therefore, was to leave the greatly indebted states to totter under a burden to which they were unequal in the indefinite expectation of a settlement, and to involve a possibility that they might never obtain relief either from the total failure of a settlement on account of the difficulties attending it, or from not receiving their just dues by the embarrassment that unavoidably rendered a settlement artificial and arbitrary.

The reference, therefore, to a settlement as the sole rule of justice without an assumption of the state debts was not likely to afford either such prompt or such *certain* justice as might be looked for from the immediate assumption of the State Debts. . . .

It will strengthen the argument for the superior justice of the assumption plan to remark that the Debts of the States represented the great mass of State effort during the War. Not much had been done by taxation. Credit had been the principal engine. . . .

Either an equitable settlement of accounts would take place or it would not—if it did not, the greatly indebted States without an assumption would certainly fail of justice and due relief; if it did, with an assumption the settlement would remedy any inequality which might have been occasioned by it and restore equilibrium. An assumption and a settlement on right principles would ensure justice—no assumption & no settlement would ensure injustice. It was to be feared a settlement might not take effect. It was precarious and contingent. An assumption of course gave the greatest certainty of Justice, by an assumption or equalization of the condition of Individuals. Pursuing mature impressions, this must be deemed of more consequence than anything which regarded the states in their corporate or collective capacities.

The most simple and satisfactory notion of Justice was to secure that individuals of the same Nation who had contended in the same cause for the same object, their common liberty, should at the end of the contest find themselves on an equal footing as to burdens arising from the contest.

Nothing could be more revolting than that the citizens of one state should live at ease free from Taxes and the citizens of a neighboring State be overburdened with taxes growing out of a war which had given equal political advantages to the Citizens of both States. . . .

The relative conditions of States depended on many artificial circumstances. These circumstances might forever have stood in the way of that equality of condition among citizens which was infinitely the most important consideration and the most desirable attainment. The measure which went most directly and certainly to this object was to be preferred. The assumption was such a measure.

By taking all the Debts upon the Union to be paid out of common Treasury defrayed by common contribution according to general rules, the citizens of every State were on an equal footing. . . .

To resume. The superiority of the plan of a joint provision over that of a separate provision in the view of justice consists in this—

That supposing a final equitable settlement of accounts between the states, either plan would produce eventual justice. . . .

But the plan of assumption was most likely to expedite justice by the immediate relief which it gave to the overburdened States.

That, setting aside the supposition of a final equitable settlement of accounts—the plan of assumption contained the best chance of success by giving relief to the overburdened States who would otherwise have remained without it, though from known circumstances there was a *moral certainty* of their being entitled to it.

That the assumption in every event better consulted justice by conducing to equalize in the first instance the burden of citizens of the same country arising from a contest in a common cause, and by securing a simultaneous and equal provision for creditors who had equal merits & who otherwise would have fared unequally.

These are the principle considerations that relate to justice—in the view of policy the argument is still more conclusive in favor of assumption.

The theory of our constitution with respect to taxation is perhaps a new example in the world—that is to say a concurrent and coordinate authority in one general head and in thirteen (now fifteen) distinct members of a confederacy united under that head to impose in detail upon all individual and upon all taxable objects. . . .

But though agreed in this general principle, they were not equally agreed in the application of the rule. Some were for a general & paramount power of taxation in the National Government and either a subordinate, or a limited by being confined to particular objects, power of taxation in the State Governments. Some were for a division of the power of taxation giving certain branches of it exclusively to the general Government, and other branches of it exclusively to the State Governments—others were for a general concurrent power of taxation in the Federal & State Governments.

The two first opinions equally presupposed a great difficulty of execution and danger of collision in a concurrent power of taxation, and sought to avoid it by different means. The last seems to have considered that difficulty and danger as less formidable than the embarrassments which belonged to either of the other schemes. And this opinion was adopted by the Convention except with regard to the duties of imports and Tonnage, which for cogent and obvious reasons was impracticable and was exclusively vested in the Federal head.

This course was, relatively to the existing state of things, the wisest. The subordination of the state power of taxation to that of the general government or the confining it to particular objects would probably have been an insuperable obstacle to the adoption of the constitution. The division of the power between the Union and the States could not have been regulated upon any plan which would not either have left the General Government more restricted than was compatible with a due provision for the exigencies of the Union, or would have so confined the State Governments as would have been equally an impediment to the success of the Constitution. . . .

But though it is admitted that the course pursued by the Convention was the most expedient—yet it is not the less true that the plan involved inherent and great difficulties. It may not unaptly be styled the Gordian Knot of our political situation.

To me there appeared but one way of untying or severing it, which was in practice to leave the states under as little necessity as possible of exercising the power of taxation. The narrowness of the limits of its exercise on one side left the field more free and unembarrassed to the other, and avoided essentially the interference and collisions to be apprehended *inherent* in the plan of concurrent jurisdiction.

Thus to give a clear field to the Government of the U States was so manifestly founded in good policy, that the time must come when a man of sense would blush to dispute it. . . .

Without an assumption of the State Debts which produced this effect, the first war with an European Power would have convinced us of the ineligibleness of our situation, of the weakness and embarrassment incident to fifteen or perhaps to 50 different systems of finance. . . .

Much clamor has been raised against the funding system on the score of *speculation*, how justly will be examined in a proper place, but what would have been the degree of it on the plan of so many different funds or stocks depending on so many different provisions? It is evident that it would have been multiplied tenfold. The legerdemain of speculation would have had full scope for its exertion.

To give as quickly as possible elevation & stability to the funds was a most important mean of raising & fixing public credit. The assumption, by equalizing the condition of every part of the public debt & placing every part on good and on equal security, was one of the most effectual expedients for that purpose. . . .

Besides the advantages to public safety and public credit, consequences very favorable to the case and satisfaction of individuals were included in the assumption—of three kinds 1 lightening the burthens absolutely of all the Citizens of the U States. 2 equalizing the condition as to burthens of the Citizens of one State with those of another. 3 bringing certain relief in the first instance to the over-indebted States & facilitating settlement of accounts. These are the incidents of the same superiority of faculty in the general Government to make a convenient provision for the whole debt.

It is curious fact which has not made its due impression that in every state the people have found relief from assumption, while an incomparably better provision than before existed has been made for the state debts.

Let the citizens of Virginia be appealed to whether they have not, in consequence of being exonerated from the necessity of providing for their debt, been relieved in degree or kind from burdens which before pressed heavily upon them. They must answer the affirmative. The same inquiry will find the same answers in every state. Men wonder at the lightness of their burthens, and yet at the capacity of the Government to pay the interest of its debt, to absorb a portion of the principal, and to find extensive resources for defense against Indian Ravages.

The solution of the enigma is in the present Financial system of the Country, intrinsically more energetic, more orderly, better directed, and more uniform & comprehensive than could possibly have been the case with __ different systems to provide for as many different loads of debt.

The effect of energy and system is to vulgar and feeble minds a kind of magic which they do not comprehend, and thus they make false interpretation of the most obvious facts. The people of several parts of the state, relieved and happy by the effects of the assumption, execrate the measure with its authors, to which they owe the blessing. . . .

It is a great recommendation of the assumption not only that it anticipated a relief which was indispensable and which might not have come from a settlement, but that it facilitated a settlement and rendered a tolerable issue far more probable. . . .

The assumption of the State Debts, by giving relief to the much indebted States, rendered the issue & consequently the principles of the settlement less important. . . .

Thus then it is one of the merits of the assumption that it facilitated a settlement of Accounts, which all the states were desirous of & so has contributed to establish their harmony. . . .

It remains to mention one consideration which naturally occurred in the reflections upon the expediency of assuming the State Debts. This is its tendency to strengthen our infant Government by increasing the number of ligaments between the Government and the interests of Individuals.

I frankly acknowledge that this tendency as far as it appeared to be founded was not excluded from the calculation, for my opinion has been and is that the true danger to our prosperity is not the overbearing strength of the Federal head, but its weakness and imbecility for preserving the union of the States and controlling the eccentricities of State ambition and the explosions of factious passions. And a measure which, consistently with the Constitution, was likely to have the effect of strengthening the fabric would have recommended itself to me on that account.

But though this was the case, though I thought too that the assumption would have in several senses a temporary tendency of the kind alluded to, and so far might serve as a prop to the Government in the infancy of its authority while there was yet a numerous party alive whose vanity and envy pledged them to opposition, and before it had acquired the confirmations of habit & age—and though weight was given to the argument where it was thought most likely to have effect—Yet upon the whole it was the consideration upon which I relied least of all.

It appeared to me in a considerable degree counterbalanced by the suggestion of an objection which has been stated—the necessity which it imposed on the government of resorting early to unpalatable modes of taxation, which jeopardized its popularity and gave a handle to its enemies to attack.

It appeared to me also entitled to the less weight on the account stated because on the supposition that this Debt was to be extinguished within a moderate term of years—its influence must then be terminated, and it had not pretensions to be considered as a permanent or lastly prop to the Government.

Besides that, it was to be foreseen that successive transfers of considerable portions of the Debt to foreigners and accumulations at home would rapidly enough lessen the number of ligaments, diminish the influence upon individuals, and, the taxes continuing, perhaps invert the effect.

Had this then been the weightiest motive to the measure, it would never have received my patronage. The great inducements with me were those which have been previously enumerated, and chiefly the giving simplicity & energy to the national finances, the avoiding the collisions of multifarious & conflicting systems, the securing to the Government for national exigencies the complete command of the national resources, the consolidation of public credit. These were the commanding motives and it is believed they were solid. . . .

The foregoing considerations appeared to me decisive for proposing an assumption of the State Debts. Experience has not led me to repent the measures. And I believe it will more & more recommend it even to its enemies. . . .

The course of the argument has stated & replied to all the objections to the assumption except one. This is that it has tended to increase the mass of the Debt.

This observation has frequently been so managed as to infuse into the minds of many a vague, confused conception that the PUBLIC Debt of the Country has been augmented in mass to the extent of the aggregate sum of State Debts assumed. But it were absurd to attempt a refutation of this idea. It is self-evident that the Assumption in this respect did nothing more than transfer the particular debts to the Union. It united fourteen sums in one and charged them upon one responsibility, that of the Union, instead of leaving them to exist separately chargeable on the separate responsibilities of the Union and the Individual states. The debt of the Union was increased, but the debts of the several members of it were proportionally decreased. The MASS of PUBLIC DEBT consequently remained the same, on the infallible evidence of a mathematical axiom that a WHOLE cannot be greater than ITS PARTS. . . .

The second feature of the plan as stated was to *fund* the entire debt, *foreign* and *domestic, original* and *assumed.*

The *funding* of the Debt has been unexpectedly the theme of much declamation and invective. A confusion of ideas has been attempted to be produced among the ignorant. The *funding* with the *assumption* have been sometimes treated as the creation of the Debt; at others the funding has been represented as its *perpetuation*, as a direct attempt to fasten the burden irrevocably about the necks of the people. A particular ingredient in the plan proposed, the rendering the debt redeemable only in certain proportions, has been pressed in to reinforce this argument & to prove the iniquitous tendency of the plan. . . .

The Revolution which gave us independence and secured us liberty left upon the country, as the price of it, a considerable Debt partly contracted by the U States in their joint capacity, partly by the individual states in their separate capacities.

What was to be done with the debt? Was it to be wiped off with a sponge or was it to be provided for?

The first ideas were the extreme of political profligacy and folly. Governments like individuals have burdens which ought to be deemed sacred, else they become mere engines of violence, oppression, extortion, and misery. Adieu to the security of property, adieu to the security of liberty. Nothing is then safe—all our favorite notions of national & constitutional rights vanish.

Everything is brought to a question of power; right is anathematized, excommunicated, and banished.

In the code of moral and political obligations, that of paying debts holds a prominent place. Tried by the test of utility, there is perhaps none of greater force or extent. Without it, no borrowing nor lending; no selling or purchasing upon time—no credit private or public; consequently a more cramped and less prosperous agriculture, fewer and more imperfect mechanic & other industrial arts, less and more embarrassed commerce, an immense contraction of national resource and strength. A most active power in the whole scheme of national happiness would be destroyed. A vast void would be created. Everything would languish and wither. . . .

The obligation to provide for the Debts for the benefit of those who were best entitled was indisputable. No arguments can enforce it. No man who has the least regard for his reputation will hazard a denial of it.

But anonymous publications have by insinuations attempted to raise doubts and prejudices. Not the mode merely of providing has been attacked, but by implication any provision whatever. The Debt itself has been sometimes treated by vague expressions as a nuisance, as a morbid excrescence in the body politic, as the creature of a wicked combination to create a monied aristocracy & undermine the republican system. A debt created by that very Revolution which gave us this Republican system has been artfully presented in these odious colors to the dislikes of a spirit of Jealousy and Avarice, and those who were disposed to uphold the integrity and credit of the Nation have been exhibited as conspirators against Democratic principles. It is afflicting that there should be a State of public information, opinion, or feeling which should encourage any man to attempt to traffic for popularity by means so absurd and so base. If they could succeed, we must renounce those pretensions to intelligence and light as a people which we claim hitherto on such just grounds. We must soon after renounce that Republican system of which these men affect to be so fond.

The plainest maxims of common sense and common honesty establish that our Governments had no option but to make a fair provision for the Debt. Justice, true policy, character, credit, interest all spoke on this head a uniform and unequivocal language.

Not to have listened to it would have been to have prostrated everything respectable among nations. It would have been an act of suicide in the Government at the very commencement of its existence. It would not have strangled the serpents which threatened, but it would have strangled itself.

The only possible question was about the nature of the provision. And to this point indeed were confined all the questions formally raised, though indirectly it has been endeavored to excite prejudices in the public mind against the debt itself & consequently against all provision for it.

But among the questions raised as to the nature of the provision, I neither recollect nor can trace that among the legislative parties, while the subject was under discussion, there was any party against the principle of *funding* the debt as contradistinguished from other modes of providing.

Indeed, but three options occurred—to pay off the principal & interest at once, which was impossible; to provide annually for the interest and occasionally for reimbursing as much of the principal as the public resources permitted—to *fund* the Debt, or in other words to *pledge* specified and adequate funds for the regular payment of interest till the principal was reimbursed, and as an auxiliary measure to constitute & pledge adequate funds for the reimbursement of the principal.

The last was conformable to the sense of America repeatedly and solemnly expressed. Different acts of Congress under the old Confederation embrace and enforce the propriety of this measure & frequently with unanimity. The states separately had all sanctioned it. The objectors were a few solitary individuals neither numerous nor significant enough by weight of talents or character to form a party.

In proposing, therefore, to fund the debt, I considered myself not only as pursuing the true principles of credit & the true policy of the case, but the uniform general sense of the Union.

I had heard no lisp from any description of men in the national legislature of an objection to this idea, and accordingly, as before observed, when the plan proposed was under discussion there appeared none in opposition to it.

The clamors, therefore, which have been subsequently raised on this head and patronized more or less directly by a whole party, are not less strong indications of the disingenuousness of party spirit than of an immaturity of ideas on the subject of public Credit.

The substance of the argument against Funding Systems is that by facilitating Credit they encourage enterprises which produce expense by furnishing in credit a substitute for revenue; they prevent the raising as much as might be raised contemporarily with the causes of expense to avoid the unpopularity of laying new taxes, and in both ways occasion a tendency to run in debt, consequently a progressive accumulation of debt and its perpetuation; at least till it is crushed beneath the load of its own enormous weight.

An analysis of this argument proves that it turns upon the abuses of a thing intrinsically good.

A prosperous state of agriculture commerce and manufactures nourishes and begets opulence, resource, and strength. These by inspiring a consciousness of power never fail to beget in the councils of nations under whatever form of Government a sentiment of superiority, pride ambition, insolence. These dispositions lead directly to War, and consequently to expenses and to all the calamities which march in the train of War. Shall we therefore reprobate and reject improvements in agriculture, commerce, and manufactures?

Again the same causes leading to opulence, increasing the means of enjoyment, naturally sharpen the appetite for it, and so promote luxury, extravagance, dissipation, effeminacy, disorders in the moral and political system, convulsions, revolutions, the overthrow of nations and empires. Shall we therefore on this account renounce improvements in Agriculture, commerce, and manufactures?

Again: Science learning and knowledge promote those inventions, discoveries and improvements which accelerate the progress of labor and industry, and with it the accumulation of that opulence which is the parent of so many pleasures & pains, so many blessings and calamities. Shall we therefore on this account explode Science, Learning & Knowledge?

Again: True liberty by protecting the exertions of talents and industry and securing to them their justly acquired fruits, tends more powerfully than any other cause to augment the mass of national wealth and to produce the mischiefs of opulence. Shall we therefore on this account proscribe Liberty also?

What good in fine shall we retain? Tis the portion of man assigned to him by the eternal allotment of Providence that every good he enjoys shall be alloyed with ills, that every source of his bliss shall be a source of his affliction—except Virtue alone, the only unmixed good which is permitted to his temporal Condition.

But shall we on this account forego every advantage which we are fitted to enjoy? Shall we put in practice the horrid system of the detestable Robespierre. Shall we make war upon Science & its professors? Shall we destroy the arts useful as well as pleasurable? Shall we make knowledge a crime, ignorance a qualification? Shall we lay in ruins our towns and deform the face of our fields. Shall we enchain the human mind & blunt all its energies under the withering influences of privation & the benumbing strokes of Terror? Shall we substitute the unmingled misery of a gloomy and destructive despotism to the alternate sunshine & storms of Liberty? Shall we exchange Science, Civilization &c.

The very objection to funding systems makes their panegyric—"*they facilitate credit*"—they give energy solidity and extent to the Credit of a Nation—They enable it in great and dangerous emergencies to obtain readily and copiously the supplies of money of which it stands in need for its defense, safety, and the preservation or advancement of its interests—They enable it to do this too without crushing the people beneath the weight of intolerable taxes, without taking from industry the resources necessary for its vigorous prosecution, without emptying all the property of individuals into the public lap, without subverting the foundations of social order.

Indeed, War in the modern system of it offers but two options—Credit or the devastation of private property. Tis impossible merely with that portion of the income of the community which can be spared from the wants, conveniences & industrious pursuits of individuals to force the expenses of a serious War during its progress. There must be anticipation by Credit, or there must be a violent usurpation of private property. The State must trench upon the Capital instead of the Revenue of the People, and thus every war would involve a temporary ruin.

Tis the signal merit of a vigorous system of national credit that it enables a Government to support war without violating property, destroying industry, or interfering unreasonably with individual enjoyments. The citizens retain their Capital to carry on their several businesses and a due proportion of its produce for obtaining their usual comforts. Agriculture, Commerce & manufactures may receive some Check, but they receive no serious wound. Their stamina remain, and, on peace returning, they quickly resume their wonted elasticity. War by the use of Credit becomes less a scourge, loses a great portion of its calamity. . . .

Thus it appears that the great objection to funding systems resolves itself into an objection to Credit in the abstract, and if listened to drives us to the alternative of a mean surrender of our rights and interests to every enterprising invader, or to the oppression of the citizens and destruction of Capital & Industry in every war in which we should be engaged and in the end, from the insupportableness of that situation, to the same surrender of our rights and interests.

Indeed as far as it is the attribute of funding systems to invigorate Credit, it is their tendency in an important particular to diminish Debt. This relates to the lower or higher rate of interest at which money is borrowed according to the state of Credit. A Government which borrows 100 Dollars at 3 percent owes in fact a less debt than a Government which is obliged to borrow the same sum at five per Cent. Interest is always a part of the debt and it is self-evident that the ultimate discharge of one which bears five per Ct will exhaust more money or income than that of one which only bears 3 per Ct. This principle runs through all the public operations in which Credit is concerned, and the difference in the result of the public expenditures and consequently its debts from a perfect or imperfect state of Credit is immense.

Every State ought to aim at rendering its credit, that is its faculty to borrow, commensurate with the utmost extent of the lending faculties of the community and of all others who can have access to its loans. Tis then that it puts itself in a condition to exercise the greatest portion of strength of which it is capable, and has its destiny most completely in its own hands. Tis then that the various departments of its industry are liable to the least disturbance & proceed with the most steady & vigorous motion. Tis then that it is able to supply all its wants not only in the most effectual manner, but at the cheapest rate. An ignorance which benights the political world and disputes the first principles of Administration is requisite to bring this position for a moment into question. The principle, on which such a question could be founded, would equally combat every institution that promotes the perfection of the Social organization, for this perfection in all its shapes, by giving a consciousness of strength & resource & inspiring pride, tends to ambitious pursuits to war expense & debt.

On this question, as on most others, evils are traced to a wrong source. Funding systems as the engines of Credit are blamed for the Wars, expenses, and debts of nations? Do these evils prevail less in countries where either those systems do not exist, or where they exist partially and imperfectly. Great Britain is the country where they exist in most energy. Her wars have no doubt been frequent, her expenses great, and her debts are vast. But is not this, with due allowance for difference of circumstances, the description of all the great Powers of Europe?

France, Spain, Austria, Russia, Prussia—Are they not as frequently at War as Great Britain, and as often of their own choice? Have not their expenses compared with their means and the state of Society been as great? Have they not all, except Prussia, heavy Debts?

The Debt of France brought about her Revolution. Financial embarrassments led to those steps which led to the overthrow of the Government and to all the terrible scenes which have followed.

Let us then say as the truth is, not that funding systems produce wars, expenses & debts, but that the ambition, avarice, revenge, and injustice of man produce them. The seeds of war are sown thickly in the human breast. It is astonishing, after the experience of its having deluged the world with calamities for so many ages, with how much precipitancy and levity nations still rush to arms against each other.

Besides what we see abroad, what have we recently witnessed among ourselves? Never was a thing more manifest than that our true policy lay in cultivating peace with scrupulous care. Never had a nation a stronger interest so to do. Yet how many were there who directly and indirectly raised and joined in the cry of War. Sympathy with one nation, animosity against another, made it infinitely difficult for the Government to steer a course calculated to avoid being implicated in the Volcano which shook & overwhelmed Europe. Vague speculations about the cause of Liberty, seconded by angry passions, had like to have plunged this young country, just recovering from the effects of the long and desolating war which confirmed its revolution, just emerging from a state little short of anarchy, just beginning to establish system and order; to revive credit & confidence into an abyss of war, confusion, and distress.

After all the experience which has been had upon the point, shall we still charge upon funding systems evils which are truly chargeable upon the bad and turbulent passions of the human mind?

Peruse the history of Europe from its earliest period, were wars less frequent or pernicious before the system of credit was introduced than they have been since? They were more frequent and more destructive, though perhaps not of as long duration at one time.

But they did not equally produce debt. This is true, yet it remains to compare the evils of debt with those which resulted from the antecedent system of War—the devastations and extortions, the oppressions and derangements of industry in all its branches, and it remains to consider whether expedients may not be devised which may preserve to nations the advantages of Credit & avoid essentially its evils. If this shall be practicable, the argument in favor of the system of Credit has no counterpoise and becomes altogether conclusive.

Credit may be called a new power in the mechanism of national affairs. It is a great and a very useful one, but the art of regulating it properly, as is the case with every new and great contrivance, has been till lately imperfectly understood. The rule of making cotemporary provision for the extinguishment of principal as well as for the payment of interest in the art of contracting new debt is the desideratum—the true panacea.

But this like most others is not an absolute but a relative question. If it were even admitted that the system of anticipation by Credit is in the abstract a bad one, it will not follow that it can be renounced by any one nation while nations in general continue to use it. It is so immense a power in the affairs of war that a nation without credit would be in great danger of falling a victim in the first war with a power possessing a vigorous and flourishing credit.

What astonishing efforts has Credit enabled Great Britain to make? What astonishing efforts does it enable her at this very moment to continue. What true Englishman, whatever may be his opinion of the merits and wisdom of the contest in which his country is engaged, does not rejoice that she is able to employ so powerful instrument of Warfare. However he may wish for peace, he will reflect that there must be two parties to the pacification, and that it is possible the enemy may either be unwilling to make peace or only willing to make it on terms too disadvantageous & humiliating. He must therefore cherish the national Credit as an engine by which war, if inevitable, can be maintained, and by which from that very possibility a better peace can be secured.

It is remarkable too that Great Britain, the only power which has uniformly cultivated an enlightened and exact plan of national credit at a juncture so critical as the present, continues to uphold the various branches of her commerce & industry in great energy and prosperity, and will in the end tax her adversary in exchange for the products of her industry with a large proportion of the expenses of the actual War. . . .

But let us still return too & keep in view this very material point already stated. Tis *Credit* in general, not funding systems in particular, against which the objections made, as far as they have foundation, lie. However obtained, it leads to exactly the same consequences which are charged on funding systems, which are no otherwise answerable for those consequences than as they are means of Credit.

Any provision, therefore, for our Revolution-Debt which from its justice and efficiency would have given satisfaction and inspired confidence, would equally have conferred national credit and would have been equally liable to the evils of an abuse of Credit.

The dilemma was either to make & continue a just and adequate provision for the debt till it was discharged, and thereby establish Credit and incur the chances of the evils incident to its abuse; or not to make a just and adequate provision for the debt and so commit national injustice incur national dishonor and disgrace, and it may be added shake and weaken the foundations of property and social security. . . .

A Government which does not rest on the basis of justice rests on that of force. There is no middle ground. Establish that a Government may decline a provision for its debts, though able to make it, and you overthrow all public morality, you unhinge all the principles that must preserve the limits of free constitutions—you have anarchy, despotism or what you please, but you have no *just* or *regular* Government.

In all questions about the advantages or disadvantages of national Credit, or in similar questions which it has been seen may be raised (and it may be added have been raised), with respect to all the sources of social happiness and national prosperity—the difference between the true politician and the political-empyric is this: The latter will either attempt to travel out of human nature and introduce institutions and projects for which man is not fitted, and which perish in the imbecility of their own conception & structure, or without proposing or attempting any substitute, they content themselves with exposing and declaiming against the ill sides of things, and with puzzling & embarrassing every practicable scheme of administration which is adopted. The last indeed is the most usual because the easiest course, and it embraces in its practice all those hunters after popularity who, knowing better, make a traffic of the weak sides of the human understanding and passions.

The true politician on the contrary takes human nature (and human society, its aggregate) as he finds it, a compound of good and ill qualities of good and ill tendencies—endued with powers and actuated by passions and propensities which blend enjoyment with suffering, and make the causes of welfare the causes of misfortune.

With this view of human nature, he will not attempt to warp or distort it from its natural direction—he will not attempt to promote its happiness by means to which it is not suited, he will not reject the employment of the means which constitute its bliss because they necessarily involve alloy and danger; but he will seek to promote his action according to the bias of his nature, to lead him to the development of his energies according to the scope of his passions, and erecting the social organization on this basis, he will favor all those institutions and plans which tend to make men happy according to their natural bent, which multiply the sources of individual enjoyment and increase those of national resource and strength—taking care to infuse in each case all the ingredients which can be devised as preventives or correctives of the evil which is the eternal concomitant of temporal blessing.

Thus: observing the immense importance of Credit to the strength and security of nations, he will endeavor to obtain it for his own country in its highest perfection by the most efficient means; yet not overlooking the abuses to which, like all other good things, it is liable, he will seek to guard against them by promoting a spirit of true national economy, by pursuing steadily, especially in a country which has no need of external acquisition, the maxims of justice, moderation, and peace, and by endeavoring to establish as far as human inconsistency allows, certain fixed principles in the administration of the finances calculated to secure efficaciously the extinguishment of debt as fast at least as the probable exigencies of the nation is likely to occasion the contracting of it.

These, I can truly say, are the principles which have regulated every part of my conduct in my late office.

And as a first step to this great result, I proposed the *funding* of the public Debt.

The quality of funding appeared to me essential in the plan of providing for different reasons.

1 First it appeared to me advisable that the nature of the provision should be such as to give satisfaction and confidence, by inspiring an opinion of security, to the Creditors. This was important not only as it regarded their advantage but as it regarded the public interest. . . .

2 It was desirable to guard the Government and the Creditors against the danger of inconstancy in the public Councils. The debt being once funded, it would require the concurrence of both branches of the legislature and of the President or of two thirds of both branches overruling the opposition of the President to shake the provision. Of this there was a moral impossibility, at least the highest degree of improbability. To make a provision annually

would require the like concurrence in its favor, of course would be continually liable to be defeated by improper views in either of the branches or departments. . . . There was good ground to apprehend that the accidental result of a single election and the accidental prevalence of ill humors in parts of the community might violate the justice and prostrate the Credit of the Nation.

It is the part of wisdom in a Government as well as in an individual to guard against its own infirmities; and having taken beforehand a comprehensive view of its duty and interest, to tie itself down by every constitutional precaution to the steady pursuit of them.

3 It appeared important to give all practicable solidity & stability to the funds or Stock which constituted the debt. The funding of the Debt was essential to this end. . . .

One effect of this was to accelerate the period which would terminate an irregular and excessive spirit of speculation in the funds

It may be remarked that it is now a considerable time since the public Stock has reached the desirable point & put an end to the excessive spirit of speculation. This has been for some time past far more active, even to intemperateness in other pursuits, in trading adventures and in lands. And it is curious to observe how little clamor there is against the spirit of speculation in its present direction; though it were not difficult to demonstrate that it is not less extravagant or pernicious in the shape of land-jobbing than in that of Stock-jobbing. But many of the noisy Patriots who were not in condition to be stock-jobbers are land-jobbers, and have a becoming tenderness for this species of extravagance. And virtuous sensible men lamenting the partial ills of all over-driven speculation, know at the same time that they are inseparable from the spirit & freedom of Commerce & that the cure must result from the disease.

Another important effect of funding the Debt was the quick appreciation of the funds from the same opinion of security. This was calculated to save immense sums to the Country. Foreigners else would have become the proprietors of the Stock at great under-values, to the loss of millions to the holders and to the Country. The loss to the holders is perceived at once, but the loss to the country, though an obvious consequence has not been equally palpable to all. . . .

It has been imagined, however, that if our debt had not been funded, its precariousness would have been a security against transfers to foreigners. . . .

Another expedient has been mentioned for preventing alienations, and consequently loss by alienations to foreigners. This was to forbid the alienations to foreigners in other words, to render them incapable of holding the Debt.

But this expedient was inadmissible and would have been ineffectual. . . .

The only effect then of the restriction would have been to depreciate the Stock of the Country the thermometer of its credit without any counterbalancing good.

Indeed if the exclusion of foreigners would have been effected *cui bono?* What harm is there that foreigners should speculate in our funds, if they give full value for them? Will not the money they give for the Stock employed in extending our commerce, agriculture & manufactures, roads, canals & other ameliorations more than indemnify the Country for the interest which they will receive upon the Stock till the principal is reimbursed? In a country with so much improvable matter in a crude state as ours, it cannot be doubted that Capital employed in those ways will incomparably more than repay the interest of the money employed.

But to overthrow this important consideration it is alleged that the money acquired by the sales of Stock to foreigners would not be employed on the objects which have been mentioned, but would be dissipated in the enjoyments of luxury and extravagance, and sent abroad again to pay for these objects to the loss *pro tanto* of the Country?

This suggestion was not founded in probability, nor has been warranted by the fact. It was true that a large increase of active Capital and augmentation of private fortunes would beget some augmentation of expense among individuals, and that a portion of this expense would be laid out on foreign articles of luxury. But the proportion which this employment of the new Capital would bear to the part of it which would be employed on useful and profitable objects would be and has been inconsiderable. Whoever will impartially look around will see that the great body of the new Capital created by the Stock has been employed in extending commerce, agriculture, manufactures, and other improvements.

Our own *real* navigation has been much increased. Our external commerce is carried on much more upon our own capitals than it was—our marine insurances in a much greater proportion are made by ourselves. Our manufactures are increased in number and carried on upon a larger scale. Settlements of our waste land are progressing with more vigor than at any former period. Our Cities and Towns are increasing rapidly by the addition of new and better houses. Canals are opening, bridges are building with more spirit & effect than was ever known at a former period. The value of lands has risen everywhere.

These circumstances (though other causes may have cooperated) it cannot be doubted by a well-informed or candid man are imputable in a great degree to the increase of Capital in public Debt, and they prove that the predictions of its dissipation in luxurious extravagances have not been verified. If a part has gone in that way, this loss has not been considerable enough to impair the force of the argument. The universal vivification of the energies of industry has laid the foundation of benefits far greater than the interest to be paid to foreigners can counterbalance as a disadvantage. . . .

A third important effect of giving solidity & stability to the Stock by funding the Debt was the rendering it useful as Capital. Those who may deny that it has even this tendency in defiance of the most manifest facts, cannot dispute that it must have it, if at all, in proportion to the security of the footing upon which it stands.

The opinion of it being a safe & substantial property is essential to that ready marketable quality which will render it expedient to invest unemployed monies in it till the opportunity of employment occurs, and certain that it can be brought into action when the opportunity arrives.

To be certain of its operation as active Capital it is only necessary to consider that it is *property which can almost at any moment be turned into money.* All property is Capital, that which can quickly and at all times be converted into money is active capital. It is nearly the same thing as if the possessor had an equal sum of money on hand. . . .

Who doubts that a man who has in his desk 10000 Dollars in good bank Notes has that sum of active capital? Who doubts any more, though there be two steps in the process, that a man who has in his hand 10000 Dollars of the notes of Merchants of unquestionable solidity and Credit which he can at any moment discount at the Banks has an equal sum, being the price of discount, of active Capital? Who can doubt any more that the possession of 10000 Dollars of funded Stock which he can readily carry into the market & sell for 10000 Dollars of these merchant's or bank notes, or gold & silver, is equally possessor of so much of active Capital?

In this Country, where the sum of gold & silver, the great organ of alienation & circulation, is comparatively more limited than in Europe, the certainty of an immediate conversion of Stock into money is not as great as in some of the great Stock markets of Europe, but the difference is not so material as to prevent the effect being substantially the same. . . .

A simple, concise, and yet comprehensive view of the effect of the funds as capital is comprised in this exhibition of it. To the mass of active capital resulting from the property and credit of all the individuals of the nation is added another mass constituted on the *joint* credit of the whole Nation and existing in the shape of the Government Stock, which continues till that Stock is extinguished by redemption or reimbursement. Is it not evident that this throwing into the common Stock of individual operations the Credit of the Nation must increase & invigorate the powers of industrious enterprise?

See what a wonderful spectacle Great Britain exhibits. Observe the mature state of her agricultural improvements under auspices of large Capitals employed to that end. Consider the extent of her navigation and external Commerce. Note the huge & varied pile of her manufactures. See her factors and agents spread over the four quarters of the Globe doing a great part of the business of other nations by force of Capital. View the great extent of her marine insurances attracting to her a considerable portion of the profits of the Commerce of most other nations. View her in fine the Creditor of the World. . . .

The third feature of my plan was to provide in the first instance for the foreign part of the general Debt in exact conformity with the contracts concerning it.

The propriety of this has been uncontested and speaks for itself. . . .

The fourth feature was "to take as the basis of the provision for the domestic part of the general debt the contracts with the Creditors as they stood at the time of the adoption of the new constitution. . . ."

To a man who thinks justly and feels rightly for the reputation of the Country of which he is a citizen, it is a humiliating reflection that it should be at all necessary to insist on the propriety of regulating the provision for the debt by the contracts concerning it.

The obligation to fulfill contracts is so fundamental a principle of private morality and social justice, so essential a basis of national Credit that nothing less than the fact itself could induce a belief that the application of the rule to our public Debt could have been controverted by leaders of parties or by any considerable portion of the community. Yet in truth it has been controverted either avowedly or virtually by a great proportion of all parties; by declarations or propositions disclaiming the application of the principle, or by the rejection of propositions necessary to give it effect.

The general proposition indeed which affirms the obligation of fulfilling contracts on Governments as well as individuals was of a nature which the most profligate politician was not shameless enough to deny.

# CHAPTER EIGHTEEN

# Articles of Association of the Merchants Bank (April 7, 1803)

*We, the Subscribers, have formed a Company or limited Partnership . . . to conduct business in the manner hereinafter specified and described, by and under the name and style of the "Merchants' Bank."*

HAMILTON DRAFTED THESE articles of association for the new Merchants Bank, the fourth in New York City, nearly two decades after he had prepared the constitution of the Bank of New York (see chapter 5), the city's first bank and the second in the United States. He had also been involved in the creation of the city's second and third banks. The second was the New York branch of the Bank of the United States, which opened in 1792. The third was the Manhattan Company, organized by Aaron Burr and chartered by the state legislature in 1799, which Hamilton had supported as a water company more than as a bank. Burr had inserted a clause into the charter that allowed the Manhattan Company to operate a bank, which may have been the real intent. Hamilton later saw this as an underhanded ruse, which contributed to the enmity between the two men.

The Merchants Bank was a project of Oliver Wolcott, Hamilton's successor as Treasury Secretary after he had served as Hamilton's number two there. Wolcott became the president of the Merchants Bank. After drawing up the articles, Hamilton became one of the new bank's attorneys.

Unlike the constitution of the Bank of New York, the articles make no mention of the intent to apply to the state legislature for a charter of incorporation. Banking over the previous two decades had become a politically charged issue as the Federalist party of Hamilton contended with the emergent Jeffersonian Republicans. By 1803, the Republicans controlled New York's legislature, and the organizers of the Merchants Bank, mostly Federalists, knew their chances of receiving a charter were slim to none. Indeed, the Manhattan Bank not only prevented consideration of a charter for the Merchants Bank; it also tried to kill the new bank. In April 1804, the Republican state legislature passed a so-called restraining act forbidding unincorporated banks from issuing banknotes. But for the Merchants Bank that was merely an inconvenience, as issuing banknotes, particularly in urban centers, was hardly necessary to carrying on a banking business based on deposits. Nonetheless, after Hamilton died as a result of his duel with Burr, in 1805 the Merchants Bank succeeded in obtaining a charter, allegedly via bribery of state legislators in return for their votes. The Merchants Bank continued in business for well over a century. It became a nationally chartered bank in 1865. Ironically, in 1920 the Manhattan Bank, which initially had hoped to kill it, absorbed the Merchants Bank.[1]

There are many similarities between the 1803 Merchants Bank's articles of association and the Bank of New York's 1784 constitution. But there are also some differences that indicate how both the times and Hamilton's thinking may have changed over those two decades.

One of the differences is that the short, one-sentence statement in the sixteenth article of the Bank of New York's constitution stating that its stockholders had limited liability—"no Stockholder shall be accountable . . . for a greater sum than the amount of his stock"—becomes a much longer and more involved statement of limited liability in the eleventh article of the 1803 articles of association. Most likely the issue of limited liability for stockholders had become a contentious one over the two decades, and Hamilton as a highly skilled lawyer had to meet objections that might be raised to the claim of limited liability in the articles. It was a bold innovation of his legal mind in the first place to assert that an enterprise not chartered by governmental authority could limit stockholder liability by making it a feature of its constitution or articles of association.

Another notable difference between the constitution and the articles relates to voting rights of stockholders. The constitution of the Bank of New York in its sixth article reduced the voting power of large stockholders by limiting their votes to fractions of the number of shares they owned. When he drafted the charter of the Bank of the United States in 1790–1791, Hamilton included a similar provision, which he termed "a prudent mean" between one vote per share, which favors large shareholders, and one vote per shareholder, which favors small shareholders. By 1803, either Hamilton had changed his position or he was carrying out the preferences of the organizers of the Merchants Bank to allot one vote per share, which eventually became the standard for shareholder voting rights.

A third difference, possibly related to the second, is in the par value of shares. The Bank of New York shares had a par value of $500 each, quite a large sum of money for 1784. Only a fairly well-to-do person could afford to buy even one share. In contrast, the par value of a Merchants Bank share was only $50, which made it far easier for a small investor to purchase a share. There were many more corporations in the United States of 1803, thanks in no small measure to Hamilton's financial reforms, than there were in 1784. The reduction in share par values may have been a measure to widen the number of investors who could participate in the stock markets of the day.

This document is not abridged.

### Articles of Association of the Merchants' Bank
[New York, April 7, 1803]

To all to whom these Presents shall come, or in any wise concern. Be it known and made manifest, that we, the Subscribers, have formed a Company or limited Partnership, and do hereby associate and agree with each other, to conduct business in the manner hereinafter specified and described, by and under the name and style of the "Merchants' Bank," and we do hereby mutually covenant, declare and agree, that the following are and shall be the fundamental Articles of this our Association and agreement with each other, by which we and all persons who at any time hereafter may transact business with the said Company, shall be bound and concluded.

I. The Capital Stock of the said Company shall consist of One Million Two Hundred and Fifty Thousand Dollars, in Money of the United States. The said Capital Stock shall be divided into Shares of Fifty Dollars each: two Dollars and fifty Cents on each Share shall be paid at the time of subscribing, and the remainder shall be paid at such times, and in such proportions as the board of Directors shall order and appoint, under pain of forfeiting to the said Company the said Shares, and all previous payments thereon: but no payment shall be required, unless by a notice to be published for at least fifteen days, in two newspapers printed in the City of New-York.

II. The affairs of the said company, shall be conducted by sixteen Directors, who shall elect one of their number to be the president thereof, and nine of the Directors shall form a board or quorum for transacting all the business of the company, except ordinary discounts, which it shall be in the power of any five of the Directors to perform, of whom the President shall always be one, except in case of his sickness or necessary absence, when his place may be supplied by any other Director, whom he by writing under his hand, shall nominate for that purpose; and until the second Tuesday in June, one thousand eight hundred and four, Oliver Wolcott, Richard Varick, Peter Jay Munro, Joshua Sands, Thomas Storm, William W. Woolsey, John Hone, John Kane, Joshua Jones, Robert Gilchrist, Wynant Van Zandt, Jun., Isaac Bronson, James Roosevelt, John Swartwout, Henry I. Wyckoff, and Isaac Hicks shall be Directors of the said Company; the Directors from and after that period, shall be elected for one year by the Stockholders, for the time being, and each Director shall be a Stockholder at the time of his election, and shall cease to be a Director if he should cease to be a Stockholder: and the number of votes which each Stockholder shall be entitled to, shall be equal to the number of shares which he shall have held on the books of the company, for at least sixty days prior to the election; and all stockholders shall vote at elections by ballot, either personally or by proxy; to be made in such form as the board of Directors may appoint.

III. A General Meeting of the Stockholders of the Company shall be holden upon the first Tuesday of June, in every year, (excepting in June now next ensuing) at such place as the

Board of Directors shall appoint, by notice, to be published in two newspapers printed in the City of New-York, at least fifteen days previous to such meeting, for the purpose of electing Directors for the ensuing year, who shall take their seats at the Board on the second Tuesday in the same month of June and immediately proceed to elect the President.

IV.  The board of Directors, are hereby fully empowered to make, revise, and alter or amend, all such rules, bye laws, and regulations, for the government of the company, and that of their officers, servants and affairs, as they, or a majority of them, shall from time to time think expedient, not inconsistent with law, or these articles of association; and to use, employ, and dispose of the joint stock, funds or property of the said Company (subject only to the restrictions hereinafter contained) as to them, or a majority of them, shall seem expedient.

V.  All bills, bonds, notes, and every contract and engagement on behalf of the Company, shall be signed by the president; and countersigned or attested, by the cashier of the company; and the funds of the company shall in no case be held responsible for any contract or engagement whatever, unless the same shall be so signed and countersigned, or attested as aforesaid.

VI.  The books, papers, correspondence and funds of the company, shall at all times, be subject to the inspection of the directors.

VII.  The said board of Directors, shall have power to appoint a cashier, and all other officers and servants, for executing the business of the company; and to establish the compensations to be paid to the president and all other officers and servants of the company respectively; all which, together with all other necessary expenses, shall be defrayed out of the funds of the company.

VIII.  A majority of the Directors, shall have power to call a general meeting of the Stockholders, for purposes relative to the concerns of the Company; giving at least thirty days notice, in two of the public Newspapers printed in the city of New-York, and specifying in such notice the object or objects of such meeting.

IX.  The Shares of Capital Stock, at any time owned by any individual Stockholder, shall be transferable on the books of the Company, according to such rules, as conformable to law, may be established in that behalf, by the Board of Directors; but all debts actually due and payable to the Company, by a Stockholder requesting a transfer, must be satisfied before such transfer shall be made, unless the Board of Directors shall direct to the contrary.

X. No transfer of Stock in this Company, shall be considered as binding upon the Company, unless made in a book or books, to be kept for that purpose by the Company. And it is hereby further expressly agreed and declared, that any Stockholder, who shall transfer in manner aforesaid, all his Stock or Shares in this Company, to any other person or persons whatever, shall ipso facto cease to be a member of this Company; and that any person or persons whatever, who shall accept a transfer of any Stock or Share in this Company, shall ipso facto become and be a member of this Company, according to these articles of association.

XI. It is hereby expressly and explicitly declared, to be the object and intention of the persons who associate under the style or firm of the "Merchants' Bank," that the joint stock or property of the said Company (exclusive of dividends to be made in the manner hereinafter mentioned) shall alone be responsible for the Debts and engagements of the said Company. And that no person, who shall or may deal with this Company, or to whom they shall or may become in anywise indebted, shall on any pretense whatever have recourse against the separate property of any present or future member of this Company, or against their persons, further than may be necessary to secure the faithful application of the Funds thereof, to the purposes to which by these presents they are liable. But all persons accepting any Bond, Bill, Note or other Contract of this Company, signed by the President, and countersigned or attested by the Cashier of the Company, for the time being, or dealing with it in any other manner whatsoever, thereby respectively give credit to the said joint stock or property of the said Company, and thereby respectively disavow having recourse, on any pretense whatever, to the person or separate property of any present or future member of this Company, except as above mentioned. And all suits to be brought against this Company, (if any shall be) shall be brought against the President for the time being; and in case of his death or removal from office, pending any such suit against him, measures shall be taken at the expense of the Company for substituting his successor in office as a defendant; so that persons having demands upon the Company, may not be prejudiced or delayed by that event, or if the persons suing, shall go on against the person first named as defendant, (notwithstanding his death or removal from office) this Company shall take no advantage by writ of error, or otherwise, of such proceeding, on that account; and all recoveries had in manner aforesaid, shall be conclusive upon the Company, so far as to render the company's said joint stock or property liable thereby, and no further; and the Company shall immediately pay the amount of such recovery out of their joint stock, but not otherwise. And in case of any suit at law, the President shall sign his appearance upon the writ, or file common bail thereto; it being expressly understood and declared, that all persons dealing with the said Company, agree to these terms, and are to be bound thereby.

XII. Dividends of the profits of the Company, or of so much of the said profits as shall be deemed expedient and proper, shall be declared and paid half yearly during the months of May and November in every year, and shall from time to time be determined by a majority of the said Directors, at a meeting to be held for that purpose, and shall in no case exceed the amount of the net profits actually acquired by the Company; so that the Capital Stock of the Company shall never be impaired by Dividends; and at the expiration of every three years, from the first Tuesday of June next, a dividend of surplus profits shall be made, but the Directors shall be at liberty to retain at least one per cent upon the capital, as a fund for future contingencies.

XIII. If the said Directors shall at any time, willfully and knowingly, make or declare, any dividend which shall impair the said Capital Stock, all the Directors present at the making or declaring such dividend, and consenting thereto, shall be liable, in their individual capacities, to the Company, for the amount or proportion of the said Capital Stock, so divided by the said Directors. And each Director who shall be present at the making or declaring of such dividend, shall be deemed to have consented thereto, unless he shall immediately enter, in writing, his dissent, on the minutes of the proceedings of the Board, and give public notice to the Stockholders, that such dividend has been declared.

XIV. These Articles of Agreement shall be published in at least three newspapers, printed in the City of New-York, for one month; and for the further information of all persons, who may transact business with, or in any manner give Credit to this Company, every Bond, Bill, Note, or other instrument or contract, by the effect or terms of which, the Company may be charged or held liable, for the payment of money, shall specially declare, in such form as the board of directors shall prescribe, that payment shall be made out of the joint funds of the Merchants' Bank, according to the present articles of association, and not otherwise; and a copy of the eleventh article of this association, shall be inserted in the bank book of every person depositing money, or other valuable property, with the Company, for safe custody, or a printed copy shall be delivered to every such person, before any such deposit shall be received from him. And it is hereby expressly declared, that no engagement can be legally made in the name of the said Company, unless it contain a limitation or restriction, to the effect above recited. And the Company hereby expressly disavow all responsibility, for any debt or engagement, which may be made in their name, not containing a limitation or restriction to the effect aforesaid.

XV. The Company shall in no case be owners of any ships or vessels, or directly or indirectly concerned in trade, or the importation or exportation, purchase or sale of any goods, wares, or merchandise whatever (bullion only excepted) unless by selling such goods, wares, and merchandise, as shall be truly pledged to them, by way of security for debts due to the said company.

XVI. If a vacancy shall at any time happen among the Directors, by death, resignation, or otherwise, the residue of the Directors, for the time being, shall immediately elect a Director, to fill the said vacancy, until the next election of Directors, to be made according to the second article of these presents.

XVII. This association shall continue until the first Tuesday of June, one thousand eight hundred and fifteen, and no longer; but the proprietors of two thirds of the capital stock of the

Company, may by their concurring votes, at a general meeting to be called for that express purpose, dissolve the same at any prior period; provided, that notice of such meeting, and of its object, shall be published in at least three newspapers, to be printed in the City of New-York, for at least six months previous to the time appointed for such meeting.

XVIII. Immediately on any dissolution of this association, effectual measures shall be taken by the Directors then existing, for closing all the concerns of the Company, and for dividing the capital and profits, which may remain, among the Stockholders, in proportion to their respective interests.

In Witness Whereof, we have hereunto set our names or firms the Seventh Day of April, one thousand eight hundred and three.

# Conclusion

## Legacies of the U.S. Financial Revolution

He smote the rock of the national resources, and abundant streams
of revenue gushed forth. He touched the dead corpse of the public credit,
and it sprang upon its feet. The fabled birth of Minerva from the brain
of Jove was hardly more sudden or more perfect than the financial system
of the United States, as it burst forth from the conceptions of
ALEXANDER HAMILTON.

DANIEL WEBSTER, AMERICAN STATESMAN, 1831

WE MAY DEFINE a financial revolution as the creation of the key
components of a modern financial system in a relatively short period
of history. The United States had the neatest, quickest financial revolution in history. It happened between 1789 and 1795, when Alexander
Hamilton served as the nation's first Secretary of Treasury. Hamilton's
writings on finance, as set forth in this book, show that he realized when
fighting in the Continental Army from 1776 to 1781 that credit was a
new power in the affairs of nations and individuals. The war dragged on
longer than it should have, Hamilton deduced, because the British had
much better financing than did the Americans.

Hamilton based his early writings on his study of financial history.
He knew that the Dutch had parlayed their financial revolution in
the first years of the seventeenth century into unprecedented wealth
and power. He knew that the British, imitating and improving on the
Dutch precedent, had done likewise a century later. He also knew that
attempted financial revolutions could fail, as France's had when John
Law's financial reforms collapsed in the popping of the Mississippi
Bubble in 1720. It led him in 1781 to advise Robert Morris, whom

Congress had just decided to put in charge of America's finances (see chapter 3), to seek a foreign loan and use it to capitalize a bank. For America to prevail in its quest for independence, Hamilton told Morris, it was more important to put its finances in order than to win occasional battles. We see all this in Hamilton's early writings.

Hamilton also knew early on that the Articles of Confederation were defective and needed to be replaced by a better plan of government. So he worked in the 1780s toward that objective, which was realized late in the decade with the writing and adoption of the Constitution. All the while, Hamilton refined his plan for financial reform. When he became Treasury Secretary on September 11, 1789, he was ready to hit the ground running. And run he did.

What were the results? We can see them by considering the changes that took place from 1789 to 1795 in each of what we have termed the key components of a modern financial system.

In terms of *public finance*, the bankrupt national government in default on its debts gave way in 1789 to the new federal government, bequeathing to it an empty treasury. While waiting for revenues from newly levied customs duties to come in, Hamilton launched the finances of the new government with loans from two of the three existing American banks. Then he unveiled his plan for restructuring the nation's debts, including assumed state debts. By 1795, public credit was established and thriving, and the federal government, with projected revenues of $6.5 million and expenditures of $5.7 million, had a surplus (see chapter 16).

In terms of *central banking*, it didn't exist in 1789. Morris's Bank of North America, chartered by Congress at the end of 1781, had morphed into an ordinary state bank with a restricted charter issued by the state of Pennsylvania. Hamilton proposed a much larger, federally chartered Bank of the United States (see chapter 10), which, despite a controversy about its constitutionality, Congress and President Washington approved. By 1795, the Bank had five offices in cities in different states. The United States thus had nationwide branch banking.

In terms of *money*, the country did not have a national currency in 1789. Instead it relied on a mixture of coins issued by other countries and fiat paper money issues of several states. Hamilton defined the U.S. dollar in his Mint Report of 1791 (see chapter 11) in terms of weights of gold and silver, and the new dollar became the nation's monetary base, into which paper currency issued by banks, not state governments, would be convertible. Although it would be refined over time, the states by 1795 had all become members of a national currency union.

In terms of *banking*, the three existing banks of 1789, each a local bank in its city and not a part of a banking system, became twenty state banks by 1795, which, along with the five offices of the Bank of the United States, were part of an American banking system. These banks received each other's notes and checks, cleared them, and lent to merchants, entrepreneurs, and governments.

In terms of *securities markets*, none that could be called "organized" existed in 1789. Someone interested in buying or selling debt securities that were priced at ten or twenty cents on the dollar in leading cities could find a broker or dealer to handle such sporadic transactions. By 1795, Philadelphia, New York, and Boston had organized, regular markets, with the first two having nascent stock exchanges. Each city made markets in what could be term national market securities: the three different Treasury bonds Hamilton issued in his debt restructuring plan and the equity shares of the Bank of the United States. In addition, each city traded the securities of its local banks, insurance and other companies, and in some cases new state debt issues.

In terms of *business corporations*, there were many more in 1795 than in 1789. Records show that only seven had been chartered in the colonial era, up to 1780. From 1781 to 1790, states chartered twenty-eight more. During the financial revolution, the numbers soared. From 1791 to 1795, 114 new corporations appeared. Over the next five years, 1796–1800, states chartered 181 more. Hamilton's Bank of the United States, by far the largest corporation of the time, had served as a catalyst to induce the states to act by chartering banks and other enterprises.

For some reason, the economic significance of the changes that took place in the U.S. financial revolution has more or less escaped the attention of historians, although the political controversies surrounding Hamilton's policies are seldom neglected. It is almost as if the historians assume that taxes, debts, the dollar, banks, bond and stock markets, and corporations have always been around, so the stance of the scholar should be to complain about them when they don't live up to expectations or when they seem to foster greedy capitalism.

Instead, these financial innovations ought to be celebrated as agents of modernization and economic growth that few countries had so early in history. Indeed, the United States, after the Dutch Republic and Great Britain, was the third nation in the world to totally modernize its finances, and those three countries successively have been the leading economies of the world for the past four centuries. All three parlayed financial modernization into economic wealth and political power. In the case of the United States, it is what Hamilton wanted his financial reforms to accomplish, and he got his wish.

Public credit financed the territorial expansion of the United States and all the wars of its history. Most of the territorial expansion came early. Jefferson's administration, using Hamilton's financial innovations, doubled the size of the country in the 1803 Louisiana Purchase. Settlers backed by rising American power induced Spain to cede Florida and the Gulf Coast to the United States in 1821. Diplomacy between Britain and the United States resolved disputes over the Canada–U.S. border in the 1840s, and in that same decade the Mexican-American War ended with the United States paying Mexico $15 million for half its territory, now the southwestern United States, in 1848. In 1853, the United States paid Mexico another $10 million for what is now the southern parts of Arizona and New Mexico. After the Civil War, the U.S. government wrote a check for $7.2 million to Russia to purchase Alaska. In all, the United States by 1867 had increased its original territory more than fourfold by employing the public credit established by Hamilton.

Hamilton's writings on finance show he realized that political power and economic power are intimately related. As he told Robert Morris in 1781 (see chapter 3):

> The tendency of a national bank is to increase public and private credit. The former gives power to the state for the protection of its rights and interests, and the latter facilitates and extends the operations of commerce among individuals. Industry is increased, commodities are multiplied, agriculture and manufactures flourish, and herein consists the true wealth and prosperity of a state.

A growing economy was good in itself, Hamilton thought, but it also helped the government by increasing the tax base—whether by increasing imports, raising property values, attracting immigrants, or other means. So his plan involved not just establishing public credit but energizing the economy by multiplying the institutions specializing in private credit. He wanted the United States to have more banks, securities markets, and corporations.

The momentum established during the financial revolution continued through U.S. history. State- and, later, nationally chartered banks mushroomed to a hundred or so by 1810, 300 by 1830, 700 in the 1830s, 1,500–1,600 by 1860, and to a historic peak of some 30,000 independent banks by the early 1920s. By the early twentieth century the U.S. banking system was far and away the largest in the world, with more deposits than the next three, Britain, France, and Germany, combined. Today the numbers are down to fewer than 6,000, but that is because of mergers and the spread of branch banking to the entire nation. The total number of bank offices is in the high tens of thousands, far above the 1920s peak.

Securities markets also expanded throughout the country's history. Today, the two largest securities exchanges by market capitalization in the world are American—the New York Stock Exchange and NASDAQ.

Corporations also multiplied. Before the Civil War the states had chartered nearly 23,000 of them with individual charters granted by their legislatures, and thousands more were being created via general incorporation laws, now the norm, by administrative offices of state governments. By the early twentieth century, the United States was home to some 270,000 corporations, 60 percent of the corporations in the world at that time. Today there are millions of corporations and related entities in the country, although only several thousand of the very largest ones are listed and regularly traded in public securities markets.

U.S. financial development after the financial revolution did not always proceed smoothly. Hamilton's central bank disappeared when Congress narrowly voted not to renew its charter in 1811. Realizing that was a mistake, Congress in 1816 reinstituted a larger version of it, the second Bank of the United States. Then President Andrew Jackson vetoed Congress's renewal of its charter in 1832, and the central bank disappeared for the second time. Its absence could not derail the momentum U.S. economic growth had attained by the 1830s, but it did make for a rockier ride than was necessary for the next seven decades, which featured many financial crises and economic recessions that a central bank might have prevented or alleviated. After such a crisis in 1907, Congress once again instituted a central bank, the Federal Reserve System, in 1913. The third central bank has now lasted more than a century. It restored a key element of Hamilton's original architecture of the U.S. financial system.

We hope that Hamilton's financial writings, as presented in this book, will be studied by citizens, financiers, and policy makers. They contain many lessons, among them the importance of fiscal and monetary responsibility; the energizing effects of money, credit, corporations, and securities markets; and the synergies of an articulated financial system. The United States was fortunate to have a Hamilton who understood all these things at the beginning of its history. He established or unleashed many of the forces that would make the United States an entrepreneurial, rich, powerful, and free nation.

# Notes

## Introduction: Hamilton and the U.S. Financial Revolution

1. MeasuringWorth, at the website https://www.measuringworth.com, provides annual estimates of both nominal and real U.S. gross domestic product, totals and per capita, and other useful long-term series, from 1790 to the present. It also provides calculators that allow one to compute the rates of growth of the various series between any two years.

2. See Peter Lindert and Jeffrey Willamson, *Unequal Gains: American Growth and Inequality since 1700* (Princeton: Princeton University Press, 2016).

3. See P. G. M. Dickson, *The Financial Revolution in England: A Study in the Development of Public Credit, 1688–1756* (New York: St. Martin's, 1967); and John Brewer, *The Sinews of Power: War, Money, and the English State, 1688–1783* (New York: Knopf, 1989).

## 1. To— (December 1779–March 1780)

1. Harold C. Syrett et al., eds., *The Papers of Alexander Hamilton*, 27 vols. (New York: Columbia University Press, 1961–1987), 2:234–36.

## 2. To James Duane (September 3, 1780)

1. For a recent account of these state cessions of land to the national government, see Farley Grubb, "U.S. Land Policy: Founding Choices and

Outcomes, 1781–1802," in *Founding Choices: American Economic Policy in the 1790s*, ed. Douglas A. Irwin and Richard Sylla (Chicago: University of Chicago Press, 2011), 259–89.

2. As noted in the introduction to this document, Hamilton's 1780 list of powers that Congress should have has considerable overlap with the powers granted to Congress in Article 1, Section 8, of the U.S. Constitution written seven years later:

Section 8

1: The Congress shall have Power To lay and collect Taxes, Duties, Imposts and Excises, to pay the Debts and provide for the common Defence and general Welfare of the United States; but all Duties, Imposts and Excises shall be uniform throughout the United States;

2: To borrow Money on the credit of the United States;

3: To regulate Commerce with foreign Nations, and among the several States, and with the Indian Tribes;

4: To establish an uniform Rule of Naturalization, and uniform Laws on the subject of Bankruptcies throughout the United States;

5: To coin Money, regulate the Value thereof, and of foreign Coin, and fix the Standard of Weights and Measures;

6: To provide for the Punishment of counterfeiting the Securities and current Coin of the United States;

7: To establish Post Offices and post Roads;

8: To promote the Progress of Science and useful Arts, by securing for limited Times to Authors and Inventors the exclusive Right to their respective Writings and Discoveries;

9: To constitute Tribunals inferior to the supreme Court;

10: To define and punish Piracies and Felonies committed on the high Seas, and Offences against the Law of Nations;

11: To declare War, grant Letters of Marque and Reprisal, and make Rules concerning Captures on Land and Water;

12: To raise and support Armies, but no Appropriation of Money to that Use shall be for a longer Term than two Years;

13: To provide and maintain a Navy;

14: To make Rules for the Government and Regulation of the land and naval Forces;

15: To provide for calling forth the Militia to execute the Laws of the Union, suppress Insurrections and repel Invasions;

16: To provide for organizing, arming, and disciplining, the Militia, and for governing such Part of them as may be employed in the Service of the United States, reserving to the States respectively, the Appointment of the Officers, and the Authority of training the Militia according to the discipline prescribed by Congress;

17: To exercise exclusive Legislation in all Cases whatsoever, over such District (not exceeding ten Miles square) as may, by Cession of particular States, and the Acceptance of Congress, become the Seat of the Government of the United States, and to exercise like Authority over all Places purchased by the Consent of the Legislature of the State in which the Same shall be, for the Erection of Forts, Magazines, Arsenals, dock-Yards, and other needful Buildings;—And

18: To make all Laws which shall be necessary and proper for carrying into Execution the foregoing Powers, and all other Powers vested by this Constitution in the Government of the United States, or in any Department or Officer thereof.


# 5. Constitution of the Bank of New York
## (February 23–March 15, 1784)

1. Albert Gallatin to Thomas Jefferson, April 12, 1804, *The Writings of Albert Gallatin*, ed. Henry Adams (Philadelphia: J. B. Lippincott, 1879), 2:184–85. The italics are Gallatin's.


# 7. Report Relative to a Provision for the
## Support of Public Credit (January 9, 1790)

1. Nations throughout history have not honored the debt of previous governments. The Communists upon assuming power in Russia repudiated the debt of the czars, and the Communists in China also reneged on the debt of the Chiang Kai-shek regime.

2. Hamilton referred to pounds and shillings because the U.S. dollar, the subject of his Mint Report a year later, was yet to be created.

3. James Madison in particular would challenge Hamilton on this, feeling that original holders should benefit from the establishment of public credit. But Madison's proposal for a discrimination in favor of original purchasers of government securities would lose by a large margin in a vote of the House in 1791, an early victory for Hamilton.

4. The settlement of state accounts along the lines Hamilton recommended took place a few years later. In it, states that had contributed more than their fair share of the costs of the Revolution were rewarded with federal bonds to make up the difference, while states that had contributed less than their fair share were not charged, but for political reasons had their deficiencies absorbed by the federal government.

## 8. To Wilhem and Jan Willink, Nicholaas and Jacob Van Staphorst, and Nicholas Hubbard (August 28, 1790)

1. Wilhelm and Jan Willink, Nicholas and Jacob Van Staphorst, and Nicholas Hubbard to Alexander Hamilton, 25 January 1790.
2. Ibid.

## 10. Second Report on the Further Provision Necessary for Establishing Public Credit (Report on a National Bank, December 14, 1790)

1. Harold C. Syrett et al., eds., *The Papers of Alexander Hamilton*, 27 vols. (New York: Columbia University Press, 1961–1987), 8:218.
2. Tench Coxe to Alexander Hamilton, March 5, 1790, in *The Papers of Alexander Hamilton*, 6:290–93.

## 11. Report on the Establishment of a Mint (January 28, 1791)

1. There would be two drafts before the final version. This phrase did not make it into the version submitted to Congress.
2. Hamilton would be off by more than half a century. Foreign coins were legal tender until abolished by the Coinage Act of 1857. For a variety of reasons, the U.S. Mint could not keep up with the demand for coins until the 1850s.

## 12. Opinion on the Constitutionality of an Act to Establish a National Bank (February 23, 1791)

1. Opinion on the Constitutionality of the Bill for Establishing a National Bank, *The Papers of Thomas Jefferson*, ed. Julian P. Boyd (Princeton: Princeton University Press, 1974), 19:276.
2. Alexander Hamilton to George Washington, February 23, 1791. Italics are Hamilton's.
3. Alexander Hamilton to Edward Carrington, May 26, 1792.

## 14. Report on the Subject of Manufactures (December 5, 1791)

1. John Nelson, *Liberty and Property: Political Economy and Policymaking in the New Nation, 1789–1812* (Baltimore: Johns Hopkins University, 1987).

2. Recent research confirms Hamilton's optimism. See Joseph H. Davis, "An Annual Index of U.S. Industrial Production, 1790–1915," *Quarterly Journal of Economics* 119, no. 4 (November 2004): 1177–1215. Davis indicates that industrial production grew at a trend rate of roughly 5 percent per year over the 125-year period of his study. The rate in the Federalist era, 1790–1800, was 5.28 percent per year.

## 15. To William Seton
### (February 10 and March 22, 1792)

1. For a detailed account of Hamilton's crisis management, see Richard Sylla, Robert E. Wright, and David J. Cowen, "Alexander Hamilton, Central Banker: Crisis Management and the Lender of Last Resort during the US Panic of 1792," *Business History Review* 83 (spring 2009): 61–86.

2. Clement Biddle to William Campbell, March 11, 1792, Clement Biddle Letterbook, Historical Society of Pennsylvania.

3. Alexander Macomb to William Constable, April 7, 1792, Constable-Pierrepont Papers, Manuscripts Division, New York Public Library, Astor, Lenox and Tilden Foundations.

## 18. Articles of Association of the Merchants Bank
### (April 7, 1803)

1. See Bray Hammond, *Banks and Politics in America: From the Revolution to the Civil War* (Princeton: Princeton University Press, 1957), 149–61.

# Index

absolute increase, of capital, 217–18
abuses: of authority, by government
  revenue collectors, 77; of credit,
  272–73, 276–77
Adams, John, 225
administration, of sinking fund, 78, 100
agriculture: economy, manufactures
  and, 197; foreign investors for,
  201; free trade argument and, 199,
  206; goods, manufacturing sector
  demand for, 198–99; importance
  of, 197; Physiocrat economists
  on, 197; private credit and, 35,
  41; promotion, from public debt
  management, 83; prosperous state
  of commerce for, 294
aid: of banks to trade and manufactures,
  123, 183; from BNA, 134–35;
  manufacturers without government,
  209–10; from sinking funds for new
  loans, 256
Alaska, purchase of, 320
alcohol: duties on, 77–78, 98–99, 109,
  113, 115; excises and taxes on, 77,
  98, 232, 240; licenses, as federal
  revenue source, 232, 236, 240;
  luxury taxes on, 77, 98
alienations, from foreign investors loss,
  303
allotment, of government
  expenditures, 34

alloys: copper with silver, 160; money
  composition of, 147, 153, 157–59,
  318
Amsterdam, as financial center, 3.
  *See also* Bank of Amsterdam
anarchy, from too little power, 48
Annapolis Convention of 1786, 4
annuities: life, for government
  creditors, 75; redeeming of, 214–16
anti-agrarian label, of banks, 172
anti-Bank advocates, on BUS
  constitutionality, 172
arbitrary rates of interest, 278
arbitrary taxes, 222
arguments: for agriculture and
  free trade, 199, 206; on BUS
  constitutionality, 122, 171–84,
  318; against national bank, 119–
  20, 126–31; second best world,
  for free trade, 199–200, 208–9;
  for state charters of incorporation,
  172, 179
army: money lack for disbanding of,
  36; states influence on, 20, 24;
  state supply requisition system for,
  20–21, 25–26
arrearages of interest, 74, 92; national
  debt and, 73, 91, 281
articles: for manufactures success, 190,
  220–21; supplied, as national debt
  source, 73, 90

of, 7, 61, 308; on malpractice
of embezzlement, 63; on senior
staff security for their trust, 61,
64; on shares, 64
Constitution, U.S., 280; Congress
powers listed in, 21; creditor
contracts at time of, 306; express
power of, 176–80; on federal
and state dual sovereignties, 275;
federal power limitations and, 173;
on government and corporations,
173, 175–78; Hamilton broad
interpretation of, 173, 174;
implied powers of, 176–77; on
police, 176, 178; political reform
and, 3–4; on powers delegated
to states, 172, 176; theory on
taxation, 285–86; writing and
adoption of, 318
constitutional convention, call to, 19,
21, 26–27, 31
constitutionality argument, on BUS,
122, 176–77, 183–84; anti-Bank
advocates reasons for, 172; ends
and means measurement criteria,
178; immediate government
powers and, 182; Jefferson on,
171, 172–73; Madison on, 171–75;
monopolies and, 179; observation
list on, 180–81; Randolph on, 171,
174–75; specific considerations for,
181–82
consumption, taxes on, 110, 113
Continental Congress: BNA bank loan
to, 66–67, 68; King Louis XVI
lending to, 105
Continental currency, depreciation of,
9, 12–13, 35
*Continentalist, The* (1781-
1782), 47–50, 53–58, 287; on
confederation revenue, 51–52;
Hamilton essays in, 4
contractual obligations: of creditors,
at time of U.S. Constitution, 306;
public credit and payment of,
70, 80
copper: alloy composition of, 147;
silver alloy with, 160

corporate charter. *See* bank charter of
incorporation
corporations: banks as legal, 7;
business, 5, 319; growth of, 5,
319, 321; increase in 1791, 185;
investors for, 186; joint stock, 35,
60, 135; limited liability of, 7; states
laws of, 179; U.S. Constitution on
government and, 173, 175–78
credit: abuses of, 272–73, 276–77;
bank, as capital liquidity, 202,
213–15; economic growth from,
34–35; entirety of, 272; as essential
to nation, 270; mixed nature of,
269; national government and,
52; as new power in world, 231,
232, 298, 317; for public safety,
238, 269, 271, 288; restriction,
for speculative trading, 224, 229.
*See also* government creditors;
national credit; private credit
currencies: depreciation of, 49, 51;
foreign loans for purchase and
retirement issues of, 10, 13–14;
public lack of confidence in, 10,
14, 318
customs duties, 110
czars, Communists debt repudiation
of, 325n1

debts: of Britain and United
Provinces, 52; Dutch investors in,
75; of France, 52, 297; Hamilton
restructuring of, 74; moral and
political obligation for payment of,
292; repudiation, 325n1; taxation
for repayment of, 74; Virginia
exoneration of, 288–89. *See also*
domestic debt; foreign debt;
funded debt; national debt; public
debts
debt securities, for liquidity, 225
debt-to-GDP ratio, 75
defaults: of Duer, 224–25; public
credit minimization of, 70
deferred: bond, 76; loans, 233
Democratic Republican party, of
Jefferson, 171

Steuart, James, 10
stockholders general meeting, of
    Merchants Bank, 310–11
stock-jobbing, 302
stocks: BUS on, 15, 121, 185, 224,
    232, 240; capital, 61–62, 224,
    304, 310; as liquidity investments,
    3; Merchants Bank Articles of
    Association on, 310–12; securities
    markets and, 5, 6–7, 319, 321;
    sequestering or confiscating, 267;
    states open subscriptions of, 30;
    subscriptions, 35, 43; transferable
    quality of, 86, 264–67, 311–12
subsidized pricing, for infant
    industries, 200
Sullivan, John, 9
Superintendent of Finance, 134;
    Morris as, 33–34, 38, 49, 53
Susquehanna river, navigation of,
    185
Syrett, Harold C., 7, 35, 197

tariffs, 50–51, 72; Congress enactment
    of, 204, 221; foreign debt
    funding from, 76–77; on foreign
    manufactured goods, 196; on
    imports, as federal revenue source,
    232, 240; protective, 200, 204, 221
taxation: of Britain, 36, 44–45; for
    debt repayment, 74; federal and
    state government power of, 275;
    of government on own funds,
    261, 266; in kind, for financing
    war, 21–22, 28; mine, 48; states,
    for revenues, 34; theory of
    Constitution on, 285–86
tax collectors, for public revenues,
    110, 112
taxes: arbitrary, 222; banks collection
    process of, 119, 126, 182;
    carriage, 232, 236, 240, 249; on
    consumption, 110, 113; excise, 77,
    98, 110, 232, 240; ex post facto,
    236; on foreign and domestic
    whiskey, 109, 111; to fund foreign

debt, 76–77, 98; heavy pecuniary
    paid in money, for war financing,
    21, 28; in kind, for war financing,
    21–22, 28; luxury, on alcohol, 77,
    98; moderate land, 48, 55, 57;
    on money balances, 237; policies,
    for domestic manufacturing base,
    221–22; poll, 57; property, 110, 113;
    snuff and sugar, 232, 236, 240, 249;
    state development via cuts in, 6; of
    states, revenues and, 34
tax on imports, 50; foreign debt
    funding from, 76–77, 98
tax revenues, federal and state
    competition for, 275
technologies: new, for manufactures,
    186; securities markets
    encouragement of new, 3
temporary duties made permanent, 234
territorial expansion, from public
    credit, 320
tontine plan, for government
    creditors, 75
trade: banks aid to, 123, 183;
    Congress regulation of, 50–51;
    extension, from public debt
    management, 83; external
    commerce and, 184; of France
    and Dutch, 50; as national
    government revenue source, 50;
    negotiation, as power of Congress,
    48, 55; as self-equilibrating, 50;
    state involvement with, 49–50, 55.
    *See also* free trade
trading companies, 17
transferable quality of stocks, 86,
    264–66; of Merchants Bank,
    311–12
Treasury, private bankers reliance by,
    67
Treasury bonds, U.S., 134, 319;
    bankruptcies from, 224; for BUS
    shares purchase, 186; investors
    inclusion of, 185; market, 1790
    securities and, 76; for SEUM shares
    purchase, 186